In the Wake of Slavery

In the Wake of Slavery

CIVIL WAR, CIVIL RIGHTS, AND THE RECONSTRUCTION OF SOUTHERN LAW

Joseph A. Ranney

PRAEGER

Westport, Connecticut
London

Library of Congress Cataloging-in-Publication Data

Ranney, Joseph A., 1952–
    In the wake of slavery : Civil War, Civil Rights, and the reconstruction
of Southern law / Joseph A. Ranney.
        p. cm.
Includes bibliographical references and index.
    ISBN 0–275–98972–0 (alk. paper)
    1. Constitutional history—Southern States.   2. African Americans—
Civil rights—Southern States—History.   3. Suffrage—Southern States—
History.   4. Women's rights—Southern States—History.   5. Southern
States—Race relations.   6. Reconstruction (U.S. history, 1865–1877)   I. Title.
    KF4541.R37   2006
    342.7302'9—dc22   2006025249

British Library Cataloguing in Publication Data is available.

Library of Congress Catalog Card Number: 2006025249
ISBN: 0–275–98972–0

First published in 2006

Praeger Publishers, 88 Post Road West, Westport, CT 06881
An imprint of Greenwood Publishing Group, Inc.
www.praeger.com

Printed in the United States of America

The paper used in this book complies with the
Permanent Paper Standard issued by the National
Information Standards Organization (Z39.48–1984).

10   9   8   7   6   5   4   3   2   1

To the memory of J. Austin Ranney, Elizabeth Mackay
Ranney, and William Robertson Mackay, Sergeant,
15th Connecticut Volunteers (1862–1865)

Contents

Acknowledgments

Many people and events have contributed to the making of this book. A child-hood spent in central Illinois, surrounded by remembrances of Abraham Lincoln and the Civil War, made a deep impression on me. Carl Sandburg's biography of Lincoln revealed that the political and social history of the Civil War era could be just as riveting and important as the military history of the war. Early life in Illinois, additional reading, and military service in North Carolina after college all taught me the truth of a central point Lincoln made in his first inaugural address: North and South are inextricably intertwined, and no one can claim a real understanding of American culture who has not tried to understand both regions.

As a young lawyer, I spent much time reading federal and state court decisions, some of which were quite old and provided tantalizing glimpses of what life's daily routine and daily concerns were like long ago. I felt called to try to make sense of these glimpses and understand how they have shaped modern-day law by assembling them into a comprehensive legal history of my home state, Wisconsin. When I did so, the central role the Civil War era played in shaping Midwestern identity once again became clear; my curiosity then shifted to the role of the war and Reconstruction in Southern legal history, and I discovered that the legal history of that era at the state level was virtually unexplored. From that discovery this book followed.

Many people have helped and encouraged me along the way. My fellow legal historian Jack Stark and Professor Austin Ranney of the University of California-Berkeley have provided helpful suggestions that have improved the quality of the book. Professor John Milton Cooper of the University of Wisconsin also provided insightful comments on an early draft of Chapter 5. I am grateful to Marquette Law School for giving me the chance to share my work as an adjunct professor, and to Dean Joseph Kearney and Professors Gordon Hylton and Daniel Blinka for the chance to share our common interest in legal history. Chief Justice Shirley Abrahamson and Justice Ann Walsh Bradley of the Wisconsin Supreme Court have also provided continuing encouragement. Thanks are due to my editor, Hilary Claggett, for her help in navigating the publishing process and her confidence that this book will be useful and interesting to legal and lay readers alike. Finally, I want to express my appreciation to the people of Wisconsin for funding the University of Wisconsin Law School library, the Wisconsin State Law Library, and particularly, the superb collections of the Wisconsin Historical Society. Without those resources, this book would not have been possible.

CHAPTER 1

Introduction: The Legal History of Reconstruction

Physically speaking, we cannot separate. We cannot remove our respective sections from each other. A husband and wife may be divorced, and go out of the presence, and beyond the reach of each other; but the different parts of our country cannot do this. . . . Suppose you go to war, you cannot fight always; and when, after much loss on both sides, and no gain on either, you cease fighting, the identical old questions as to terms of intercourse, are again upon you.

—Abraham Lincoln (1861)

It would be only fair to the reader to say frankly in advance that the attitude of any person toward this story will be distinctly influenced by his theories of the Negro race. If he believes that the Negro in America and in general is an average and ordinary human being, who under given environment develops like other human beings, then he will read this story and judge it by the facts adduced.

—W.E.B. Du Bois (1934)[1]

In August 1865, 100 Mississippians traveled from their homes in the Delta, the northeastern hills, the central piney woods, and the Gulf coast to a constitutional convention at Jackson where they hoped to put their state's war-shattered government back together. The delegates' thoughts during the trip to the capital must have been grim. On every side they could see the destruction war had inflicted on their land and their people. Slavery, a central pillar of their lives, was gone and a new system would have to be devised to take its place.

Debate in the convention was often sharp and bitter. Diehards urged resistance to the new order because "if we abolish slavery . . . we shall then be tormented and tortured upon other and new exactions." William Yerger, a former chief justice of the state, had little patience with such talk. "Why . . . contend for constitutional rights and constitutional guarantees, that we have no more power to grasp, than we have to grasp the rays of the moon?" he asked. Edmund Goode closed the debate on a note of resignation that expressed the feelings of most delegates. "There was a wager of law, as well as of battle," he said, "and the preamble [of the proposed constitution] declares that the question was decided against us."[2]

Goode spoke greater truth than he realized. A new and larger wager of law was about to be placed. Reconstruction was nothing less than a revolution: its primary goal was the legal restructuring of Southern race relations in the wake of emancipation, but it also created significant changes in the social hierarchy of the white South and in the Southern economy. Northern lawmakers' efforts to restructure race relations in the South also forced the North to recognize and ameliorate many of its own racial injustices.[3]

The Civil War and Reconstruction played a particularly crucial role in shaping modern American law, so much so that one legal historian has suggested American legal history can be divided into three eras: the years up to 1860, the decade of 1860–1870, and the years since 1870.[4] New constitutions, statutes, and case law had to be developed to accommodate emancipation and the numerous economic problems that followed the Civil War, and supporters of Reconstruction came to believe that legal change represented their best hope of creating permanent change in the Southern social order.

Throughout American history, most legal developments have taken place at the state level, primarily because the American constitutional system gives the federal government limited enumerated powers and reserves all remaining powers to the states and the people. Even though the Civil War and Reconstruction marked a dramatic expansion of federal power and influence, daily life after the war for Southern blacks and whites was defined at least as much by state laws as by federal laws. But surprisingly, little attention has been paid to the postwar evolution of law in the South at the state level and to the different ways in which each state modified its legal system in order to accommodate emancipation and address the economic challenges created by wartime destruction. This book makes a beginning effort to fill the gap.[5]

It is useful to begin with a political and social overview of Reconstruction and the events that preceded and followed that era.

THE ANTEBELLUM ERA: A DIVERSE SOUTH

Apart from the shared institution of slavery, the Southern and border states in 1860 were quite diverse. The legal systems of the original Southern states along the Atlantic seaboard (Maryland, Virginia, the Carolinas, and Georgia) bore a colonial stamp that the newer Southern states did not have. The sea-board states relied heavily on English common law and were slower to adopt American reforms such as direct popular election of judges, homestead exemptions, and married women's property rights laws. The newer Southern states were more receptive to such reforms.

The Deep South remained predominantly agricultural through the first half of the nineteenth century. Land ownership remained the chief determinant of social and economic status in the region; demand for slave labor remained steady and there was little reason for Deep South states to modify their legal systems to accommodate the forces of industrialism and entrepreneurialism that were gaining ground elsewhere. The transition to a commercial and industrial economy had proceeded farther in the Upper South and border states, particularly Maryland and the portions of Virginia, Kentucky, and Missouri that bordered the Ohio and Mississippi rivers. These regions relied heavily on trade with Northern states, and trade brought Northern political and social influences with it. The most important influence was the "free labor" doctrine: in simplified terms, a belief that humans were happiest and most productive, and created the best possible society, when they were allowed to work by their own choice and for their own benefit. The free labor doctrine formed an important part of antislavery sentiment; border-state residents never subscribed to abolition in any significant numbers, but it is likely that the doctrine gradually helped erode their commitment to slavery.

Economic changes also eroded the institution of slavery in many areas. For example, between 1760 and 1820, Maryland and Delaware moved from an agricultural economy based on tobacco, a crop heavily dependent on year-round intensive labor and thus ideally suited to slave labor, to a mixed economy dominated by shipbuilding and other trades requiring labor skills not associated with slavery and by production of wheat and corn, seasonal crops equally unsuited to slave labor. As a result, by 1860, both states had more free blacks than slaves, and it was widely believed slavery would soon become extinct in both. The same forces were working in a milder form in Kentucky, Missouri, western Virginia, and Tennessee.[6]

There were also deep cultural differences among Southern whites. The Tidewater and Piedmont areas of the Southern seaboard states were first settled by migrants from south and west England, loyal to the Anglican church and generally supportive of the monarchy in its struggles with Parliament for power during the seventeenth century. In the New World, these sentiments translated into a planter-dominated society that was culturally conservative and highly hierarchical. The Appalachian hill country, comprising the western portions of Virginia and the Carolinas and northwest Georgia, was largely settled by Scots-Irish (Scots and north Englanders who had colonized northern Ireland after the Protestant reformation). They were religious dissenters who viewed all forms of governmental authority with suspicion and desired only to be left alone; they had few slaves but had no great love for blacks.[7]

Hill and lowland cultural divisions were replicated as new southwestern states, including Alabama, Mississippi, Tennessee, Kentucky, Missouri, and Arkansas, were settled after American independence. In addition to their religious and political differences, hill and lowland regions in the newer states had fundamentally different views of the American union. Hill people in Kentucky and Tennessee took great pride in the fact that they had been the first Americans to settle the trans-Appalachian region and had held it for the United States during the American Revolution. This legacy created a unique bond to the Union. States carved out of areas first settled by Spain and France added unique elements to the Southern cultural mix. Texas and Louisiana borrowed heavily from Spanish and French civil law systems; they also had large Catholic populations that supported slavery but favored a more humanistic view of slaves than their Protestant Anglo neighbors. Spanish and French officials in colonial Louisiana permitted the development of a substantial free black community, which was augmented at the beginning of the nineteenth century by a large influx of free blacks fleeing war and revolution in Haiti and Dominica. The New Orleans free black community gained early experience with black self-governance and would eventually play an important role in shaping Louisiana's Reconstruction policies.[8]

WAR AND THE RESTORATION PERIOD

The war also affected the Southern and border states in different ways. The Deep South states were the first to secede. In the Upper South states of Virginia, North Carolina, Tennessee, and Arkansas, Unionists from the hill regions and elsewhere had sufficient strength to block secession until the bombardment of Fort Sumter in April 1861. The outbreak of war forced Southern Unionists to choose sides. Most stayed with their states and reluctantly supported secession, but in the four border slave states (Missouri, Kentucky, Maryland, and Delaware), economic and personal ties to the North proved strong enough to defeat secession. Unionists in western Virginia formed a loyal government that was admitted to the Union in 1863 as the state of West Virginia. Because they remained loyal, the border states were not occupied or subjected to Congressional Reconstruction after the war, but like their Confederate sisters, they had to modify their legal systems to accommodate emancipation and to remedy wartime destruction. In many cases, their modifications were strikingly similar to those of the ex-Confederate states.

The war brought different degrees of destruction to different states. Most of the war's major battles were fought in the border and Upper South states, and as a result, those regions experienced heavy wartime destruction. The western border states were plagued by guerrilla warfare as well. Missouri's wartime government largely ceded the task of keeping order to federal troops and a newly expanded state militia, but Kentucky, which in many respects followed a unique path during the war and Reconstruction, tried to use civil law to control the whirlwind of war. Only Texas and Florida escaped the war without serious damage, and this was reflected in their reaction to the new order of things at the end of the war: five months before Appomattox, the Texas legislature proclaimed that Texans "were free to govern themselves as they, and not as others saw fit . . . we are forbidden to admit a thought of further association with the people of the North."[9]

Reconstruction began in late 1863 when Abraham Lincoln introduced a plan to bring the seceded states back into the Union as they were retaken by Union forces. Under Lincoln's plan, state residents could take an oath pledging loyalty to the federal government and supporting abolition of slavery; whenever the number of oath-takers equaled 10 percent of the number of votes cast in the last prewar election, the state could reorganize if it agreed to abolish slavery. Arkansas and Louisiana met this requirement and created new governments and constitutions in 1864; Tennessee followed suit in early 1865.

After the Confederacy collapsed in April 1865, Andrew Johnson quickly adopted a presidential reconstruction plan similar to Lincoln's: he granted amnesty to all who would take an oath similar to the 10-percent plan oath and instructed the conquered states to call constitutional conventions to abolish slavery, with the expectation that the states would then resume full participation in the Union. The period that followed (1865–68) is referred to in this book as the Restoration period because most of those who took the reins of power were sincere Unionists but were also members of the prewar elite in their states. They accepted the reality that the war had destroyed slavery, and they abolished the institution with little hesitation, but they also enacted black codes largely adapted from prewar slave and free black codes, thus making clear that Southern whites could not easily view blacks in fundamentally new ways. Several state codes were so similar to prewar slave codes that they attracted extensive and unfavorable attention in the North and in Congress.[10]

During 1866, Johnson and Congressional Republicans waged a fierce struggle over the extent to which the Southern social and legal system should be reformed before the former Confederate states were readmitted to full participation in the Union. The Republican majority in Congress was divided between Radicals and moderates. Radicals had long believed that unless Southern blacks were given civil and political rights fully equal to those of whites the sacrifices of the war would have been in vain; that the South could not be trusted to give blacks full equality; and that Congress must create permanent guarantees of such rights. Moderates were more reluctant to impose reform from above: they hoped that oath laws and other measures promoting Unionist control of state and local governments would eventually result in state governments creating meaningful equality on their own. The black codes and continuing reports of widespread violence and mistreatment of blacks in the South eventually led many moderates to side with the Radicals, and in April 1866, Congress passed over Johnson's veto the first great civil rights act of the Reconstruction era. The 1866 Act guaranteed certain basic civil rights to all United States citizens, regardless of color, including the right to hold and inherit property and to sue and testify in court. Later the same year, Congress prepared the 14th Amendment to the United States Constitution. The amendment, which has become a cornerstone of Ameri constitutional law, was a compromise between Radicals and moderates: it protected blacks against state infringement of civil rights enjoyed by United States citizens, but it left open the question of whether it extended to other civil rights traditionally conferred by state law, such as the right to vote and to marry, and to infringement of civil rights by individuals.[11]

Except for Tennessee, Southern Restoration legislatures refused to ratify the 14th Amendment, mainly because of a combination of racist impulses and genuine concern for the preservation of state rights. The Civil War had forced the federal government to expand its role in American life dramatically: in addition to raising armies on an unprecedented scale, the government had nationalized the currency system, enacted the first income tax, and passed other measures that made it a permanent central force in the nation's economy. The federal government remained a major force in Southern local government during the Restoration period. The federal Freedmen's Bureau, created in 1865 to provide economic relief to destitute Southerners and ease friction between the races in the transition from slavery to freedom, actively intervened in state and local justice systems when it believed blacks were not being treated fairly, and local military commanders did the same. Southern legislators feared the 14th Amendment would pave the way for a permanent federal role in local and state law.[12]

CONGRESSIONAL RECONSTRUCTION

In March 1867, the core period of Reconstruction began when Congress passed a series of laws requiring a governmental transformation of the ex-Confederate states. The Reconstruction Acts placed the South under temporary military control, and the states were directed to frame new constitutions. Only persons willing to take a loyalty oath could participate in the process, and the constitutions must provide for black suffrage. The states would not be readmitted to representation in Congress until these conditions were met.

Unlike the Restoration constitutional conventions, most of which had made only minor changes to prewar constitutions, the Reconstruction conventions that met in 1867–68 created completely new documents. Their changes were not confined to civil rights: many conventions adopted other social and economic reforms such as homestead exemptions and married women's property rights, which had gained popularity before the war but had not penetrated the South completely. The conventions contained substantial numbers of black delegates, and provided the first opportunity in American history for blacks to have a real say in shaping the legal system under which they lived.[13]

Reconstruction legislatures in many states abolished the most obnoxious features of the Restoration black codes, but few of the legislatures aspired to create a social revolution. Whites across the political spectrum found integration distasteful and many black leaders, aware of this reality, chose not to press the point but instead devoted their energies to shoring up basic civil and political rights for blacks such as suffrage and jury service. For example, laws against interracial marriage remained on the statute books during Reconstruction in all states except Mississippi and South Carolina; on another front, legislatures responded to black demands for education by creating common school systems (though most failed to provide adequate funding), but only in Louisiana was a serious effort made to create integrated schools.[14]

There was less change in the courts than in other branches of government during Reconstruction. Most state supreme courts experienced a complete turnover of personnel under the new constitutions, but the border state courts and North Carolina's court did not. Reconstruction judges spent most of their time addressing issues unrelated to civil rights; challenges to debtor relief laws, questions of how to value wartime Confederate money transactions in federal currency, and everyday disputes over wills, contracts, accidents, and other matters made up the bulk of their workload. Some Reconstruction courts regularly broke with Restoration precedent in an attempt to inculcate federalist values in their constituents, but most did not.

Conservative whites reacted to Congressional Reconstruction in a variety of ways. The years between 1867 and 1871 marked the rise of the Ku Klux Klan and other white vigilante organizations that systematically harassed and assaulted blacks and white Republicans, particularly in areas where the races were roughly equal in number. After severe outbreaks of violence and disorder in the Carolinas in 1870–71, Congress enacted a new series of civil rights laws, which, along with the 1866 Act, formed the core of civil rights laws on which the second great civil rights movement of the mid-twentieth century would be based. The 1870–71 laws prohibited racial discrimination in voting rights and, more broadly, any action to deprive citizens of constitutional rights under color of state law. Congress gave the president broad powers to enforce the laws and also created a new cabinet-level agency, the Justice Department, which prosecuted Klan leaders and was able to obtain a substantial number of convictions despite the deep hostility of local whites.[15]

THE REDEMPTION PERIOD

The 15th Amendment to the federal Constitution, ratified in 1870, permanently guaranteed black suffrage throughout the United States but also put in motion a series of events that led to the "redemption" of the South from Reconstruction. In a sense it is astonishing that the amendment was ratified: as late as 1868, only a handful of states, mostly in New England, allowed blacks to vote. But the course of Reconstruction changed minds in both North and South. Most Northerners came to believe that federally guaranteed black suffrage was necessary to preserve basic civil rights for Southern blacks, and black suffrage at home no longer seemed so fearsome. Southern conservatives grudgingly recognized that in order to be free from military and Congressional control, they too must accept permanent black suffrage. But they also saw a political opportunity: sentiment was growing throughout the United States for "universal suffrage and universal amnesty," and conservatives hoped the 15th Amendment could be used to persuade state legislatures and Congress to lift remaining suffrage restrictions on ex-Confederates. By 1872, virtually all such restrictions had been eliminated, thus paving the way for conservatives' political resurgence.[16]

The resurgence came quickly. Congressional Reconstruction had never taken hold in Virginia and Georgia, where coalitions of conservatives and moderates gained control of state government in 1870. Between 1870 and 1873, conservatives regained full control of Texas and partial control of several other states; between 1873 and 1876, they regained complete control of North Carolina, Alabama, Mississippi, and Arkansas. The border states followed a similar pattern: Republicans who espoused goals similar to those of the Reconstruction governments lost control of Maryland in 1867, of Tennessee and Missouri in 1870, and of West Virginia in 1872. Kentucky and Delaware remained under conservative control throughout the Reconstruction era. In Louisiana and South Carolina, both of which had large and politically active black populations, and in Florida where Republicans had tried with some success to ally with moderate whites, conservative "redemption" took longer. In 1876, conservatives won close elections marred by violence and intimidation; and in early 1877, as part of a tacit bargain made in the disputed national election, the new Republican president, Rutherford Hayes, withdrew most remaining federal troops from the South, thus ensuring conservative control and permanently weakening the federal government's role as a deterrent to abuse of Southern blacks' civil rights.[17]

The effects of Reconstruction did not disappear after 1877. Some Redemption governments immediately enacted new constitutions in order to formalize their repudiation of Reconstruction, but many nonracial reforms of the Reconstruction era proved popular and in states where Reconstruction conventions had approached civil rights reform with caution, new constitutions were a matter of less urgency. Most Redemption governments quickly replaced Reconstruction supreme court judges but the reaction of the new judges to their predecessors' handiwork was measured: a few Reconstruction-era decisions concerning civil rights and federalism were overturned but many other decisions were upheld. Redemption judges generally refrained from overtly criticizing their predecessors: respect for precedent and a felt need for judicial consistency outweighed any impulse to express condemnation, even of an era that Southern conservatives would long regard as one of foreign occupation.

The Redemption era, which lasted in most Southern states until the mid-1890s, was marked by gradual erosion of blacks' civil rights at both the federal and state levels and by a modest readjustment of legal relations between the white upper and working classes. Redemption lawmakers developed an accommodation with black leaders based partly on paternalistic impulses and partly on a desire to minimize the risk of renewed federal intervention. Redemption legislatures repealed some of the more advanced civil rights measures their Reconstruction predecessors had enacted, such as Louisiana's school integration law, but most civil rights laws were left intact: racial control was achieved through custom and informal coercion rather than statutes. Some Reconstruction-era economic measures were also modified: for example, many states altered crop lien laws to favor landowners and merchants rather than sharecroppers. But Redemption legislatures devoted most of their attention to new matters, particularly regulation of railroads and limitation of state and local subsidies to railroads and other private enterprises. Redemption courts dealt primarily with economic issues but when civil rights cases came before them, they generally enforced the remaining Reconstruction-era laws faithfully.[18]

THE STRAIGHT-OUT ERA

After 1877, Northern interest in the plight of Southern blacks declined and interest in reconciling with Southern whites increased. Working-class Southern whites, many of whom viewed blacks as a threat to their livelihood and social status, gradually pressed Redemption leaders for more direct, "straight-out" measures against the perceived threat, including violence if necessary. By 1900, the "straight-out" era produced a variety of voting laws that were racially neutral on their face but effectively eliminated black suffrage in the South. The era also swept away the remaining Reconstruction constitutions, although the new constitutions preserved many nonracial reforms of the Reconstruction era, and it produced a wave of Jim Crow laws mandating segregation in public places and institutions. These laws were largely upheld by the federal Supreme Court in cases such as *Plessy v. Ferguson* (1896) and *Berea College v. Kentucky* (1908). There was little that Southern blacks and their white supporters could do to stop these trends. They had to content themselves with public protests and acts of witness, such as the debate during South Carolina's 1895 constitutional convention between Senator Ben Tillman, one of the founders of the "straight-out" movement, and former Reconstruction leaders Robert Smalls and William Whipper. Protest and witness would remain the lot of Southern blacks for another half-century until the second civil rights revolution started to bear fruit in the 1940s.[19]

It is no easy task to weave the legal changes of the Reconstruction era and the decades that followed into a coherent historical narrative. Most of the chapters that follow are devoted to a single aspect of law; different aspects of law were prominent at different times during the Reconstruction era, and where possible, they are presented in the order in which they rose to prominence. The book begins (Chapter 2) with an overview of the prewar social and legal conditions that shaped the views of Reconstruction-era lawmakers, including a brief summary of differences in the law of slavery among the Southern states and the various paths by which the Southern Unionist judges who presided during Reconstruction arrived at their views. Chapter 3 reviews the legal dislocations the Civil War caused in the Southern and border states and the use of loyalty oaths to define the struggle between Unionists and conservatives for postwar control of their states.

The book then turns to changes in Southern law during the Restoration and Congressional Reconstruction periods. Chapter 4 surveys the evolution of civil rights law during Reconstruction. It analyzes the black codes of 1865–66 and the movement to gain federal compensation for freed slaves, and asks whether these were at bottom a form of mourning for the lost institution of slavery. The chapter also examines the approaches that Reconstruction and Redemption legislatures took to civil rights laws, particularly laws concerning miscegenation and equality of access to trains, hotels, and other public places. Chapter 5 analyzes the South's reaction to the "new federalism" of the postwar era: concerns about increased federal power were articulated mainly by state supreme courts, which reacted in a variety of ways ranging from enthusiasm to muted opposition. Chapter 6 turns to the constitutional history of Reconstruction: it reviews Restoration and Reconstruction constitutions and explains how the latter made a permanent imprint on Southern legal history.

The book then turns to several nonracial areas of Southern law that changed in important ways during Reconstruction. Chapter 7 examines economic laws. Southern legislatures devoted a great deal of attention to debtor relief laws and laws governing the comparative rights of tenant farmers, landowners, and supply merchants to crops; state courts likewise expended much effort considering the constitutionality of such laws and attempting to reconcile them with traditional contract rights. Corporation law (discussed in Chapter 8) also played an important role in Reconstruction: lawmakers often were torn between the impulse to provide governmental assistance to railroads and other corporations and their desire to limit the risks of providing such assistance and control corporate abuses of economic power. Chapter 9 describes the advance of married women's property rights in the South during Reconstruction and the efforts of Southern women to obtain the vote.

The final section of the book surveys the legal aftermath of Reconstruction. Chapter 10 explains that Redemption-era lawmakers and courts pruned but did not entirely eliminate Reconstruction-era reforms. Chapter 11 surveys the "straight-out" era, particularly efforts to restrict black suffrage and civil rights without running afoul of the 14th and 15th Amendments, as well as the courts' reaction to such efforts and Southern blacks' acts of protest and witness against new laws. The book concludes (Chapter 12) by offering some thoughts on the major themes of Southern law during Reconstruction. It considers in particular the extent to which Reconstruction statutes and case law left a permanent imprint on Southern and American law, and the role Southern courts played in keeping the door to justice open at least a crack for Southern blacks until the coming of a second civil rights revolution.

The themes sounded by Abraham Lincoln and W.E.B. Du Bois in the quotations at the beginning of this chapter shape the sensibility of this book.

The Civil War and Reconstruction were products of fundamental differences in Northern and Southern culture, differences that have persisted in modified form to this day. Lincoln's insight that the North and South are in the end inseparable and therefore must come to understand each other and achieve enduring "terms of intercourse" in order for larger American ideals to prevail was ahead of its time in 1861 and, sadly, is still ahead of its time today. Du Bois's insight that Reconstruction is best understood by viewing black Americans not through the blinders of liberal or conservative stereotype but as "average and ordinary human beings" applies to nineteenth-century white Southerners as well. To view Americans of either race otherwise denigrates their essential humanity and impedes true understanding of the legal legacy of Reconstruction. This book tries in a small way to honor Lincoln's and DuBois's visions by illuminating a corner of Southern and American legal history that is little known but is vitally important to understanding the evolution of modern America.

Traveling the Political Dial: Political and Cultural Forces That Shaped Reconstruction-Era Lawmakers

> Some gentlemen have said to me, "Rather than permit free negroes to vote and hold office, we are ready for another war." I tell them, "No." Let us have peace, the war nearly ruined us—another war will finish the job. Let us try to make the most of a bad bargain, and not make bad worse.
> —Chief Justice Richmond Pearson (North Carolina), 1868

> I know it is difficult to get out of a net, to change ideas after you are fifty or sixty years old . . . but they have no right to force us younger people, who have new ideas and are to live under a new system, to hold their exploded views. . . . They must not expect me to go the gait they paced fifty years ago; they must not expect to make the Eastern Shore [of Maryland] like a province of China, where men do the same things, father and son, for a thousand years.
> —Judge Hugh L. Bond (Maryland), 1867[1]

In early 1861, Georgia governor Joseph Brown urged secession upon his constituents in fiery terms. The North, Brown argued, was "deadly hostile to the institution of slavery, and openly at war with the fundamental doctrines of the Constitution." If Georgia remained in the Union, "they will say that we have again blushed and submitted, as we always do." Brown's governorship ended with the Confederacy's defeat in 1865, and it appeared that his political career was over. But three years later, as a newly minted Republican, Brown was appointed to the Georgia supreme court. Chief Justice Brown then supported federal primacy using language that would have made Governor Brown blanch. In response to an argument that Georgia automatically regained its state rights at the end of the war, he retorted: "[This] is not only a practical absurdity, but is contrary to the usages which govern the intercourse between civilized nations, if not contrary to equity and common sense. . . . [T]he conqueror had the right to dictate the terms of settlement to the conquered, who were bound to submit to and carry them into effect."[2]

Brown's change of views was dramatic but hardly unique. Like their constituents, Southern lawmakers had to make their personal peace with emancipation and military defeat. The ways in which they did so were shaped in large part by the views they and their states had taken of slavery and the Union before the war, and also by an American legal culture that put a high value on continuity and predictability of the law and encouraged judges and lawyers to look for guidance to national treatises and court decisions. The nature of lawmakers' personal journeys played an important part in shaping postwar Southern law.

PREWAR LEGAL APPROACHES TO RACE

American slavery rested on two main pillars: a realization that the South's economic dependence on black labor made control of such labor essential, and a deep-seated desire among whites for racial homogeneity that could only be achieved through social separation.[3] But the proper degree of control was a subject of constant debate. As Georgia jurist Thomas R. R. Cobb explained, "the law looks favorably upon such conduct as tends to the proper subordination of the slave; but at the same time looks with a jealous eye upon all such conduct as tends to unnecessary and cruel treatment." Southern judges wrestled continuously with these competing considerations of economic interest and humanity and often struck very different balances between the two.[4] After the war, Reconstruction-era lawmakers were asked to determine what civil, political, and social rights blacks should be given that they did not have before the war. In order to answer this question, they again had to balance considerations of interest and humanity. Freedmen were no longer property, but were they fully human?

In order to understand the different responses these questions elicited, it is useful to examine how prewar black codes addressed the humanity of blacks. Three legal issues shed particular light on white attitudes to black humanity: protection of slaves from abuse by masters and other whites, restrictions on manumission, and the extent to which slaves were allowed to improve their condition through education and business enterprise.

Southern states recognized that controlling owner abuse of slaves presented perhaps the most direct conflict between considerations of interest and humanity. Judge Thomas Ruffin of North Carolina expressed this most famously in *State v. Mann* (1829):

The power of the master must be absolute to render the submission of the slave perfect. I must freely confess my sense of the harshness of this proposition; I feel it as deeply as any man can; and as a principle of moral right every person in his retirement must repudiate it. But in the actual condition of things it must be so. . . . The slave, to remain a slave, must be made sensible that there is no appeal from his master.[5]

All Southern states imposed at least minimal limits on slave punishment, for example, by making murder or life-threatening injury of slaves a crime, and a few states allowed slaves a limited right of self defense.[6] Louisiana's unique civil law system, based on the French Code Noir and the state's early Spanish code, provided comparatively generous rights and protections to blacks. Louisiana slaves were granted limited rights to own property and protect themselves from abuse; free blacks were granted more substantial liberty and property rights. The Code Noir prohibited slaveowners from breaking up black families by sale either as punishment or in order to satisfy creditors; some Upper South states later followed Louisiana's lead in this respect.[7]

Manumission was an equally contentious subject throughout the antebellum era because conceptually, it was only one step removed from general emancipation and a potential end to the slave system. Because slaves were property, the law created a presumption that slave owners could free their slaves at will. But as Cobb noted, "considerations of public policy have imposed restraints upon, and in some cases prohibited entirely, the exercise of this right."[8]

Prior to 1800, there were few restrictions on manumission anywhere in the South. There was a surge in manumissions in response to new concepts of freedom disseminated during the American Revolution. In the late 1700s, jurists in Virginia and Georgia went so far as to publicly propose gradual emancipation with compensation to owners. Kentucky's constitutional conventions of 1792 and 1799 seriously considered emancipation, and Virginia and Tennessee continued to debate emancipation seriously as late as the 1830s.[9] But shortly after 1800, a reaction took place in the Deep South: Georgia, Louisiana, and South Carolina prohibited manumission except with legislative consent. Other slave states enacted milder limitations: for example, in 1801 Tennessee adopted a system requiring court approval for manumission but allowing such approval on a variety of grounds so broad as to make approval almost routine.[10]

After 1830, a second reaction took place. Spurred by Nat Turner's 1831 slave rebellion in Virginia and by the steady growth of antislavery and abolition sentiment in the North, many slave states imposed new restrictions on manumission, required slaves to leave if they were freed, and even encouraged free blacks to return to slavery.[11] Some Upper South states resisted this trend. Arkansas enacted only sporadic restrictions on emancipation after 1830; Kentucky never modified its basic emancipation law of 1794. Maryland placed no restrictions of any sort on manumission, and in 1810 Delaware followed the pattern set by several Northern states in the late eighteenth century by requiring gradual emancipation of future-born children of manumitted slaves, thus "firmly setting physical and permanent slavery in Delaware on course for permanent extinction." The abolition sentiment that had bloomed briefly during the Revolution never completely died out in the border states: small but vocal abolition groups persisted in Kentucky, Tennessee, and Maryland to the eve of the Civil War.[12]

Surprisingly, several Deep South judges continued to defend manumission after 1830. The South Carolina supreme court, led by Chief Justice John Belton O'Neall, issued a series of decisions in the 1830s and early 1840s approving "quasi-emancipation" devices fashioned by Southern Quakers and other opponents of slavery to get around statutory restrictions on emancipation. For example, in *Carmille v. Carmille's Executors* (1842), the court upheld a deceased slaveowner's will that conveyed slaves to his heirs on condition that the heirs allow the slaves to have the use of their own time and labor. The court reasoned that the slaves' payment of a nominal annual fee to the new owners was sufficient to keep them in slavery, thus the state's 1820 antimanumission law did not apply. The court may have been motivated in part by a desire to preserve slaveowners' rights to full control of their property, but O'Neall also argued that broad freedom to manumit was necessary to save slavery itself: "Nothing will more assuredly defeat our institution of slavery, than harsh legislation rigorously enforced. . . . If it was so that a man dared not make provision to make more comfortable faithful slaves, hard indeed would be the condition of slavery. For then no motive could be held out for good conduct; and the good and the bad would stand alike."[13]

Courts in other states with emancipation restrictions, including Virginia and Georgia, also upheld quasi-emancipation devices; but as the Civil War approached, they began to retreat from their positions. The Virginia supreme court began to divide in the 1850s: several judges, including Richard Moncure, who would later serve on the state's Reconstruction court, consistently voted in favor of a broad right of manumission, but by 1858 a majority of the court generally opposed quasi-emancipation devices. Georgia's supreme court followed a similar pattern starting in 1853.[14]

Southern states varied greatly in the extent to which they allowed slaves and free blacks to improve themselves before the war. The South Carolina black code of 1740, which served as a guide for many Deep South states, prohibited masters from teaching their slaves reading, writing, or arithmetic; it reflected the fear of many whites that education would foster slave discontent and, eventually, rebellion. Beginning in the early 1830s, several Deep South states augmented their education restrictions and others, including Virginia, enacted restrictive laws for the first time.[15] The Upper South and border states felt less need to formally restrict slave education, preferring to leave the issue to individual masters. In those states, less dependent on agriculture than the Deep South, many masters believed they could make more money by teaching slaves a trade and hiring them out to local businesses.[16]

Southern states divided over the scope of entrepreneurial freedom to be given to blacks. Many planters believed slaves with special skills would be more productive and profitable if they were allowed some choice of employment and were allowed to keep a share of their earnings. Likewise, many planters believed field slaves should be allowed to farm small plots of their own and sell or barter their produce as an incentive to perform their regular work more productively. A few states forbade such practices outright, but most simply required the master's consent for such activities.[17]

Because of their sizable free black populations and declining slave populations, antebellum Maryland and Delaware foreshadowed what life would be like in the South after general emancipation. In 1810 Delaware enacted a liberal manumission law ensuring that the state would eventually become free, and by 1860 the same result was generally expected for Maryland.[18] But the approach of freedom triggered reactions in these states that found analogs in the rest of the South during Reconstruction. Delaware tried to ensure that freed blacks would not become an economic burden: it allowed the courts to punish blacks convicted of theft by hiring them out to masters for up to a year, and in 1849 the legislature enacted a harsh vagrancy law allowing similar temporary reenslavement of unemployed blacks.[19] During the colonial era, free blacks in Maryland had virtually the same civil rights as whites, but that began to change in the 1790s as the wave of Revolutionary-era manumissions receded. Between 1795 and 1810 Maryland enacted vagrancy laws similar to Delaware's; required free blacks to obtain certificates of good character from local officials in order to sell products or keep hunting equipment; and allowed its courts to apprentice children of destitute or unfit black parents to white masters.[20]

Maryland and Delaware thus demonstrated that whites could accept black freedom when changing economic or social conditions made that inevitable, but they could not accept too rapid a transition to freedom. Controls such as vagrancy and apprenticeship laws would be put in place and stoutly defended. Such controls were not merely transitional: many whites hoped they would encourage freed blacks to move elsewhere, thus eliminating the need to grapple with the deeper problems of racial integration and equality that would inevitably follow emancipation. St. George Tucker, an eminent Virginia jurist, expressed this sentiment when he proposed a gradual emancipation scheme for his state in 1803. "By denying [freed blacks] the most valuable privileges which civil government affords," said Tucker, "I wish to render it their inclination and their interest to seek those privileges in some other climate. . . . Under such an arrangement we might reasonably hope, that time would either remove from us a race of men, whom we wish not to incorporate with us, or obliterate these prejudices, which now form an obstacle to such incorporation."[21]

THE SCARS OF SOUTHERN UNIONISM

A large majority of Reconstruction-era judges had been Unionists before the war, but there were several varieties of Unionism in the South.

Some Southerners, particularly prewar Whigs, shared a vision of a diversified national economy bound together by roads, railways, and other public improvements sponsored by the federal government. Some supported the Union for more idealistic reasons: they viewed the United States as a grand experiment in democratic government and feared that secession would doom the experiment to failure.[22]

As their states seceded, Southern Unionists faced an agonizing choice whether to remain loyal to their principles or to their homes. For most, loyalty to their state and their neighbors proved more compelling than political principles, but they reached widely varying conclusions as to the extent of service they owed the Confederacy. Some Unionists joined the Confederate armies or served as high Confederate officials; some retired to private life and declined to associate with the Confederacy in any way; others compromised by serving as low-level officials or aiding the war effort as civilians.[23] A smaller group of unconditional Unionists continued to adhere to the Union after Sumter. In some states, they were forced into exile; in other states, they retreated to Unionist hill areas where they could find protection from draft officials and other Confederate authorities. The most prominent exiles, including Andrew Johnson of Tennessee and Andrew Jackson Hamilton of Texas, spent the war either administering occupied areas or raising and leading Union regiments composed of fellow exiles.[24]

PRAGMATISTS, CONSERVATIVES, AND OUTSIDERS: A COLLECTIVE PORTRAIT OF RECONSTRUCTION JUDGES

Reconstruction judges came to the bench after the Civil War with a wide variety of views about the meaning of the war and the postwar social order. Some were pragmatists who wanted to use the law to forge an accommodation between their constituents and the new order; others viewed themselves as souls outside the mainstream of Southern thought and advocated a radical reshaping of Southern law. Many of the "outsider" judges had gone through personal spiritual struggles that led them to embrace the Republicans' reform program; others embraced Republicanism because their secessionist neighbors had forced outsider status upon them.

Judicially Stable States: Virginia and North Carolina

Virginia and North Carolina had significantly less court turnover during Reconstruction than other ex-Confederate states. This was so partly because Unionists had a strong presence on both states' courts before the war. Richard Moncure of Virginia and North Carolina's Richmond Pearson were the only Southern judges who served throughout the war and Reconstruction periods.

Moncure, the son of a prominent Virginia family, served on his court almost continuously from 1851 until his death in 1882. He generally favored humanity over interest in prewar slave cases; a Whig Unionist, he remained with Virginia after Fort Sumter but was more interested in law than politics and favored accommodation to the new order after the war. The conservative government that took control of the state in 1870 retained Moncure, and its other appointees were mostly Whig Unionists who had stayed with the South during the war but had engaged in local government service or private practice rather than military service.[25]

North Carolina's Reconstruction court included Pearson, one of the South's leading pragmatists, and Thomas Settle, one of the leading "outsider" judges. Pearson had a brief political career before the war but gained his principal fame as a legal scholar and educator. He was appointed to the North Carolina supreme court in 1848, became chief justice in 1858, and served until his death in 1878. Pearson was a member of the planter class but like Moncure, he generally emphasized humanity over economic interest in slave cases. During the war, he consistently defended North Carolina's state prerogatives against the central government at Richmond; during Reconstruction, he tried to shape North Carolina law to accommodate the new order by showing due respect for federal power and protecting the basic civil rights of blacks, but at the same time he tried to prevent any economic or political retaliation against former Confederates. Pearson's philosophy made him unpopular in many quarters: when Governor William Holden was impeached in 1870 for declaring martial law in the central part of the state in order to quell Ku Klux Klan activity, Pearson presided over the trial, was accused of being too supportive of Holden, and as a result, was nearly impeached himself.[26]

Settle joined Pearson on the court in 1868. Settle gravitated to his outsider sensibility as naturally as Pearson gravitated to pragmatism: in the words of one commentator, "the major part of his life was passed in opposition to the prevailing current of opinion." As a young man, Settle advocated increased rights for North Carolina's working-class whites and small farmers. He served briefly in the Confederate army but for him, as for many Southerners, the war became "a clarifying moment that altered his life and placed him on a path utterly unthinkable a few short years earlier."[27] Settle was deeply disturbed by the violence and destruction of war: he accepted the war's outcome as a divine judgment that North Carolina's prewar slave society must be thoroughly uprooted, and he concluded the Republicans offered the best hope of furthering that ideal. Slavery, Settle proclaimed, was "a blight and mildew upon every land it ever touched. Educated labor and machinery are what we now need, to make this country what it should be." Like virtually all Southern whites, Settle opposed social equality between the races, but he was disturbed by the widespread resistance to even minimal civil rights for blacks and argued that "forty millions of the great Anglo-Saxon race should . . . be

Chief Justice Richmond Pearson, North Carolina. Courtesy of the Commissioners of Yadkin County.

willing to give to four millions of poor, ignorant, slave-ridden Africans an equal and fair race in the contest of life" and "pull down none, but . . . elevate all." Settle resigned in 1876 to pursue an unsuccessful campaign for the governorship; President Hayes then appointed him to a federal district judgeship in Florida, where he served until his death in 1888.[28]

The Fluctuating States

There was very little judicial continuity in the Deep South after the war. Supreme court judges appointed during the Restoration period gave way to new courts and judges under Congressional Reconstruction, and they in turn gave way to Redemption courts and judges. The philosophies and experiences of each group differed greatly; the judges within each group were also far from monolithic.

During the Restoration period, many Southern states retained wartime judges on their courts and most felt free to appoint judges who had actively sympathized with the Confederacy. Charles Dupont and William Forward of Florida and Mississippi's William Harris, Henry Ellett, and Alexander Handy were leading examples of secessionist judges who remained on their courts after the war. Judge Handy arguably represented the outer limit of how far ex-Confederate states were willing to go in retaining judges who would preserve traditional values: he was "immovably Southern in his views," had supported secession "both as a right and a necessity," and had performed special service in 1861 as Mississippi's official envoy to his native Maryland in an unsuccessful effort to persuade that state to join the Confederacy.[29]

A few states, most notably Georgia, limited themselves after the war to judges who possessed Unionist credentials or had remained aloof from politics. Chief Justice Joseph Lumpkin, who had served on Georgia's supreme court since its inception in 1845, had acquired a national reputation that enabled him to continue his service after the war. Lumpkin's colleagues Iverson Harris and Dawson Walker had spent most of their careers as lawyers and circuit

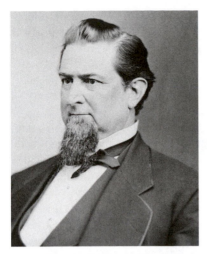

Judge Thomas Settle, North Carolina.
Courtesy of the Library of Congress.

judges and had not been enthusiastic about the Confederacy. Even states less shy about retaining Confederate sympathizers chose for their courts some moderates who had not actively supported the Confederacy during the war. William Byrd and Thomas Judge of Alabama and Arkansas's chief justice David Walker were leading members of this group.[30]

There was also considerable variation among Deep South judges during the Congressional Reconstruction period. A number of Reconstruction judges were unconditional Unionists who, like Thomas Settle, viewed themselves as Southern outsiders. Unlike Settle, however, their outsider status was as much externally imposed as self-imposed. Andrew Jackson Hamilton, Amos Morrill, Lemuel Evans, and Wesley Ogden of Texas spent the war in enforced exile from their state and actively aided the Union war effort. Thomas Peters of Alabama took refuge from the war among fellow Unionists in the north of his state and James Taliaferro of Louisiana, one of the few delegates to vote against secession at his state's 1861 convention, was imprisoned by Confederate authorities for much of the war.[31]

Hamilton was the most prominent and most colorful of the Deep South's outsider judges. His career in many ways was a frontier counterpart of Settle's. Hamilton moved to Texas from Alabama in 1846 and became a committed Unionist in a state where few shared his views. In the late 1850s, he allied with Sam Houston to combat the rising tide of secession sentiment in Texas; his outspoken views earned him the partly humorous, partly derisive, nickname "Colossal Jack." On the eve of the war, Texas was still a frontier state, "a world where the consciousness of war and killing was ever present." This sensibility led many Texans to view persons with opposing opinions as enemies to be destroyed; as a result, after Lincoln's election, Hamilton and other Unionists were given a choice between silence and exile. Hamilton fled to Washington, where he spent the war raising troops among fellow exiles and dramatizing their plight in speeches to Northern audiences in order to promote enthusiasm for the war.[32]

After the war, Hamilton dedicated the remaining 10 years of his life to restoring Texas to the Union spiritually as well as politically. Andrew Johnson appointed him provisional governor of Texas at the end of the war, and in 1868 he was appointed to the Texas supreme court. During his two years of service on the court, Hamilton used his position to defuse the cult of

Judge Andrew Jackson "Colossal Jack" Hamilton, Texas. Courtesy of the Library of Congress.

the Lost Cause as much as possible, urging Texans to accept the new postwar order and reject the "confederation of states entered into in hostility to the national authority and for its final overthrow . . . illegal and treasonable in [its] character."[33]

Most Reconstruction judges, however, were prewar Unionists who took little part in the war. Some, such as Florida's James Westcott, served as district judges or in other civil positions not related to the war effort; others, such as Florida's Ossian Hart and Texas's Albert Latimer, simply rusticated themselves for the war's duration.[34] Georgia presented an unusual case: Joseph Brown, the ex-secessionist, tried to lead the Reconstruction court to full acceptance of the postwar order, but his colleague Hiram Warner, a prewar Unionist, counseled caution.

During his long career, Brown, in the words of one Georgia historian, "travelled the political dial from doctrinaire states' rights Democrat and secessionist to Radical Republican scalawag and finally to Bourbon Democrat without more than temporary loss of face or fortune or his essential popularity in Georgia." Brown was elected governor in 1857 as a states' rights Democrat; he came out for secession immediately after Lincoln's election, but during the war he lobbied the Richmond government persistently for the right to control Georgia troops, to the point where he was regarded by Richmond as an impediment to the war effort. Sherman's 1864 campaign through Georgia gave Brown a personal taste of the destruction the war visited upon his state, but at the end of the war Brown, like Pearson, wasted little time mourning the Confederacy: he jettisoned his prewar views on slavery and states' rights and adopted economic recovery as his paramount goal. Brown cultivated federal officials and Georgia Unionists, mainly because he believed recovery could be achieved more quickly by cooperation than resistance. When Georgia's new Reconstruction constitution went into effect in 1868, Governor Rufus Bullock rewarded Brown by appointing him chief justice.

The Georgia supreme court was little more than a way station for Brown, but during his two years on the bench he made a significant impact on Georgia law, consistently rejecting legal challenges to Reconstruction economic reforms. Ironically, Brown held that many of the measures of his own wartime administration were invalid: he stated bluntly that the result of the war compelled such decision. After leaving the court in 1870, he worked actively for economic development and amnesty for ex-Confederates; he allied with conservatives as he sensed the end of Reconstruction growing near, and in 1877, once more a Democrat, he won election to the United States Senate.[35]

Hiram Warner was Brown's opposite in many respects. Like Pearson, Warner tried to forge through law a smooth transition from the old order to the new during Reconstruction, but he based his jurisprudence more on abstract principle and less on pragmatism than did Pearson. Warner's life and views were shaped by an unusual mix of regional forces. Born and raised in New Hampshire, he moved to Georgia as a young man to take a teaching post but quickly gravitated to the law. He rose to prominence in the Georgia bar and served on the state's supreme court from 1845 to 1855. Warner's politics reflected a mix of Northern and Southern influences: he opposed South Carolina's nullification movement in the 1830s as a young man and remained a Unionist throughout his life, but he also became a planter and consistently defended slavery. Warner was a lonely voice of opposition at Georgia's 1861 secession convention, but he ultimately chose to support his state and sign the ordinance of secession.

Warner believed devoutly in legal process and social order; his beliefs perhaps intensified at the end of the war when a Union raiding party occupied his plantation and made him the subject of a mock hanging, cutting the noose around his neck only at the last moment. He was reappointed to the court near the end of the Restoration period; Bullock renewed the appointment under the Reconstruction constitution because of Warner's judicial reputation and because there were few other proven Unionists available for the post. Warner was not prepared to nullify acts of the Confederacy as readily as Brown, and he was considerably more skeptical of Reconstruction economic reforms. Brown argued that Georgia's Reconstruction legislature should be given great leeway in light of the need to relieve postwar poverty and repair wartime destruction, but Warner made clear that for him sanctity of contract trumped all other considerations. Brown usually persuaded the court's third member, Henry McCay, to side with him but Warner prevailed in the long run: on several occasions the United States Supreme Court upheld his views and overturned his colleagues' decisions. Warner's conservatism won him reappointment to the court after Reconstruction ended, and he remained there until his death in 1881.[36]

Horatio Simrall of Mississippi, like Warner, was a product of interregional forces. He was born in Kentucky in 1818, attended college there and in Indiana, and moved to Mississippi in 1838, where he became a lawyer and state legislator. Simrall displayed a strong progressive streak early in his career as a leader of the movement for free public schools in Mississippi, and in 1857, perhaps preferring the more mild system of slavery that existed in the border states, he moved back to Kentucky. But when the war came, he went against his native state and sided with the South, serving as lieutenant governor of

Kentucky's short-lived Confederate government that was established when Confederate general Kirby Smith occupied Lexington in 1862. After Smith's invasion failed, Simrall returned to Mississippi. He was elected to the state's first postwar legislature and took a centrist position: he supported basic civil rights for freedmen and opposed the most egregious features of the black code enacted by his colleagues but he also led a successful fight to prevent Mississippi from ratifying the 14th Amendment.

In 1870, conservative Unionist governor James Alcorn appointed Simrall to Mississippi's Reconstruction court, where he remained until 1878. Simrall played an important role in the Mississippi court's decision to steer a moderate course. He voted to uphold many Reconstruction reform measures, including one of the first American laws granting blacks equal access to public accommodations, but like Warner, he firmly defended property and contract rights against reform laws when the two conflicted. Simrall ended his career on a characteristically mixed note. In 1890 he was one of only two Republicans elected to Mississippi's Redemption constitutional convention, but rather than protest the convention's avowed purpose of disfranchising black voters, he prepared the main committee report recommending disfranchisement and explained how that might be done without violating the 14th and 15th Amendments.[37]

Only a handful of Reconstruction judges were "carpetbaggers," that is, Northerners who had moved South after the war. Postwar governors and legislatures preferred to appoint native Unionists wherever possible, and they selected recent Northern immigrants only when the pool of natives not disqualified by Confederate service was simply too small to yield good candidates. Like their native Unionist colleagues, carpetbag judges were far from monolithic. South Carolina's Ammiel Willard and Florida's Edwin Randall deliberately hewed a moderate course and took pains to cultivate a respectable image among conservatives. As a result, each remained on his court after Reconstruction ended in his state. Moses Walker of Texas and Jonathan Tarbell of Mississippi were somewhat more supportive of reform measures but did not view themselves as true reformers or as career jurists.[38]

The only carpetbag judge who actively involved himself in reform politics, and the only one whom Southern conservatives truly reviled, was Chief Justice John McClure of Arkansas. McClure, a native Ohioan, entered Arkansas with Union forces in 1863; he remained after the war, bought a plantation, became active as a Republican politician and editor and was appointed to Arkansas's Reconstruction court in 1868. While on the court, he vocally supported Radical governor Powell Clayton: when Clayton was impeached in 1870, McClure issued an injunction preventing Clayton's lieutenant governor from taking his place. As a result, McClure was also impeached and avoided removal from office only narrowly. Undeterred, he remained politically active throughout the remainder of the state's Reconstruction period; after Reconstruction ended, he remained in Arkansas and continued to speak out on public matters until his death in 1915.[39]

Like Warner, a number of Reconstruction judges had been born in the North but had moved to the South as young men and made their careers there. They were in no way carpetbaggers: because of their Northern upbringing most were Unionists, but they remained loyal to their adopted states during the war. The sharp economic and social shifts that followed the war sent them in different political directions. Some, such as Alabama's Elisha Peck and Mississippi's Ephraim Peyton, found no difficulty making the transition to the Republican Party and actively supported the new order but several, most notably Warner, concluded it was important to preserve as much of the prewar social order as possible, and they were often less supportive of Reconstruction reform measures than their colleagues. Chief Justice John Ludeling of Louisiana was an unusual hybrid: he was a native of his state but his parents had immigrated to Louisiana from France and Dominica respectively, and he maintained close ties with his wife's family in New York. Ludeling's status as a double outsider reinforced his inclination to support Republicanism and reform in his state.[40]

The Border States

Although the border states were not subject to formal reconstruction, several of them experienced postwar political and judicial shifts similar to those of ex-Confederate states. Republicans gained control of Missouri, Tennessee, and Maryland during the war and also created the new state of West Virginia; they retained control of Maryland until 1867 and of the other states until the early 1870s. Reconstruction judges in these states were divided between Republicans such as Sam Milligan and James Shackelford of Tennessee, who had supported Union efforts to retake their states and viewed support of Republican aims after the war as a logical extension of their crusade, and moderates such as their colleague Alvin Hawkins, who sided with the South during the war and afterward gradually drifted toward the conservatives.[41] Redemption courts in the border states were closely divided between men such as Tennessee's A.O.P. Nicholson and West Virginia's Alpheus Haymond, who had enthusiastically supported the Confederacy and had bided their time in political exile during Reconstruction, and hill conservatives such as Tennessee's Thomas A. R. Nelson, who opposed the Confederacy during the war and Republican reforms after the war with equal fervor.[42]

The Civil War and Reconstruction had a particularly striking effect on two border state judges who became important figures in the history of American civil rights, Hugh Bond of Maryland and John Marshall Harlan of Kentucky. Both men started their careers as conservative Unionists who were comfortable with slavery, but the turmoil of war and emancipation impelled both men to advocate black rights in ways that previously would have been unthinkable to them.

Bond was born in Baltimore in 1828; he was educated in New York, returned to Maryland to practice law and was appointed Baltimore's criminal court judge in 1860. As slavery decayed in Maryland, Bond's attachment to the system declined correspondingly. During the war, he became an active Unionist and eventually endorsed emancipation, recognizing that the war would end slavery in Maryland regardless of its military outcome. Soon after Maryland emancipated its remaining slaves in 1864, Bond received an opportunity to give emancipation practical meaning and he took it. Maryland state courts apprenticed thousands of newly freed slave children to white masters even though Maryland's apprenticeship laws required that parents' wishes be consulted and allowed only illegitimate children and children whose parents suffered from "extreme indigence or poverty" to be apprenticed. The apprenticeship abuses offended Bond deeply. Bond believed blacks did not have the inherent ability to achieve social or economic equality with whites, but he also believed they had a right to try. "If [a black person] can get a living," said Bond, "let him get it; if he cannot, let him go without; only throw no obstacles in his way."[43]

When Maryland's supreme court rejected a challenge to the apprenticeship law, Bond stepped in. He worked with the federal Freedmen's Bureau to discourage apprenticeship abuses and regularly issued habeas writs from his court directing the release of apprenticed black children. His efforts were sufficiently effective that Maryland's conservative 1867 legislature deprived his court of jurisdiction over apprenticeship cases. Bond responded by adhering even more firmly to his creed. Like Settle, he ran unsuccessfully as the Republican candidate for governor at the end of his state's Reconstruction period, and like Settle, he soon reappeared on the federal bench: in 1869, President Grant appointed him the first judge of the newly created federal Fourth Circuit Court of Appeals. During the early 1870s, Bond presided over several of the first major trials for violation of federal civil rights laws, and he was instrumental in ensuring that despite fierce local resistance to federal law enforcement, the trials were completed and convictions were enforced.[44]

John Marshall Harlan's personal journey was similar to Bond's. Harlan was born into a prominent political family in Louisville in 1833; like Bond, he started his career as a conservative Unionist and a slaveowner. Harlan opposed secession in 1861, but unlike many of his fellow Kentuckians, he believed his state must actively support the Union war effort rather than remaining neutral. Harlan was commissioned a brigadier general and saw extensive combat service before returning to civilian life in 1864. His war experience put him more firmly on the side of the Union and convinced him that emancipation was inevitable. When Kentucky Unionists split into Republican and conservative factions at war's end, Harlan knew he had to make a fundamental choice, and he sided with the Republicans.

Harlan viewed this decision as a crossroads in his life and once he made it, he did not look back. In an astonishingly short time he not only shed his remaining doubts about the wisdom of emancipation but fully embraced black civil and political rights, including suffrage, both as a practical necessity for the postwar South and as a moral good. Harlan built up Kentucky's Republican

Party and tried to improve civil rights for black Kentuckians; he had more political than legal success, and like Settle and Bond, he narrowly lost a race for his state's governorship. In 1877 President Hayes, seeking a strong Southern Unionist for the United States Supreme Court, chose Harlan, who served on the High Court until his death in 1911. Throughout his judicial career, Harlan was an often-lonely voice on the Court for civil rights, most notably as a dissenter in such cases as the *Civil Rights Cases* (1883) and the *Plessy* and *Berea College* cases. Harlan consistently protested his colleagues' narrow construction of the scope of Reconstruction civil rights laws and their propensity to delegate civil rights enforcement to the states.[45]

SOUTHERN JUDGES AND AMERICAN JUDICIAL CULTURE

Southern judicial behavior was heavily influenced by a broader American judicial culture containing strong elements of nationalism and judicial conservatism. The culture was conservative in that it encouraged judges from all regions to insulate themselves from politics as much as possible, to decide legal issues based on a highly standardized process of reasoning, and to follow the decisions of their predecessors wherever possible in order to promote certainty and stability in the law. It was nationalistic in that it encouraged judges to take guidance, where appropriate, from jurists throughout the United States and Europe. The culture, which had developed after the American Revolution, was well entrenched on the eve of the Civil War and continued to thrive after the war, so much so that three-quarters of a century later, a leading authority on the American legal profession commented: "Tenacity of a taught legal tradition is much more significant in our legal history than the economic conditions of time and place. . . . [There has been] a *communis opinio* over the country as a whole on the overwhelming majority of legal questions, despite the most divergent geographical, political, economic, social and even racial conditions."[46]

Judicial conservatism and nationalism rested on several pillars, including the British common law tradition, a national body of legal literature, and the intersectional experiences of many judges. During the colonial era, American judges generally followed British common law, and this continued after independence. As a separate body of American law developed, state courts, including those of the South, had ready access to published decisions from other states and looked to them for guidance as to novel and difficult issues of law. These bonds were reinforced by nationally circulated legal treatises such as Sir William Blackstone's *Commentaries on the Law of England* (1765–69), New York Chancellor James Kent's *Commentaries on American Law* (1826), and Justice Joseph Story's *Commentaries on Equity Jurisprudence* (1836). Likewise, judges in all regions were schooled in the standard modes of judicial analysis the Anglo-American system had created. Their duty was to listen to and weigh competing arguments and evidence and make a decision, and they were expected to explain in detail the reasons and authorities that supported their decision. Such forces were instrumental in shaping among judges a common, national conception of many areas of law.[47]

Many Southern judges also had personal experience with other regions of the United States that their constituents did not. Some had spent time at Northern colleges, primarily Princeton and Yale; others attended Transylvania College in Lexington, Kentucky, which enjoyed a national reputation for excellence and a national student body.[48] A surprising number of Southern judges—Warner is a leading example—were born in the North and moved to the South as young men; though they quickly adapted to slavery and other Southern institutions, their early Northern experience often provided a moderating influence when the sectional crisis came. The role of Northern-born judges long resident in the South increased after the war: because many of them were prewar Unionists, they were less likely to be disqualified from holding office on account of Confederate service and they were attractive candidates to the Unionists who controlled Reconstruction-era state governments.

In short, Southern lawmakers brought a wide variety of sensibilities, connected by a strong Unionist thread, to their task of responding to the new postwar order. Southern Unionism put an enduring stamp on Southern legal history, but the many legal dilemmas that Unionist judges had to address during Reconstruction would send them down different paths. For many lawmakers that journey began with the effort to preserve basic civil order during the Civil War and to adjust to the new central government at Richmond.

CHAPTER 3

Law and the Wartime South

> Everyone has something unpleasant to remember, and many have wrongs to revenge. . . . The denunciations of parties, the hazard of costs and damages, and the inflictions of punishments, would not only keep alive these evils, but would cause them to spread like a pestilence. . . . [I]t will be a great public good if the past can be forgiven and forgotten.
> —Chief Justice Richmond Pearson (North Carolina), 1867

> The insurgents secure immunity to themselves, in proportion as their numbers are formidable, their deeds unlawful, and as they increase their own necessities for converting the private property of unoffending citizens. . . . If this be the true rule, the peaceful private citizen may be plundered without redress. . . . [Amnesty] would offer a premium to treason, and beset the pathway of peace and loyalty with difficulty and danger.
> —Judge George Loomis (West Virginia), 1867[1]

In early 1861, Simon Bolivar Buckner, a West Point graduate and former army officer, was one of a small group of trained military professionals whose services both the Union and the Confederacy urgently desired. Buckner cast his lot with the Confederacy but his state, Kentucky, did not. The Confederacy quickly made Buckner a general, but he had a difficult war: he was forced to surrender Fort Donelson to U.S. Grant in early 1862, and after his release, he spent the rest of the war serving in equally unsuccessful campaigns. Buckner's misfortunes did not end with the war: in 1861 Kentucky's Unionist legislature passed a law making Confederate soldiers legally liable for their wartime actions, and the Louisville & Nashville Railroad obtained a judgment against Buckner for the cost of a bridge his troops had destroyed in the Fort Donelson campaign. The L&N took virtually all of Buckner's property to pay the judgment and Buckner exiled himself from Kentucky. But in 1866, with the threat of rebellion and destruction at an end, the legislature repealed the liability law. The L&N was forced to return Buckner's property to him and he returned home; five years later, Kentucky's supreme court required the railroad to compensate him for his lost income from the property as well.[2]

Although Buckner ultimately obtained vindication, he and many other Confederates were buffeted during the war and Reconstruction by shifting opinions as to the rights and liabilities supporters of the rebellion should have. Should Confederate supporters and returning Confederate troops be excluded from suffrage and other political and civil rights? Should former combatants be held liable for damage they had caused during the war? These were particularly urgent matters in the border and Upper South states, which were closely divided politically. State lawmakers had to strike a balance between punishment and leniency. The approaches that different states took to these issues provided useful clues to the approaches they would take to other political and legal issues during Reconstruction.

THE DRAFT LAW CONTROVERSY

The Civil War triggered dramatic, if temporary, changes in Southern states' legal business. With many Southerners away on military service, the number of civil and criminal cases in the courts decreased dramatically; in addition, many courts had to close down as Union forces approached. Southern legislatures and courts turned their attention away from peacetime legal issues and focused on military matters, including the validity and scope of the Confederate draft that began in 1862.

The Confederate draft laws were highly unpopular. Despite the intense pressure placed on Southern men to join the armed forces, many did not want to risk their lives. The draft laws exempted overseers and planters who owned more than 20 slaves, thus triggering complaints that the Confederacy was waging "a rich man's war and a poor man's fight." Confederate conscripts sent Southern courts a steady stream of *habeas corpus* petitions for release from military custody, claiming that the draft infringed their personal liberties or that they had unfairly been denied exemptions. The petitions and the Richmond government's attempt to conscript state officials into military service highlighted a fundamental dilemma of the Confederacy: did the principle of strong central government have a place in a society that owed its existence to secession from a central government?[3]

Southern courts were virtually unanimous in upholding the draft laws, but they did so with different degrees of enthusiasm. In two important test cases decided in late 1862, the Georgia and Texas supreme courts defended the draft on pragmatic rather than ideological grounds. They conceded the draft inevitably interfered with liberty and state sovereignty but emphasized that without it, the Confederacy could not survive. "If . . . in deference to state sovereignty the Confederate Government must depend upon the separate, unconcerted action of the several States," reasoned Georgia's Charles Jenkins, "it is but the shadow of a government, the experiment of confederated republics must inevitably fail, and the sooner it is abandoned the better." Not all judges agreed. James Bell of Texas argued that Confederate conscription was contrary to the original intent of the United States Constitution, incorporated into the Confederate constitution, that the central government would be limited to powers enumerated in the constitution and all other powers would be reserved to the states. George W. Stone worried that his colleagues on the Alabama supreme court were adopting a "mistaken theory of the oneness of our distinct [federal and state] governments." Stone hoped that after the war, when the Confederacy became permanent, the federalist "heresies which aided in overthrowing the old Union will not be allowed to enter into the sanctuaries of the new."[4]

Richmond Pearson was the most prominent skeptic. In 1863 Pearson and his colleagues on the North Carolina supreme court confirmed that because the Confederate central government had never established a fully functioning federal court system, state courts would have the final word on conscription cases and need not defer to military authorities. Confederate Secretary of War George Randolph and his successors repeatedly complained of Pearson's decision but reluctantly went along with it. Pearson was also disturbed by the Richmond government's decision in early 1864 to revive the draft eligibility of men who had previously procured substitutes. He felt the revival broke the contract the government had made with procurers of substitutes and in early 1864, he released a number of draftees for that reason. Later in the year his colleagues overruled him, but Pearson refused to recant in the face of criticism. He commented sardonically that "if the Courts assume the government may act on that principle . . . [that] 'necessity knows no law,' . . . [w]e may put aside the books and indulge the hope, that when peace again smiles on our country, law will resume its sway. *Inter arma, silent leges.*"[5]

Governors such as Joseph Brown of Georgia and Zebulon Vance of North Carolina became increasingly hostile to conscription as the war went on, and disputes arose as to how broadly they could use their powers to exempt state officials from the draft. Southern state courts struck a balance. They held that the Richmond government could not conscript truly essential state officials, but in a highly publicized clash with Brown, Georgia's supreme court rebuffed his efforts to induce Georgians to join the state militia rather than Confederate federal forces. In matters of troop disposition, the Richmond government was supreme.[6]

By upholding the draft law and the central government's authority, Southern courts were able simultaneously to confirm their loyalty to the Confederacy and keep the nationalistic prewar judicial culture in good repair. In so doing, they laid a foundation for judicial support of reconciliation and deference to federal authority after the war.

LAW AND ORDER IN THE WARTIME UPPER SOUTH

Union forces secured control of Missouri, Kentucky, and West Virginia in late 1861, but Confederate sympathizers continued to put up armed resistance in those states. Some organized guerrilla units that were loosely under the Richmond government's control; others engaged in bushwhacking and looting without Richmond's sanction and used the war as an excuse to settle personal grudges. Hangings, shootings, burnings, and forcible appropriation of civilian property were common. Regular and irregular troops often struck innocent targets, and in the heat of war, they wasted little time worrying about their mistakes. Confederate armies under Kirby Smith, Braxton Bragg, John Bell Hood, and Sterling Price repeatedly tried to win back Missouri, Kentucky, and Tennessee, and their advances and retreats contributed to the breakdown of law and order. A similar pattern of irregular fighting and violence unfolded in the hill regions of the Confederacy where Unionist sentiment endured. The pace of destruction accelerated and attitudes hardened as the war went on. Even Abraham Lincoln was not immune: as he explained to border Unionists in the summer of 1862, the war could not be fought "with elder-stalk squirts, charged with rose water. . . . The enemies [of the Union] must understand that they cannot experiment for ten years trying to destroy the government, and if they fail still come back into the Union unhurt."

As the war went on, military authorities took increasingly harsh measures to suppress guerrilla activity. "Tolerance, permissiveness, and even protection of the civil populace leading to reconciliation did not work. . . . Soon, loyalty oaths, confiscation and destruction of property, imprisonment, exile, and even some executions (for questionable acts conveniently labeled espionage) replaced the policy of lenience." These measures succeeded for the most part, but they inflicted scars and contributed greatly to lingering bitterness that played an important role in shaping postwar law and politics in the border and Upper South states.

The wartime governments of Missouri, Tennessee, and West Virginia were created hastily in order to replace Confederate-leaning administrations; they concentrated on military measures necessary to ensure their survival. Kentucky was the only border state that made a serious effort to regulate wartime violence through its civilian legal system.[7] In 1861 the Kentucky legislature enacted an expatriation law making participation by state citizens in any invasion of the state a felony; the following year, it enacted a broad sedition law criminalizing membership in secessionist societies and other acts that aided the Confederacy. Kentucky also prohibited its citizens from encouraging Confederate enlistments, penalized those who encouraged Confederate troops or guerrillas or failed to warn authorities of their approach, and gave victims of Confederate attacks the right to sue their attackers and collect damages.[8] But at the same time, Kentucky attempted to preserve its prewar social order and check the expansion of federal authority as much as possible. Early in the war, it petitioned the Lincoln administration to limit the war's objective to preservation of the Union rather than emancipation, and the legislature objected loudly when emancipation of slaves in Confederate-controlled areas and recruitment of black troops became part of the Union war strategy. Many Kentuckians resented the Lincoln administration's imposition of martial law on parts of the state and were disappointed by the federal government's failure to compensate them for wartime damage. After the war, as Confederate sympathizers returned and Kentucky Unionists felt free to express their resentment of federal wartime control measures, the legislature quickly repealed the expatriation and sedition laws. Other antiguerrilla laws remained on the books but became dead letters.[9]

AMNESTY FOR WARTIME ACTS

Bitterness over wartime destruction did not end with the war: during Reconstruction, Southern courts handled a steady stream of claims against former soldiers. Such claims forced Southern lawmakers to decide whether combatants should be held liable for wartime crimes and damage or whether they should receive amnesty.

Most states chose amnesty; some did so more readily than others. North Carolina and Mississippi adopted amnesty laws shortly after the end of the war, which they made applicable to both Union and Confederate veterans. Courts in both states held that Confederate forces were not outlaws but were belligerents who enjoyed all the rights international law accorded to forces of combatant nations. However, the courts also made clear that under the belligerency doctrine, soldiers were entitled to amnesty only for acts truly related to military purposes, or, in the case of enlisted men, acts carried out in response to military orders. The North Carolina and Mississippi courts also extended amnesty to civilians who had acted in defense of their homes and families. The amnesty laws remained in effect even after the Restoration governments that enacted them were replaced by Reconstruction governments. Judge Simrall of Mississippi explained, "It is not to be expected . . . that those who acted under military orders were at all times discreet and forbearing," and that more practically, abrogation of the state's amnesty law "would flood the courts with suits for compensation." In North Carolina, Chief Justice Pearson noted that in addition to the difficulty of judging whether wartime acts were justified, damage lawsuits "would cause [lingering bitterness] to spread into a pestilence." In the same spirit, he upheld a portion of North Carolina's law extending the amnesty period past the end of the war to the beginning of 1866. "Just as the ocean is angry, long after the storm has passed," Pearson explained, "so the passions of men do not become calm in a day, after a war." But Pearson and his colleagues made clear that amnesty would be strictly limited to belligerent acts. For example, they held that a Confederate deserter who looted a house near the end of the war was not protected, but that a Union soldier who shot another during a dispute over recruitment of black troops was protected.[10]

In some states, few war damage lawsuits were filed and lawmakers did not feel a need to enact amnesty laws. In the case of states such as South Carolina, Alabama, Louisiana, and Texas, this was not surprising: they were not primary theaters of war, the Unionist presence in each state was small and they suffered less destruction than other Southern states. But the failure of states such as Virginia and Georgia to enact amnesty laws is curious: they were primary theaters of war and suffered severe damage. Several factors likely account for their lack of interest in such laws. Virginia's most adamant Unionists were now located in a new state, West Virginia, and the Unionists remaining in Virginia were moderates more interested in reaching a postwar accommodation with their secessionist neighbors than in revisiting wartime wrongs. Georgia's small band of Unionists did not have sufficient political power to make life difficult for ex-Confederates. In the handful of war damages cases that came before the Virginia and Georgia supreme courts, both courts readily applied the belligerency doctrine.[11]

In the border states, close political divisions and extensive wartime destruction made amnesty a matter of intense concern, and the evolution of amnesty laws in these states followed a very different pattern than it did farther south. The Republicans who controlled Tennessee and West Virginia at the end of the war rejected amnesty because it would weaken their still precarious hold on power; the trauma caused by wartime divisions and guerrilla activity was still fresh. The only hope of relief for ex-Confederates lay in persuading their courts to adopt the belligerency doctrine, and they had little success in that quarter. In 1867 the Tennessee supreme court limited the belligerency doctrine to situations posing "immediate and impending danger" to soldiers: mere action for military purposes was not enough to shield ex-soldiers from liability for damages. West Virginia's supreme court went further: in *Hedges v. Price* (1867) it refused to give ex-Confederates any benefit of the belligerency doctrine. The court held that although Confederate soldiers might technically be belligerents, they were also rebels and traitors. It noted that in most wars the losing government indemnified the victors for war damages as a condition of peace, and reasoned that because the Confederate government no longer existed, its soldiers must pay for war damage instead. Amnesty, warned Judge George Loomis, would "offer a premium to treason, and beset the pathway of peace and loyalty with difficulty and danger."[12]

Missouri and Kentucky were less rigid. In the few war damage cases that came before it, the Missouri supreme court indicated it would apply the belligerency doctrine more broadly than Tennessee or West Virginia. Kentucky had followed its own legal path during the war, and it continued to do so after the war ended. The Kentucky supreme court quickly made clear that it would use the belligerency doctrine to shield Confederate troops from liability for military actions notwithstanding the state's broad wartime liability laws. The court reasoned that Kentucky soldiers "became constituent elements of the Confederate army, the national law defined their belligerent rights [and] over these rights of war no state has any right to interfere." However, like

North Carolina, the Kentucky court defined the scope of military action narrowly: for example, it held that John Hunt Morgan's troops were liable for the 1862 burning of the Christian County courthouse in southwest Kentucky because the courthouse had no strategic or military value, and it held that Morgan's raids on banks were robbery, not legitimate impressment of property. In 1867, after thousands of Kentucky Confederate veterans had returned home, the legislature enacted a general amnesty law applying to both Confederate and Union veterans. The legislature took pains to explain that "it is not intended . . . to declare that the rebellion was justifiable, or that all acts done [by Union forces] were right" but that the law was necessary to "giv[e] tranquility to the State."[13]

Tennessee and West Virginia conservatives aligned their states with Kentucky and Missouri after they gained political power in the early 1870s. Tennessee's Redemption court expanded the scope of the belligerency doctrine well beyond the cases of "immediate and impending danger" accepted by its Reconstruction predecessor, but indicated that it was doing so for practical more than ideological reasons. "The power of military commanders backed by bayonets, and the organization of courts martial, and the not unfrequent punishment administered without trial or opportunity of defense, and upon the mere order of a military satrap, soon taught subordinates and citizens that resistance was futile," explained Judge Thomas Turney. "To require individuals or corps to resist or disobey a military organization supported by a government, is to change the law and require an impossibility." Both West Virginia and Missouri amended their constitutions to extend amnesty to Confederate as well as Union soldiers. West Virginia's Redemption court confirmed that these new provisions effectively restored the belligerency doctrine.[14]

TESTS OF FAITH: LOYALTY OATHS AND SUFFRAGE

One of the most important postwar issues, and one that preoccupied state and federal lawmakers throughout the Reconstruction era, was the extent to which ex-Confederates would be allowed a voice in postwar government. Northerners and Southerners, Radicals and conservatives alike recognized the answer would play a key role in shaping the South's future. The debate began during the war, when officials in the border states and Union-occupied areas of the South had to determine how to treat paroled Confederate prisoners and other Confederates living within Union lines. It continued after the war over two closely related issues: first, whether Southerners should be required to take an oath of loyalty to the Union and what form the oath should take; and second, the conditions under which ex-Confederates should be allowed to vote, hold office, practice law, and participate in other public professions. Again, the Deep South and Upper South took strikingly different approaches to this issue.

Loyalty oaths usually flourish during periods when a nation is concerned about its underlying strength and unity; thus, it is not surprising that oath requirements proliferated both during and after the Civil War. Early in the war, Congress enacted a series of oath laws in reaction to widespread defections of federal soldiers and civilian employees to the Confederacy at the war's commencement. The first law, enacted in August 1861, imposed a comparatively mild "pledge" oath, which required federal civilian employees to swear future loyalty to the federal Constitution but did not require them to affirm past loyalty. After it became clear that the war would be long and hard, Congress enacted stricter oath laws, culminating in the "ironclad oath" of July 1862, which required pledges of both past and future loyalty. Federal employees were required to swear that they had never "voluntarily borne arms against the United States," had "given no aid, countenance, counsel or encouragement to persons engaged in armed hostilities thereto," had never sought or accepted office under a hostile government, and had "not yielded a voluntary support to any pretended government" hostile to the United States. Near the end of the war, Congress imposed a similar oath on attorneys as a condition of practicing law in the federal courts. Conservative senators, led by Thomas Bayard of Delaware, objected that the ironclad oath laws were unconstitutional because they were *ex post facto* laws, that is, they unfairly imposed penalties for conduct that took place before they were enacted, but such objections were ignored.[15]

Nineteenth-century Americans took oaths very seriously, and military authorities found loyalty oaths and parole oaths (which allowed Confederate prisoners to regain freedom by swearing not to take up arms against the United States in future) to be useful tools for determining whether Confederate sympathizers living in occupied areas would behave peaceably or not. Many Southern Unionists who had stayed with their states after Fort Sumter had taken minor Confederate government positions to avoid conscription, and as a result, they could not honestly take the ironclad oath. They echoed Bayard's protest and complained that the oath unfairly penalized them for doing what was necessary to survive. But their objections were also ignored, and Union commanders imposed prison terms and other harsh penalties on Southerners who refused to take oaths or broke them.[16]

The Republican governments that held power in Missouri, Tennessee, West Virginia, and Maryland at the end of the war also found oath laws useful as a means of controlling political opposition. Border Republicans viewed oaths not merely as tactical weapons but as indispensable to the survival of Unionism in their states. Missouri, which suffered the fiercest guerrilla fighting and the most violence of any border state, enacted the most draconian oath laws. In 1862 the legislature enacted an ironclad oath that went beyond the federal oath: in addition to federal limitations, it required affiants to swear they had never taken up arms against the United States voluntarily or otherwise. The Missouri oath applied not only to government officials and public professionals such as lawyers, teachers, and clergy, but also to bank and corporate officers and "every other person assuming to discharge the duties pertaining to his avocation under the laws of this State." In 1864 the legislature called a constitutional convention and instructed it to consider measures "necessary to preserve in purity the elective franchise to loyal citizens." The convention was closely divided between Radicals who wanted the ironclad oath continued and moderates who preferred a milder "pledge" oath addressing only future loyalty to the federal and state constitutions. The Radicals prevailed by a narrow margin, and oath laws and suffrage limitations became the centerpiece of the new Missouri constitution. The 1863 oath was expanded: voters would now be required to affirm they had never "in any manner adhered" or "disloyally held communication" with the Confederacy, had never associated with any organization "inimical" to the Union, had never avoided the draft, and had never encouraged others to do so. Concerned that the expansion of the wartime oath might jeopardize passage of the constitution, Radical delegates added a provision authorizing the legislature to eliminate the oath and related suffrage restrictions, if it wished. Missouri voters ratified the constitution by a narrow margin.[17]

Farther east, Tennessee and Maryland enacted similar oath and suffrage requirements. Tennessee Radicals inserted a relatively mild version of the ironclad oath in the state's 1865 constitution, requiring voters to swear they would support the federal Constitution and had been active supporters of the Union and opponents of the Confederacy during the war, but the Tennessee legislature restricted suffrage further. The state's new voting law barred all ex-Confederates from voting, with two exceptions: Confederate conscripts could vote if two qualified voters vouched for their loyalty, and the disabilities of other Confederates would expire in 5 or 15 years, depending on their wartime military rank. Maryland's 1864 constitutional convention prescribed an ironclad oath similar to Missouri's but limited it to voting and officeholding. As in Missouri, the restrictions were highly controversial and Maryland's 1864 constitution passed by a very narrow margin. West Virginia imposed the mildest oath requirement, perhaps because Unionists had a larger base of support than in other border states and felt more politically secure. In 1861, before it was clear that Union forces would be able to hold northwest Virginia, organizers of the new state enacted an ironclad oath for voters and officeholders very similar to Missouri's oath; but by 1863, with Union control and separate statehood assured, the founders chose not to incorporate oaths or loyalty-based suffrage limitations into the new state constitution. Statutory oath requirements for officeholders and public professionals remained in effect after 1863, but at the end of the war, the legislature allowed returning Confederates to vote if they swore loyalty to West Virginia's constitution and took the "pledge" oath prescribed by Andrew Johnson for persons seeking a presidential pardon.[18]

As a practical matter, election officials in all Southern states had great leeway in determining whether voters met statutory suffrage requirements. Tennessee Radicals officially encouraged officials to marginalize Confederate sympathizers: they inserted in the 1865 constitution a provision that persons "well known to the judges of the election to have been unconditional Union men" and "true friends of the Union" could vote even if they were unable to take the voters' oath. Control of the process for selecting election officials was often critical to political control of a state, and both Radicals and conservatives readily modified election laws to help their cause. Generally, Radicals favored laws allowing state officials to appoint all local election officers, reasoning this would help them keep control even in regions hostile to their cause; conversely, conservatives favored local appointment of officials in order to solidify their pockets of support.[19]

Oath laws and loyalty-based suffrage laws remained controversial in the border states throughout their short lives. In Missouri, conservatives repeatedly challenged the laws, resulting in two United States Supreme Court decisions that became the leading American cases in the field: *Cummings v. Missouri* (1867) and *Blair v. Ridgely* (1870). John Cummings, a priest, was barred from administering religious rites after he declined to take the oath prescribed by the 1865 constitution. Cummings's main argument against Missouri's ironclad oath was that it was an unconstitutional *ex post facto* law because it imposed penalties for conduct occurring before its enactment. The Missouri supreme court rejected his position, reasoning that the *ex post facto* doctrine applied only to criminal laws and that Missouri's oath law prescribed no criminal penalties. The court concluded the oath clause merely required professionals to affirm they were not guilty of treason or disloyalty: if they were guilty of either, it was reasonable to conclude that allowing them to practice public professions and vote was not in the public interest. Cummings appealed and two years later, a closely divided United States Supreme Court reversed the Missouri court by a 5–4 vote. The High Court held the *ex post facto* doctrine applied to all laws punitive in nature, and it rejected the Radical position that past service to the Confederacy was relevant to the issue of fitness to practice a profession.[20]

Soon thereafter, Frank Blair, who had founded Missouri's Republican Party and had played a vital role in the military effort to save Missouri for the Union but had sided with Johnson against the Radicals after the war, argued that the *Cummings* decision applied equally to loyalty-based suffrage restrictions. The Missouri supreme court reluctantly accepted the High Court's *Cummings* decision as binding, but it drew a distinction between voting and the practice of a profession: the latter was a natural property right that could not be taken away arbitrarily, but American courts had long agreed that states had broad power to prescribe limitations on voting. Judge David Wagner tartly noted that in the past other states had first given and then withheld the vote from free blacks; he concluded that by the same token Missouri could "consider [ ] that those who had betrayed our flag, and exhibited their hostility to the Government, were, for the time being, unsafe and unfit repositories of political power." Blair appealed, and Republicans and conservatives throughout the nation anxiously waited for the High Court's decision: if it extended *Cummings* to suffrage requirements, ex-Confederates would be reenfranchised and Reconstruction might come to a quick end. But in early 1870, the High

Court announced it was deadlocked: four justices would uphold the Missouri court's decision and four would reverse it. Thus the Missouri court's decision would stand.[21]

Except for Kentucky, where lingering resentment of wartime Union occupation contributed to ready acceptance of returning Confederate soldiers into the electorate, courts in other border states also upheld loyalty-based oaths and suffrage restrictions, even to the point of defying the *Cummings* decision. In West Virginia, Charles Faulkner, a leader of the northwest Virginia bar who had stayed with Virginia during the war but returned to his native region after the close of hostilities, challenged his new state's oath requirement for lawyers and other public professionals. The West Virginia supreme court rejected the challenge: Judge James Brown stated that lawyers who sided with the Confederacy were "public enemies" who should not be allowed to "avail themselves of the use of the courts they were fighting to destroy" or "expound[ ] the laws which the expounders set at defiance." Brown noted the United States Supreme Court's *Cummings* decision but flatly stated that it was not persuasive and was not binding on West Virginia's courts. The Maryland and Tennessee supreme courts also rejected challenges to their states' voting oaths and agreed with the Missouri court's conclusion in *Blair* that the *Cummings* decision was not applicable to suffrage limitations. "How far those of her people who united in this effort to destroy the Union and assisted in bringing the war . . . within her borders . . . were to be deemed safe depositories of the right of suffrage," said Maryland judge Daniel Weisel, was a matter for the state alone.[22]

The situation was considerably different in the ex-Confederate states. In 1864, provisional Union governments formed in Virginia and Arkansas required voters and officeholders to take "pledge" oaths, but Virginia softened its oath requirement by giving the legislature broad authority to restore the suffrage of ex-Confederates and in 1866 Arkansas' Restoration court struck down most of that state's oath law, reasoning that it contained *ex post facto* elements and that prewar voters could not be deprived of suffrage without a hearing. No other ex-Confederate states enacted oaths or loyalty-based suffrage requirements of any sort during the Restoration period: Restoration leaders believed the oath many Southerners had taken to obtain Johnson's presidential pardon should be sufficient.[23]

After 1867, many Reconstruction governments were reluctant to impose oath requirements because they hoped to form long-term political coalitions that included ex-Confederates. Some Republicans also opposed oaths on principle, reasoning that the ideals of equality they had fought for in the war meant that both ex-Confederates and blacks should be allowed to vote. Most states enacted "pledge" oath requirements; some also provided that the suffrage limitations Congress had imposed under the Reconstruction Acts and in the 14th Amendment would remain in effect until lifted by Congress. A few states went further because their leaders concluded they had no realistic chance of gaining conservative support and therefore need not conciliate conservatives. Alabama and Arkansas' Reconstruction constitutional conventions required voters to affirm that they accepted "the civil and political equality of all men" and that they would not persecute Unionists or deprive others of their civil rights. Both states excluded from suffrage Confederates who had "violated rules of civilized warfare," but also provided that the legislature could remove such disabilities. Louisiana adopted constitutional restrictions nearly as draconian as Tennessee's: its 1868 constitution excluded from the polls Confederate officials and those who had preached or written in support of the Confederacy, as well as anyone who had "notoriously levi[ed]" war against the United States or given aid to the Confederacy. However, any ineligible person could regain the vote by taking an oath "acknowledg[ing] the late rebellion to have been morally and politically wrong, and that I regret any aid or comfort I may have given it."[24] Federal judges in Georgia, west Tennessee, and Alabama anticipated *Cummings* by refusing to enforce the 1865 federal attorneys' oath law; the United States Supreme Court later endorsed these rulings in *Ex parte Garland* (1867).[25]

The ratification of the 15th Amendment marked the beginning of the end for loyalty oaths and suffrage restrictions. Many Unionists believed the 15th Amendment would protect Southern blacks from future interference with their voting rights and would guarantee a permanent base of Union support in the South; they now found common ground with conservatives in supporting suffrage for both blacks and ex-Confederates. Even federal Chief Justice Salmon Chase, a reliable Radical, reflected this change of political mood: he commented privately that "there was so much injustice and needless harshness in the extent of the right to challenge, and in the oath by which the challenged voter could relieve himself of the challenge, that one was naturally inclined to go as far as possible against it."[26]

Missouri had taken the lead in creating loyalty-based oaths and suffrage requirements, and it now took the lead in eliminating them. In 1870 a coalition of conservatives and moderate Republicans took control of the legislature and repealed the 1865 constitution's oath and suffrage restrictions. Thereafter, Missouri required only a pledge oath. Between 1870 and the end of Reconstruction in 1877, every Southern state repealed its remaining ironclad oaths and suffrage restrictions, sometimes replacing them with pledge oaths and sometimes eliminating oaths altogether. Reconstruction governments in Arkansas and West Virginia eliminated oaths voluntarily, but most oaths were eliminated only after Redemption governments came to power.[27]

By 1872, ex-Confederates were fully reassimilated into the Southern electorate. West Virginia's Redemption constitution, enacted in that year, pronounced an epitaph on loyalty-based oaths and voting restrictions and indicated that the Republicans' time to hold power in the South was passing. It banned all oaths, stating that "Political tests, requiring persons . . . to purge themselves by their own oaths, of past alleged offences, are repugnant to the principles of free Government, and are cruel and oppressive."[28]

Debates over the legal dilemmas of war were important because they provided early indicators of the course of postwar legal change in the South. The border states, where political divisions were close and Republican control was tenuous, enacted the most sweeping oaths and suffrage limitations, and it was natural that the leading United States Supreme Court decisions on the constitutionality of oath and suffrage laws all came from closely divided states where opponents of the laws had much to gain if their challenges were successful. Oath laws provided a good measure of the nation's postwar mood. They flourished while the passions roused by the war were still fresh; they died quickly and signaled the coming end of Reconstruction as the passions of war started to recede.

Wartime legal dilemmas also gave Southern courts an opportunity to affirm the primacy and value of a central government and maintain the nationalistic judicial culture, even under the Confederacy. Southern courts defended the need for central authority at Richmond in the face of widespread states' rights sentiment, and after the war, virtually all Southern courts—Restoration, Reconstruction, and Redemption courts alike—applied established national and international standards in addressing liability for wartime damage, holding that Confederate and Union soldiers were exempt from damage liability when they acted as belligerents but not when they acted outside that role.

Suffrage laws and issues of deference to central authority affected Southern blacks as well as whites. Loyalty-based suffrage criteria disfranchised many whites but no black Southerners because blacks did not participate in the rebellion; thus, the strictness of suffrage oath laws directly affected the racial balance of power in each state. Suffrage was just one of a panoply of issues Southern lawmakers had to consider in addressing the most fundamental legal dilemma of the Reconstruction era: what civil, political, and social rights should they give to Southern blacks? How would postwar lawmakers redefine and balance the competing considerations of humanity and interest their predecessors had pondered during the slave era, now that slavery had been stripped out of the legal system? The next chapter addresses these questions.

CHAPTER 4

The Great Wreck of Property: Coming to Grips with Emancipation

> [Georgia's Restoration government] acted on the theory, that colored men were not a portion of the people for whom the government was organized, but an anomalous class . . . whose rights depended solely on the legislation of that class whose rights came from God. . . . [T]he very object and intent of the reconstruction laws, was to repudiate this idea.
> —Judge Henry McCay (Georgia), 1869

> Admit us into the sanctum sanctorum of justice—the jury box—give us a fair show in the courts. The idea of giving a negro justice, in a court where the judge has sucked the milk of prejudice from his mother's breast, where the lawyers, though they may be the most thorough radicals extant, honestly believe me immeasurably their inferior, and the jurors there assembled . . . do not believe that I have any right to be protected from the encroachment of that class looked upon as my superiors!
> —William Grey (Arkansas), 1868[1]

In 1864, as the Civil War moved toward its close, several border states and conquered Confederate states called constitutional conventions to consider emancipation of their slaves. In the Maryland convention, held as Confederate forces gathered to attack Washington and Baltimore, Unionist delegates predicted emancipation would usher in a new era of growth and prosperity because "[t]he very essence of the American idea is that labor is respectable [whereas] slavery makes labor *disreputable*." A conservative delegate demanded that slaveowners be compensated for their freed slaves and complained that "property, henceforth . . . is but a shuttle-cock, to be bandied here and there."

Another delegate closed the debate by warning conservatives that further efforts to preserve the prewar system would be futile. "These gentlemen may as well quit it and go home," he said, "because *the thing is dead.* They may galvanize the corpse, and make it grin hideously, but to bring it to life is an utter impossibility."[2]

The Maryland delegates reflected the mixed feelings with which Southern lawmakers approached the task of adjusting to emancipation. Many Southerners viewed their military defeat as a divine judgment against slavery and accepted emancipation peaceably. Others, particularly in the border states, saw emancipation as a betrayal of their wartime loyalty. But Southerners of all political views had grown up under a system that viewed blacks as less than fully human. Southern states had granted slaves and free blacks limited rights before the war, and some courts had adopted a more expansive view than others of the humanity of blacks, but the task of fitting the South's legal system to emancipation was immense. History and legal precedent offered little guidance to Southern lawmakers; their task was complicated by internal divisions and by the fact that Congress and the Northern public, familiar only with a free labor system, often held sharply contrasting views of how that task should be performed.

INITIAL ADJUSTMENTS: THE RESTORATION CONSTITUTIONS AND THE BLACK CODES

In late 1863, Louisiana and Arkansas Unionists organized new governments under Abraham Lincoln's "10 percent" plan; they enacted new constitutions abolishing slavery in 1864, as did Maryland and Virginia's Unionist governments. Tennessee and Missouri followed suit in early 1865. At the end of the war, Andrew Johnson urged the former Confederate states to enact new constitutions and restore their governments as quickly as possible. Johnson emphasized that the states were expected to abolish slavery and repudiate Confederate war debts, but otherwise he left them free to restructure their postwar order as they saw fit. All of the ex-Confederate states held conventions in late 1865: some were content to enact the minimum measures Johnson had specified and leave the details of postwar restructuring to their legislatures, while others took the opportunity to enact more thoroughgoing reforms.[3]

Most Restoration conventions accepted the end of slavery without apparent regret, but there were notable exceptions. Mississippi's convention took pains to state that it was enacting emancipation only because the federal government had destroyed slavery; other Deep South states used equally grudging language. Some delegates believed the courts would overturn wartime emancipation and that if their states acceded to emancipation they would "then be tormented and tortured upon other and new exactions." Others warned that resistance would "place an argument in the mouth, and a weapon in the hands of those who wish not only to strike down the institution of slavery, but to strike down the social and political superiority of the whites." Conventions in several states expressed their belief that emancipation would create more problems than it solved; they instructed their legislatures to "guard [freedmen] and the State against any evils that may arise from their sudden emancipation." A few conventions imposed explicit restrictions on blacks, providing clues to the aspects of black freedom that most concerned white Southerners: Georgia and Alabama proscribed miscegenation and Florida and Texas limited blacks' ability to testify against whites.[4]

Beginning in the fall of 1865, Restoration legislatures enacted black codes to fill in details omitted by the conventions. The codes quickly attracted unfavorable attention in the North and laid the groundwork for Congressional Reconstruction. The codes may be viewed from many perspectives. Two that are crucial to understanding their place in Southern and American history are often ignored. First, the codes were not created in a vacuum: they were part of a continuum of Southern regulation of race relations extending from the early 1600s to the mid-1900s, and they must be viewed in the context of the regulations that came before them. Second, the black codes varied substantially from state to state and the variations illuminate broader differences in Southern states' approaches to Reconstruction.

CIVIL RIGHTS: LABOR CONTRACTS, VAGRANCY, APPRENTICESHIP LAWS, AND THE RIGHT TO TRAVEL

Postwar lawmakers divided the task of regulating freedmen into three areas: civil, political, and social rights. The concept of "civil rights" had a narrower scope in the 1860s than it does today: it was limited to a basic core of rights that Republicans and conservatives alike agreed were essential to the survival and basic dignity of all free persons regardless of race. South Carolina's legislature defined such rights by stating that blacks "are not entitled to social or political equality with white persons but they shall have the right to acquire, own and dispose of property; to make contracts; to enjoy the fruits of their labor; to sue and be sued; and to receive protection under the law in their person and property." Most states included similar provisions in their codes.[5]

Restoration-era lawmakers spent much effort creating controls over black labor. The most common controls were labor contract, vagrancy, and apprenticeship laws. Planters needed tight controls over labor to make their operations profitable; small farmers and workers needed such controls to limit the competitive threat blacks posed in the marketplace. Northern opinion also favored close regulation of black labor. During the first years of Reconstruction, military authorities and the Freedmen's Bureau shared concerns of many white Southerners that newly freed slaves would not be able to adjust to a free labor system or see the inherent link between virtue and work, and therefore must be compelled to do so. The Bureau prodded blacks to enter into labor contracts with white planters and, in some cases, intervened to settle disputes and enforce the contracts.

Most black codes required that contracts between planters and black workers be in writing and that their provisions be explained to workers, many of whom were illiterate, before the contracts would be effective. The codes also included antienticement laws that imposed penalties on employers who hired black workers already under contract to another. Many Deep South states reenacted other restrictions in their prewar free black and slave codes, prompting United States Supreme Court Justice Samuel Miller to complain that the new codes "do but change the form of the slavery."[6]

The South Carolina, Mississippi, and Texas labor codes were the most deserving of Justice Miller's charge. South Carolina required agricultural laborers to work from sunrise to sunset and to rate themselves as "full hands" or fractional hands, preserving the classification system many slaveowners had used. The legislature also required employers, openly referred to in the code as "masters," to assign tasks commensurate with a worker's rating. The legislature assumed that freedmen would remain under control of their employers while off duty: workers were not allowed to leave their plantations without permission except on Sunday, when they were required to return by sunset. They were also forbidden to receive visitors without the employer's consent. Employers were allowed to administer "moderate correction" to difficult workers, a phrase taken directly from antebellum slave laws. Workers who quit without "good cause" lost all right to compensation. As under slavery, black workers were not allowed to sell agricultural products without their employers' consent, and South Carolina preserved portions of its prewar free black code requiring black artisans to obtain licenses to practice their trades. Texas adopted most of South Carolina's restrictions; in addition, it encouraged blacks to work in family units and allowed employers to dock workers' wages in case of "sickness feigned for purposes of idleness." Mississippi did not attempt to preserve slave labor regulations as extensively as its sister states, but it formulated harsh new restrictions: blacks were required to obtain a certificate from local officials that they had a lawful home or employment, and any worker who quit employment was subject to arrest upon complaint by the employer that there had been no good cause for quitting.[7]

All three states relied heavily on vagrancy laws to enforce their labor codes. Vagrancy laws were more popular than direct labor restrictions because they were common throughout the United States before the war and were viewed by Northerners and Southerners alike as an acceptable means of protecting society from unsatisfactory behavior. Vagrancy laws could easily be phrased in racially neutral terms, thus further shielding them from Northern criticism; even so, Mississippi and South Carolina chose to enact special vagrancy laws for blacks. Mississippi enacted perhaps the harshest laws. Blacks who did not have a work certificate would be subject to fine or imprisonment; those who could not pay fines for labor code violations or certain other petty criminal offenses could be hired out to pay their fines, with their employers having

Hiring Out of Debtor, Monticello, Florida. Courtesy of the Library of Congress.

first preference. Mississippi defined the term *vagrant* to include all persons who "neglect their calling or employment" or "do not provide for the support of themselves and their families," as well as all persons who failed to pay an annual poll tax. Unlike whites, black offenders were subject to immediate arrest and hiring out for failing to pay the tax. South Carolina defined vagrancy in broader terms and preserved a 1787 statute that established special vagrancy tribunals for blacks. Alabama, Louisiana, and several Upper South states enacted vagrancy laws phrased in nonracial terms; other Southern states relied on prewar vagrancy laws and apparently did not feel a need to revise their laws in response to the dislocations of war and emancipation.[8]

Apprenticeship laws were another popular means of controlling freedmen, but they triggered more controversy than vagrancy laws, perhaps because children were a more natural subject of sympathy than adults. Like vagrancy laws, apprenticeship laws had a long history: since colonial times it had been common practice to bind out poor and orphaned children of both races to employers who could provide them a rudimentary education and basic vocational skills. After the war, a few Southern states simply applied existing apprenticeship laws to children of freed slaves without change, but others enacted new laws specifically aimed at black children. The new laws provided for apprenticeship in the traditional cases of poverty and orphanhood, but South Carolina also required apprenticeship of children of parents of "notoriously bad character." North Carolina, Mississippi, and Kentucky attracted unfavorable attention by giving preference to masters who wanted to take on their former slave children as apprentices.[9]

Even laws racially neutral in their wording were often applied in a discriminatory manner. Maryland provided one of the best examples. Between 1864 and 1867, state courts apprenticed thousands of children of newly freed slaves with little or no regard to the wishes and financial situation of their parents, even though Maryland law required that "the inclination of the . . . parents . . . shall be consulted" and that poverty must be "extreme" to justify apprenticeship. Such abuses soon attracted the attention of the Freedmen's Bureau, which publicly criticized and prosecuted state officials under the 1866 Civil Rights Act. Maryland's supreme court rejected a challenge to the apprenticeship law based on arguments that it created a form of slavery and denied blacks equal protection of the law, but Hugh Bond, who at that time presided over Baltimore's criminal court, cooperated with the Bureau and regularly issued habeas writs releasing apprenticed black children. The Maryland legislature responded in 1867 by depriving Bond of his jurisdiction in such cases, but during the same year, federal Chief Justice Salmon Chase, sitting as a district judge in Maryland, rejected the arguments Maryland's supreme court had accepted and held that the prevailing apprenticeship practices violated the 1866 Act.[10]

Some courts attempted to protect black families against the worst abuses of the apprenticeship system. They required strict compliance with statutory notice requirements and other procedural safeguards for apprenticeship hearings, and some courts independently required that black parents be given a chance to appear and object to apprenticing of their children. Surprisingly, Deep South courts expressed more concern for black families than Upper South and border state courts. Georgia's supreme court cautioned that "public functionaries should be vigilant in preventing any one, under the name of master, from getting the control of the labor and services of such minor apprentice, as if he were still a slave . . . slavery is with the days beyond the flood." Mississippi's supreme court expressed similar sentiments. In North Carolina, Judge Edwin Reade gave a more pragmatic reason for procedural fairness: "It is best," he said, "that the colored populations should be satisfied that they are liable to no unlawful impressments, and that they should see that what is required of them has the sanction of the law. It may then be hoped that they will be contented, and will cheerfully submit to what they might otherwise mischievously resist." Kentucky's supreme court struck the only discordant note: in direct contrast to North Carolina, it held that good character and industrious habits were not sufficient to avoid apprenticeship and that the preference that state law gave to former masters would be strictly enforced.[11]

No such concerns surfaced as to protection of adult workers, perhaps because the most egregious features of the black codes were eliminated during Congressional Reconstruction. South Carolina's and Alabama's anti-enticement laws were challenged on the ground that they impaired workers' liberty rights and discriminated against blacks, but both challenges were rejected. The South Carolina supreme court explained that restrictions on enticement had been an established feature of American law before the war and noted that "the loss of agricultural labor, for even a few days, might often prove of irreparable injury to the crop."[12]

Another feature of prewar black codes that carried over into many postwar codes was restrictions on interstate travel. Before the war, white Southerners had generally viewed free blacks as potential catalysts of slave rebellion; accordingly, many states had prohibited free blacks in other states from settling within their borders and had required newly freed slaves to leave. No state attempted to expel freedmen after the war, because whites recognized black labor would continue to be vital to the Southern economy, but many states preserved prewar restrictions on black immigration. For example, black immigrants were allowed to settle in South Carolina only if they furnished a bond as security, and black immigrants to Arkansas were allowed to stay only if they had come in with the Union armies.[13]

POLITICAL RIGHTS: COURT TESTIMONY, JURY SERVICE, AND CRIMINAL PENALTIES

Much of the controversy over black codes involved the issue of what political rights should be granted to Southern blacks in the wake of emancipation. Should blacks be given a full voice in the operation of their states, no voice, or something in between? Many white Southerners feared that giving blacks voting and office-holding rights, the right to sit on juries and testify against whites, and other tools for gaining a voice in state government commensurate with their numbers would lead to black political domination, social intermingling, and the gradual decline and fall of the white race. They agreed wholeheartedly with Georgia judge Charles Jenkins's characterization of political and social equality as "a fatal delusion." Conversely, as delegate William Grey explained at Arkansas's 1868 constitutional convention, Southern blacks worried that white lawmakers "do not believe that I have any right to be protected from the encroachment of that class looked upon as my superiors." Southern blacks viewed the rudimentary civil rights granted in the black codes as tokens seldom enforced and perpetually at risk of repeal; thus they believed they must have political rights as a matter of basic self-protection.[14]

The primary political issues lawmakers addressed in formulating the black codes were the rights of black Southerners to testify in court, serve on juries, and enjoy equal treatment under criminal laws. (Black suffrage would later become a fundamental issue of Reconstruction, but in 1865 and 1866, when the black codes were enacted, it did not have a critical mass of public support.) On the eve of the Civil War, Southern states allowed blacks to testify only in exceptional situations. At the end of the war, most states expanded blacks' testimonial rights modestly: in addition to being allowed to sue for wrongs done to them, blacks were allowed to testify in their own lawsuits and black criminal defendants were allowed to call other blacks as witnesses for the first time. Several border and Deep South states allowed blacks to testify in all civil lawsuits and allowed black crime victims to testify against white defendants; other states were not willing to go that far.[15]

Controversy over testimonial rights played an important role in the enactment of the first great federal civil rights law in 1866. The 1866 Act allowed unrestricted black testimony in all federal courts and permitted defendants in state courts that did not allow black testimony to remove their cases to federal court.[16] Southern lawmakers quickly recognized that the 1866 Act was a blow against the black codes and, more fundamentally, was a warning that unless Southern states accepted a broader concept of black rights, there would be further federal intervention. Moderates, including Horatio Simrall in Mississippi, had warned at the time the black codes were enacted that testimonial restrictions would attract Congressional attention, and their predictions were now fulfilled.

Some states voluntarily repealed testimonial restrictions in the hope they could avoid further Congressional intrusions but others resisted, most notably Kentucky. Between 1865 and 1871, the Kentucky legislature repeatedly rejected efforts to eliminate limits on black testimony; as a result, many black litigants removed their cases to Judge Bland Ballard's federal district court and such cases soon made up a large part of Ballard's docket. In *United States v. Rhodes* (1866), federal Supreme Court justice Noah Swayne, sitting as a district judge, rejected a challenge to the 1866 Act's removal provisions. Swayne commented bluntly that if the courts were to "[b]lot out this act and deny the constitutional power to pass it . . . the worst effects of slavery might speedily follow. It would be a virtual abrogation of the [13th] amendment." But the following year, in *Bowlin v. Commonwealth* (1867), Kentucky's supreme court sharply criticized Swayne's reasoning and argued that the 13th Amendment "gave the colored race nothing more than freedom." Chief Justice George Robertson, speaking for the court, neatly expressed the combination of racism and genuine state sovereignty concerns that underlay opposition to the 1866 Act. The Act, complained Robertson, "would place the black race, in all the States, under the pupilage of Congress, free from the control of the local sovereign that governs the white race, and ought to have the same jurisdiction over all citizens, black as well as white."[17]

Judges in other states disagreed with Robertson. Delaware's supreme court upheld the 1866 Act; Georgia's Restoration court held that a state law similar to the Act "made [blacks] entitled to all the civil rights enjoyed by white persons" and stated that it did not "feel disposed to fetter the enjoyment of those rights by technical criticism." All Southern states except Kentucky eliminated their remaining testimonial restrictions during Congressional Reconstruction, and the few courts that considered testimonial issues after 1868 made clear that they viewed the elimination of restrictions as being "in favor of truth and liberty."[18] But in the late 1860s, a new challenge came out of Kentucky. In *United States v. Blyew* the defendants, who were charged with a particularly vicious murder of a black family in Kentucky, argued that federal courts could not take jurisdiction over state crimes simply because Congress disliked state testimonial restrictions. While the case was pending, a number of Kentucky leaders concluded that removal of such restrictions was the best means of reducing the federal government's presence in the state, and in 1872, the legislature finally agreed. Shortly after Kentucky's testimonial restrictions were repealed, the United States Supreme Court decided *Blyew*, holding that state cases could be removed to federal court under the 1866 Act in cases where state officials directly failed to enforce black citizens' rights but that the mere denial of the right to testify did not amount to such a failure.[19]

The right to serve on juries received less attention than testimonial rights because it was subsumed in suffrage issues: most Southern states provided that jurors were to be chosen from lists of eligible voters. A few states explicitly barred blacks from jury service during the Restoration period, but most such restrictions terminated between 1868 and 1870 when blacks were permanently enfranchised. Most states eliminated jury restrictions simply by retaining existing laws allowing voters to serve on juries; a few went further and explicitly prohibited racial discrimination in jury selection.[20]

The role of race in criminal laws was a sensitive issue for both whites and blacks. Many prewar black codes had prescribed special crimes and punishments applicable to blacks only. For example, many states had prohibited slaves from selling goods without their master's permission on the assumption that slaves had a propensity to steal and resell crops and equipment, and many had prohibited sales of weapons and alcohol to blacks. The codes had also allowed liberal use of whipping as punishment at a time when American and world opinion was rapidly turning against such punishment, and the death penalty was more extensively prescribed for blacks than whites. Many Southern whites believed black crime would increase with emancipation as freedmen experimented with their newfound liberty; they therefore resisted liberalization of criminal laws for blacks. Conversely, blacks viewed race-based criminal laws as a direct affront to their freedom and dignity, and their position received substantial support in the North.

Generally, Restoration legislatures tried to preserve as many prewar restrictions as possible while making at least a slight bow to Northern public opinion. Most black codes recited that with limited exceptions, criminal laws would apply equally to both races. But the exceptions were telling: many states continued to impose harsher penalties on blacks for assaults against whites, particularly sexual assaults on white women, than on whites who committed the same crimes. Several preserved whipping as a punishment and preserved prewar restrictions against black acquisition of firearms, and several states extended the hiring-out concept embodied in black labor codes to petty criminal offenses, thus giving Southern magistrates a powerful tool to remind recalcitrant freedmen that the specter of bondage had not been completely eliminated.[21]

SOCIAL RIGHTS: INTERMARRIAGE AND PUBLIC ACCOMMODATIONS

The issue of social mixing of the races was the far outpost of the civil rights debate during Reconstruction. Conservative and Republican whites alike agreed blacks should be granted basic civil rights necessary to survival, but both groups also agreed the law should not encourage mixing of the races. Social mixing touched on whites' deepest racial fears: in the words of historian Leon Litwack, many whites believed equal access to public places "would eventually open the door to the home, the parlor, and the bedroom . . . [and would] prepare the way for no distinctions at all." Judge Robert P. Dick of North Carolina, a staunch Republican, confirmed the consensus on this point when he explained to a grand jury in 1875 that federal civil rights laws did not mandate social equality:

Every man has a natural and inherent right of selecting his own associates, and this natural right cannot be properly regulated by legislative action, but must always be under the control of individual taste and inclination. . . . The hope and expectation that there will ever be a nation on earth in which all men will associate upon terms of social equality is a wild dream of fanaticism, which can never be realized. . . . These social prejudices naturally resulted from the condition of things and are too deeply implanted to be eradicated by any legislation.[22]

Black leaders recognized the depth of white resistance to social equality and responded by giving it lower priority than other objectives. Many black leaders assured whites they did not wish to transform Southern society completely, but only wanted to live peaceably alongside whites. They agreed with John Montgomery, a delegate to Arkansas's 1868 constitutional convention, that: "The question . . . is that of political equality merely. The people will arrange the question of social equality for themselves, irrespective of anything that we may do." Montgomery's colleague William Grey also emphasized that social separation was acceptable as long as the same rules and penalties were applied to both races, but he could not resist a gibe: "It does seem strange to me that gentlemen oppose it [miscegenation] only when it takes place in a legitimate [that is, marital] form."[23]

The debate over social equality during the Reconstruction era comprised two phases. Up to about 1870, the primary focus was on miscegenation, but after that time, the debate shifted to the issue of whether accommodations laws should be enacted mandating equal access to public transportation and public places such as restaurants, hotels, and theaters.

Both during and after slavery, interracial sexual relationships were common in practice but officially abhorred. Many whites throughout the United States believed blacks were genetically inferior: Chief Justice Brown of Georgia spoke for many when he stated interracial relationships could only produce offspring "sickly and effeminate . . . inferior in physical development and strength to the full-blood of either race." At a deeper level, miscegenation touched whites' deepest fears of losing their racial identity and the sense of superiority that went with it. During the Restoration period, most states reenacted prewar miscegenation laws. Some states were careful to specify equal penalties for whites and blacks who married or cohabited illegally, but a few chose to be selective: for example, Florida penalized only relationships between black men and white women. Small cracks appeared in the wall of antimiscegenation sentiment during Congressional Reconstruction. In Mississippi, Louisiana, and South Carolina, where blacks made up the highest proportion of the population, black lawmakers quietly used their new power to block reenactment of prewar miscegenation laws. They were less successful in other states.[24]

Official disapproval of interracial sexual relationships was no more effective in ending such relationships than it had been before the war, and a small but steady stream of miscegenation cases came before Southern courts throughout Reconstruction. Many of the cases presented white judges with opportunities to shape the law to accommodate popular distaste for miscegenation, but to a surprising extent, they resisted such temptation. For example, in *State v. Ross* (1877), a mixed couple eloped from North Carolina, married in South Carolina where interracial marriages were legal, returned to North Carolina, and was then prosecuted under the state's miscegenation law. The North Carolina supreme court was faced with the question of whether to honor the South Carolina marriage under traditional rules of comity (requiring that each state uphold valid legal actions taken in sister states) or to hold the marriage was not enforceable in North Carolina because it violated state policy. The court adhered to comity, albeit with great reluctance. "However revolting to us . . . such a marriage may appear," said Judge William Rodman, "such cannot be said to be the common sentiment of the civilized Christian world." Judge Edwin Reade protested that North Carolina "must be its own judge of what is an evil [because] [s]elf preservation requires it." In *Ross*, the couple did not intend to return to North Carolina when they married; but in a companion case where the couple did intend to return, the court voided the marriage without hesitation.[25]

Southern courts divided over the validity of miscegenation laws. Couples in several states argued that federal civil rights laws extended to racial discrimination in marriage. North Carolina firmly rejected the challenge: Judge Reade reasoned that the state's miscegenation law "is no discrimination in favor of one race against the other, but applies equally to both," that the law "has the sanction of both races" and that "neither the Civil Rights Bill nor our state constitution was intended to enforce social equality." Courts in Georgia and Texas concurred, although Texas courts were divided as to whether the state was permitted to impose penalties on whites only.[26] But

Mississippi's, Louisiana's, and Alabama's Reconstruction courts disagreed. The Mississippi court, though conservative in many respects, held that a provision in the state's Reconstruction constitution legitimating blacks' prewar cohabiting relationships applied to interracial relationships; the court stated firmly that "as a question of policy or propriety, people may differ, but this is a view of the case which the court cannot entertain." The Louisiana court held that the 1866 Act terminated all civil restrictions on interracial marriages.

Alabama's handling of the issue attracted the most controversy. In *Ellis v. State* (1868), Alabama's Restoration court held the 1866 Act did not invalidate miscegenation laws but only required that penalties for miscegenation apply equally to both races. Four years later, in *Burns v. State* (1872), the Reconstruction court disagreed. Speaking for the court, Judge Benjamin Saffold took a strikingly modern view of federal civil rights laws: the 1866 Act, he said, was "intended to destroy the distinctions of race and color in respect to the rights secured by it. It did not aim to create merely an equality of the races in reference to each other." The *Burns* decision was widely denounced, and in 1877, the Redemption court reversed it, denouncing miscegenation as "abhorrent" and criticizing Saffold's view as "narrow and illogical." Southern states that did not have miscegenation laws enacted such laws soon after Reconstruction ended in 1877, and the laws remained in effect in most Southern and many Northern states well into the twentieth century. They were not completely eliminated until 1967.[27]

The public accommodations issue arose relatively late in the Reconstruction era because it involved a more direct challenge to segregation than any other civil rights issue. Segregation was taken so much for granted that few states North or South found it necessary to enact laws on the subject before the Civil War: custom was sufficient to enforce it. That continued to be the case after the war: the only references to public accommodations in the early black codes were Mississippi and Texas laws prohibiting blacks from sharing railroad cars with whites and a Florida law prohibiting either race from entering railroad cars or church services reserved to the other race. Black leaders in St. Louis and Baltimore—border state cities more susceptible to nascent Northern notions of integration than other parts of the South—mounted efforts in the late 1860s to allow blacks equal access with whites to streetcars and railroad cars, but they were mostly unsuccessful.[28]

The accommodations issue rose to prominence in 1870, when Massachusetts Senator Charles Sumner introduced a bill in Congress guaranteeing blacks the right of access to hotels, restaurants, theaters, railroad cars, and other carriers and places open to the public. The bill failed to pass, but Sumner reintroduced it at every subsequent session until it was enacted in watered-down form in 1875 as the last major Reconstruction-era civil rights law, largely as a personal tribute to Sumner who had died the year before. The accommodations movement also gained a foothold in several Southern states during Reconstruction. Louisiana led the way, mandating integrated schools and equal access to public places in its 1868 constitution, and between 1870 and 1873, Georgia, Florida, Mississippi, and Arkansas enacted similar laws as to public places only. Except for Tennessee, the border and Upper South states declined to enact such laws. Black voters were less numerous there than in the Deep South; most likely, white Republicans, most of whom did not personally favor racial mixing, took a realistic view of the opposition they would face in advocating steps toward social equality and decided to concentrate on political and economic reform instead.[29]

Reconstruction accommodations laws were challenged only in Mississippi and Louisiana. Ironically, the challengers relied primarily on an argument that the laws could not stand because they interfered with federal laws. Both states' supreme courts rejected the argument. In Mississippi, Judge Simrall concluded that the 14th Amendment should not be construed broadly to preempt local legislation: state legislatures had traditionally enjoyed broad power to regulate public places and public carriers, and he and his colleagues declined to change the rule even for laws whose wisdom they questioned.

But the Louisiana case turned out differently. In *DeCuir v. Benson* (1875), a prosperous Creole couple traveling by steamboat from New Orleans to their upriver plantation challenged their restriction to the portion of the vessel reserved for blacks. A majority of the Louisiana supreme court agreed with Simrall that federal laws did not restrict the Louisiana legislature's right to prohibit segregation on carriers. Judge W. G. Wyly, who dissented, argued that Louisiana's accommodations law violated the commerce clause of the United States Constitution, which gave the federal government primary control over interstate commerce. Wyly reasoned that although Congress had not mandated segregation on steamboats, segregation was the universal custom on the lower Mississippi River: only Congress could require integration along paths of interstate commerce. The United States Supreme Court agreed with Wyly and overturned Louisiana's law. *DeCuir* was a serious setback for accommodations laws in the South: the 1875 federal accommodations law required that blacks be given access to carriers and public places but despite Sumner's pleas, Congress was not prepared to prohibit segregation of blacks and whites. Redemption legislatures in the South objected vociferously to even the watered-down version of the federal law that was ultimately passed, and during the decades following Reconstruction, they replaced remaining state accommodations laws with an elaborate system of Jim Crow laws mandating separation that remained in effect for nearly a century.[30]

SOUTHERN REACTION TO THE FEDERAL CIVIL RIGHTS LAWS

The Northern public's views on civil rights and the South shifted repeatedly during Reconstruction. The shifts produced the 14th and 15th Amendments to the United States Constitution and the great federal civil rights acts of the Reconstruction era, described in Chapter 1. The history of the federal laws has been ably recounted elsewhere and is not a subject of this book, but the federal laws affected legal developments at the state level following the war, and it is useful to consider briefly just what these effects were.

The federal government began its role as an overseer of Southern law almost immediately after the close of the war. During the interregnum between the collapse of the Confederacy and the creation of Restoration governments, federal military authorities provided the only source of law and order in the South. Local commanders were active in that role: they issued numerous civil regulations in the form of military orders and established military courts for the handling of both civil and criminal disputes. Some commanders, most notably General Daniel Sickles in South Carolina, struck down portions of the early black codes they found egregious and warned local officials against going too far in restricting black rights. The Freedmen's Bureau created its own local courts and frequently intervened informally in labor disputes, forcing many black workers to enter into less-than-satisfactory contracts with white employers but at the same time protecting workers against many employer abuses. White Southerners viewed Bureau courts as a usurpation of their civil justice system, but in Alabama, a bargain was struck that served as a model for other states: the Bureau agreed to close its local courts on condition that state courts allow black testimony. Bureau policies played a major part in inducing many states to eliminate testimonial restrictions from their black codes even before Congressional Reconstruction.[31]

When Congress adopted the 14th Amendment and sent it to the states for ratification in 1866, Southern states faced a dilemma. They were profoundly uneasy about the fundamental changes they sensed the amendment would bring, but it was clear to many Southerners that the ex-Confederate states would not be readmitted to representation in Congress unless they ratified the amendment. Nevertheless, every Restoration legislature except Tennessee's refused to ratify. Lawmakers denounced the amendment for a variety of reasons; by far the most common was a belief that the amendment would concentrate power over black rights in the federal government at the expense of the states and create the potential for drastic interference with states' control of their internal affairs. In Mississippi, Judge Simrall, then in the legislature, believed the amendment's creation of substantial new rights would "tend to create distrust and jealousy between the white and black races, and perpetually to disturb and keep alive these evil passions," and he worked actively to defeat the amendment. Sentiment in the border states was much the same: even Delaware, whose loyalty to the Union had never been in doubt, denounced the amendment as an unwarranted alteration of the original balance of power between the states and the federal government and as an impediment to lasting reunion.[32]

In the South, only Tennessee, Missouri, and West Virginia ratified the 14th Amendment prior to Congressional Reconstruction. Tennessee did so primarily to avoid Reconstruction and secure early readmission to Congress: in his message urging ratification, Governor William Brownlow argued that as the victor in the war, the federal government could impose any terms of reunion it wished and that, as a measure of conquest, the 14th Amendment was relatively mild. Reconstruction legislatures naturally viewed the amendment more enthusiastically than their predecessors: between 1868 and 1870 most ex-Confederate states ratified the amendment, but in Texas and Arkansas, ratification efforts failed even at the high tide of Reconstruction, and on the border, Kentucky, Maryland, and Delaware consistently refused to ratify.[33]

Congressional Reconstruction also witnessed the rise of the Ku Klux Klan and a host of similar organizations dedicated to control of blacks and white Republicans by intimidation where possible and violence where necessary. After 1868, the use of violence rose rapidly, particularly in areas where whites and blacks were roughly even in numbers. In several states particularly plagued by violence, Reconstruction legislatures enacted anti-Klan laws, many of which resembled the antiguerrilla measures Kentucky had enacted during the war. Mississippi, Alabama, and Tennessee imposed severe penalties on persons who committed crimes of violence against persons or property while disguised; in order to discourage sheltering of Klansmen, they also provided that counties in which atrocities occurred would be liable for the victim's damages in cases where the perpetrators could not be found and held to account. North Carolina and South Carolina enacted narrower laws that did not hold local communities liable. Arkansas, whose Reconstruction government was embroiled in a near-war with a statewide network of guerrillas, enacted the most sweeping law: in addition to creating drastic penalties for persons who practiced intimidation and violence in disguise, the legislature provided rewards for informers and imposed individual liability for damages on persons sheltering vigilantes. Kentucky was the only border state that experienced severe postwar race-based violence; conservatives, who controlled the state, were reluctant to acknowledge the problem, but eventually Kentucky also enacted an anti-Klan law in 1872.[34]

The anti-Klan laws had only limited success. By 1870 murder, arson, and attacks on blacks and white Republicans were endemic in many Southern states. In that year, North Carolina Governor William Holden declared martial law after an outbreak of severe violence in the central part of his state, but he was impeached and removed from office in the ensuing political storm. In 1871, after efforts of local officials to stem violence in South Carolina failed, President Ulysses Grant declared federal martial law in nine counties and sent federal troops to take control of law enforcement. Soon afterward, Congress enacted the Ku Klux Klan Act of 1871: it carefully tailored the act to take aim at Klan activities while avoiding any hint of direct interference with states' rights by defining interference with federal constitutional rights as a new crime. Many Southern lawmakers recognized that the Klan Act represented another step increasing federal control over civil rights; they denounced the act accordingly, but public concern over violence was such that their complaints went unheeded.

Under federal Attorney General Amos T. Akerman, a Georgia Unionist who had stayed with his state but had accepted the war's result as a mandate to change Southern society, the federal government prosecuted Klan Act cases throughout the South. Most prosecutions took place in the Carolinas and Mississippi, culminating in a series of Klan trials in South Carolina presided over by Hugh Bond, now a federal judge. Largely because of energetic prosecution and Bond's firm hand in maintaining courtroom order, the federal government convicted many Klansmen, but it also encountered widespread resistance. Some defendants fled before trial or were sheltered by their communities, and some could not be convicted because no one would testify against them. In 1872, Akerman's successor, George Williams, faced with limited resources and increasing Congressional reluctance to prolong federal involvement in the South, signaled to Southern leaders that he would agree to prosecute only egregious cases of violence if local officials would discourage violence generally. The bargain succeeded, largely because local officials had become increasingly concerned that Klan violence was threatening their authority as well as federal authority. Many officials also saw that Reconstruction was coming to an end and that there would be new opportunities to use nonviolent measures to control the role of blacks in Southern postwar society. Most states kept anti-Klan laws on the statute books after the end of Reconstruction because they were a useful sop to Northern public opinion, an insurance policy against active federal civil rights enforcement, and occasionally, a useful tool to suppress excessive white violence. As Tennessee's Redemption court explained in 1878, state anti-Klan laws "have proved themselves wholesome in the partial suppression already of one of the greatest of the disturbing elements of social order in this state."[35]

MOURNING THE END OF SLAVERY: SLAVEOWNER COMPENSATION AND SLAVE SALES CONTRACTS

Two additional issues of the Reconstruction era—state efforts to obtain compensation for owners of emancipated slaves and the enforceability of installment payment obligations under prewar slave sales contracts—have received little attention from historians. They are important because they show that many white Southerners went through a kind of mourning process before finally accepting emancipation. Southerners had developed a level of comfort with slavery over several centuries, and they could not reverse course quickly, and therein lay one of the central problems of Reconstruction.

The linkage between freedom for slaves and compensation for slaveowners had a long history in the South. By the early nineteenth century, Revolutionary-era sentiment for manumission had largely receded, but many Southerners were still morally uneasy about slavery, and they hit upon the creation of African colonies for freed slaves as a possible solution. Colonization societies flourished throughout the South from 1810 to the eve of the Civil War; many raised substantial sums to purchase slaves from willing masters and send them to Liberia and other African settlements. Colonization also found much support in the North: as late as 1863, Abraham Lincoln seriously proposed that the federal government subsidize a massive colonization scheme as a means of making the border states free and solidifying their loyalty to the Union.

As Frederick Douglass and other black leaders pointed out, mass colonization was hopelessly impractical. The number of slave children born each year alone outstripped the ability of white Americans to buy slaves' freedom. Nevertheless, the colonization movement reinforced loyal slaveowners' belief during the war that if emancipation occurred, they were entitled to compensation from either their state or the federal government. They soon became disillusioned. Many slaves in the border and Upper South states took advantage of the advance of Union armies to escape to freedom; others stayed with Union forces and were protected by them. As a result, the slave population of the border states fell rapidly throughout the war, and it became increasingly clear that slavery was doomed there regardless of the war's outcome.[36] Congress accelerated the process by enacting what turned out to be the only federal slaveowner compensation law: in 1864, it authorized military authorities to offer freedom to slaves as an inducement to enlist, with compensation of $300 per slave to their owners. As additional incentive, Congress later provided that families of black recruits would also be freed.[37]

The border states reacted to these events in different ways. Missouri and Maryland came to grips with emancipation quickly: at the end of the war, both states enacted new constitutions emancipating all slaves. Missouri's convention approved emancipation by a near-unanimous vote. The delegates acted in part for economic reasons: many accepted the free-labor argument, long made by Northern opponents of slavery, that America could reach its full economic potential only under a legal system that offered all workers, including blacks, the chance to advance through their own efforts. A few delegates also praised emancipation as a moral good. The Maryland convention voted for emancipation by a closer margin and only after extended debate from which talk of the morality of slavery was conspicuously absent. When West Virginia formed as a state, it initially declined to consider emancipation, but it reluctantly agreed to insert a gradual emancipation plan in its constitution when Congress made clear that such a plan would be required as a condition of statehood.[38]

Kentucky again was an exception among the border states, resisting emancipation to the end. The Kentucky legislature made several refinements to the state's fugitive slave laws during the war in a futile effort to stem slave defections to Union lines. The Kentucky supreme court declared that the federal laws allowing slave enlistments and freeing black recruits' families were unconstitutional because they deprived slaveowners of property without due process of law: many escaped slaves were worth more than the $300 federal limit on compensation. "Under what pretense," Chief Justice Robertson asked plaintively, "could Congress assume power to abolish slavery in Kentucky, a devoted union State, always for a restoration of the union, and nothing more or less?" Judge Rufus Williams, the lone dissenter, argued that the laws at issue were legitimate war measures. More practically, he pointed out that Kentucky slaveowners stood to receive about $30 million for their slaves under the laws and that such payments would be "the only savings possible out of the great wreck of [their] property incident to the rebellion." Williams, unlike most Kentuckians, recognized that by 1865 the prospect of compensation was rapidly disappearing.[39]

Compensation for emancipated slaves was also important to many Marylanders, but the issue received very little attention in Missouri. Maryland's 1864 convention prohibited the state from compensating slaveholders but left the way open for efforts to obtain federal compensation. Conservatives revived the issue after they regained control of the state: the 1867 legislature formally petitioned Congress for compensation "for the inconveniences, public and private, produced by such changes of system . . . according to the faith of the federal Government solemnly pledged." However, when the legislature called a convention to prepare a Redemption constitution, it required that the 1864 constitution's prohibition of state compensation be continued. The 1867 convention inserted a statement in the new constitution exhorting Congress to pay, but several delegates openly admitted that the passage of time had made the cause hopeless and that it should be abandoned. Tennessee's legislature also submitted a compensation petition in 1865. The 14th Amendment ended all hope by explicitly prohibiting compensation for freed slaves, although curiously, West Virginia asked Congress to consider compensation two years after the amendment was ratified.[40]

Unlike the border states, the ex-Confederate states entertained no hopes of compensation after the war. Even conservatives who rejected any but the most minimal changes in the legal status of freed slaves accepted emancipation and the loss of the slaves' value as the price of the war. At Redemption, conservative legislatures in North Carolina and Tennessee underscored this position by stating that no further requests for compensation should be made.[41]

Another issue that illustrated the mourning process for slavery was whether slave sale contracts should be enforced. Many prewar contracts called for installment payments over periods that extended past 1865, and Southern state courts were frequently called upon to decide who should bear the loss caused by emancipation. Many Southern Republicans viewed the issue as a final chance to drive home the evils of slavery, and Reconstruction constitutional conventions in most Deep South states declared slave contracts void and prohibited any further enforcement of them. These provisions were promptly challenged as an unconstitutional impairment of contract rights, and Southern supreme courts split over the issue. Most courts agreed that because slave sales contracts were not against public policy at the time they were made, they could not be voided: buyers must complete their payments and bear the loss. Louisiana's Reconstruction court disagreed, holding

that the voiding of slave contracts was a fundamental matter of state policy and that "the prohibition against the enactment of laws impairing the
obligations of contract has no application to the sovereign power." Texas's
Military Court agreed to enforce slave contracts by a narrow 3–2 margin:
Jack Hamilton, always a judicial Radical, argued in dissent that laws voiding
slave contracts should be upheld because they comported with the Emancipation Proclamation, which represented a fundamental federal decision in
favor of freedom and was binding on the ex-Confederate states by right of
conquest.[42]

Georgia provided the final answer to the issue. The Georgia supreme court
upheld the voiding clause in the state's Reconstruction constitution in a series
of decisions, one of which, *White v. Hart* (1869), was appealed to the United
States Supreme Court. In 1872, the High Court held that contract rights
took priority over the states' interest in retroactively condemning slavery
and that slave contracts must be enforced because they were not invalid at
the time they were made. Litigants in a number of states adopted variants of
Hamilton's position and argued that, at the least, slave contracts made after
the effective date of Lincoln's Emancipation Proclamation (January 1, 1863)
should be voided, but this argument was uniformly rejected: Restoration
and Reconstruction courts alike held the Proclamation was a military measure only and that wartime slave contracts were not void unless made within
areas controlled by Union forces. Again, only Louisiana disagreed.[43] Thus
slave sales contracts lingered and, in a modest way, prolonged the process of
mourning for slavery.

CONCLUSION

The prewar Southern struggle to balance considerations of humanity
and economic interest in setting the rights of black Southerners continued
unabated after the war, but with two crucial new participants: blacks themselves and Northern public opinion as reflected by Congress. The hope that
Reconstruction would realize the full potential of emancipation by elevat-
ing black Americans to true equality with whites ultimately was dashed, but
Reconstruction resulted in some permanent gains. The gains seem modest to
modern eyes, but given the immensity of the task of overcoming a centuries-
old culture of slavery, they were significant.

Restoration black codes have been accurately criticized as thinly disguised attempts to preserve the substance of the slave system, but they also
reflected subtle but real shifts in the South's legal treatment of blacks. The
fact of emancipation forced even the most recalcitrant Restoration legislatures to eliminate many prewar restrictions on blacks' activities, and most
state codes extended a small core of basic civil rights to blacks and added
some additional protections, most notably requirements that employment
contracts be in writing and be explained to illiterate workers and provisions

for resolving disputes before local tribunals. Few black workers were able to take real advantage of these protections: community prejudice, informal coercion, and occasional violence were all too effective as deterrents. But at a minimum, the nascent protective provisions provided a small opening for free-labor values and eventual acceptance of blacks as full human beings with full civil rights—an opening that would be more fully exploited a century after Reconstruction.

Congressional Reconstruction and the death of the dream of slaveowner compensation widened the opening a little. Reconstruction constitutional conventions and legislatures eliminated many black code restrictions and, in some cases, explicitly affirmed that black Southerners would henceforth enjoy vital civil and political rights previously denied them, such as the right to testify against whites, vote, and serve on juries. Some of this legacy was later erased: as will be seen in Chapter 11, post-Reconstruction lawmakers found many ways to restrict suffrage, jury service, and other black rights without provoking Congressional reaction. But some Reconstruction-era guarantees of basic rights remained embedded in Southern state constitutions and statutes long after their creators passed from the political scene.

Reconstruction permanently changed the tone of debate in the South over black rights. Post-Reconstruction lawmakers could no longer rely on the universal prewar presumption that blacks were less than fully human and were automatically to be subordinated to whites. A critical mass of Southerners now viewed restrictions on blacks as matters of political and economic interest that could be changed if necessary, rather than as immutable parts of the natural order of things. This was a vital if obscure legacy of Reconstruction. Furthermore, Southern judges served notice from the earliest postwar years that, in general, they would enforce racially neutral laws as written and would ensure that blacks received at least minimal due process when authorities sought to enforce restrictive laws against them. The courts also made clear they would enforce Reconstruction reform laws, no matter how repugnant, except in cases where such laws were clearly invalid under well-established constitutional and legal principles. Judge Rodman's decision to honor South Carolina's policy of allowing interracial marriage, though made reluctantly, signaled perhaps more clearly than any other Reconstruction decision that the prewar tradition of judicial conservatism and nationalism would continue.[44] The tradition was of little use to the vast majority of black Southerners who could not take their cases to the highest level because of lack of money or intimidation, but it provided another small opening for black rights.

The background presence of the federal government also shaped Southern states' responses to emancipation. Southern blacks and their white allies made use of federal laws and federal courts frequently and often successfully to protect and extend black rights. Even after the end of Reconstruction, Southern lawmakers had to pay heed to federal laws and to a risk of renewed federal intervention if they restricted black rights too tightly or too blatantly. Open defiance of federal authority in cases of conflict was now legally untenable as well as impracticable. Southern courts played a central role in reconciling their states to the new postwar federal order, which is described in the next chapter.

CHAPTER 5

Cleaning up after the Confederacy: The New Federalism and Allocation of Losses of War

> This new and beautiful organism is yet in the course of practical development, which may soon prove whether its fundamental equilibrium of local and national power is in most danger of disturbance from the centrifugal tendencies of the states, or the centripetal attractions of the central government.
>
> —Chief Justice George Robertson (Kentucky), 1865[1]

It is a truism that the balance of power between the state and federal governments underwent a fundamental change during the Civil War and the Reconstruction era. The Lincoln administration expanded on an unprecedented scale the armed forces and the bureaucracy that organized and supplied them. The war also made the federal government a major force in the nation's economy for the first time: in order to finance the war, Congress federalized the nation's currency system, created the nation's first income tax, and made the government a major participant in national and international credit markets. Faced with the specter of disunion, most people in the North and a surprising number of Southern Unionists developed a stronger sense of national union. The federal military machine shrank substantially after the war, but the government's role in the economy and the new sense of union did not. Congress, backed by Northern public opinion, expected the South to accept the new federal order as a condition of full participation in national affairs.[2]

Southern state courts played a vital role in that transition. Most Southern courts believed they had a duty to reconcile their constituents to the demise of the Confederacy and the concept of states' rights the Confederacy had embodied, but they took a surprising variety of approaches to this task.

FEDERALISM BEFORE THE CIVIL WAR

The American debate over the proper balance of power between state and federal governments began with the nation. In the *Federalist Papers* (1788), Alexander Hamilton neatly summarized the nationalist position, arguing that the new federal government was the creation of the American people directly, not of the states. "The national and State systems are to be regarded as *one whole*," said Hamilton, with state courts as "auxiliaries to the execution of the laws of the Union." Ten years later, Thomas Jefferson summarized the states' rights position when he prepared a resolution for use by Kentucky's legislature in opposing the federal Alien and Sedition Act. Jefferson argued that the right of "interposition," that is, a state's right to determine the validity of federal laws independently of the federal government, is an essential component of liberty. He also proclaimed that the federal government "was not made the exclusive or final judge of the extent of the powers delegated to itself . . . but that, as in all other cases of compact among parties having no common judge, each party has an equal right to judge for itself, as well of infractions, as of the mode and measure of redress."[3]

The debate continued during the early nineteenth century in response to several unpopular United States Supreme Court decisions written by Chief Justice John Marshall, a Hamilton ally and committed federalist. In 1816, Judge Spencer Roane of Virginia urged defiance after Marshall rejected a Virginia supreme court decision limiting the rights of heirs of a large British landholder in Virginia. In 1823, after Marshall ruled that newer states such as Kentucky could not impose restrictions on landowners who had purchased land within their borders when the land was part of another state, Kentucky and Ohio seriously considered adopting interposition as their official state policy. "What chance for justice have the states," complained Kentucky governor Joseph Desha, "when the usurpers of their rights are made their judges?" In 1832–33, South Carolina argued that it had the right to nullify a federal tariff within its borders; it backed down only under threat of military force by President Andrew Jackson, and at the same time, Georgia successfully defied a series of Marshall decisions adverse to the state's policy of allowing white settlement of Cherokee lands before the federal government had acquired them through treaty.[4]

Antebellum Southern courts, reflecting their nationalistic judicial culture, were considerably more restrained in their enthusiasm for states' rights than were their constituents. Roane was highly respected as a jurist but his decision to speak out for states' rights was a judicial anomaly. Kentucky's supreme court distanced itself from Governor Desha and conceded it was bound by decisions of the Marshall court as to matters clearly within the scope of federal power. Likewise, Georgia's supreme court affirmed that the federal Constitution and federal laws took precedence over Georgia laws and Chief Justice Joseph Lumpkin indicated that, like Hamilton, he viewed the federal government as an instrument of the American people rather than the states.[5]

THE *AB INITIO* DOCTRINE

Concepts of federalism in the postwar South were forged largely in debates over a doctrine devised by Senator Charles Sumner of Massachusetts. In early 1862, during the war's first winter, Sumner introduced resolutions declaring "[t]hat any vote of secession . . . becomes a practical abdication by the State of all rights under the Constitution" and "works an instant forfeiture of all those functions and powers essential to the continued existence of the State as a body politic." Sumner's doctrine became known as *ab initio* because it would require seceded states to follow the procedure for gaining statehood from the beginning. Sumner also foreshadowed Congressional Reconstruction by arguing that the clause of the federal Constitution guaranteeing the states a republican form of government gave Congress the right and duty to "assume complete jurisdiction of such vacated territory" and to prescribe the terms on which such territory was to be readmitted to the Union.

Ab initio never had a realistic chance of popular acceptance in either the North or the South: ultimately, as even its defenders perceived, secessionists "cannot afford to lose the nation, and the nation cannot afford to lose them." Nevertheless, the doctrine played an important role in the South's postwar transition to the new federalism because it challenged the remaining bonds of loyalty to the prewar order. Any Southern court that adopted or even flirted with *ab initio* would send its constituents a strong message that the old order had truly passed away and that the federal government should now be unreservedly accepted as supreme.[6]

Two 1869 United States Supreme Court decisions, *Texas v. White* and *Thorington v. Smith*, also played an important role in shaping postwar views of federalism. In *White*, the High Court buried *ab initio* once and for all—or so it thought. The Court held that although "the rights of the [Confederate states] as a member, and of her people as citizens of the Union, were suspended" during the war, the states never lost their identity as members of the Union. "The Constitution," said Chief Justice Salmon Chase, "looks to an indestructible Union, composed of indestructible States." Chase confirmed a line already drawn by many Southern courts: Confederate governmental acts "necessary to peace and good order among citizens, . . . must be regarded, in general, as valid," but "acts in furtherance or support of rebellion against the United States, or intended to defeat the just rights of citizens, . . . must, in general, be regarded as invalid and void."[7]

In *Thorington*, the Court addressed the issue of whether wartime transactions involving Confederate currency were valid. During the war, the value of Confederate currency declined in tandem with the Confederacy's military fortunes. According to North Carolina's official scale, the Confederate dollar was nearly at par with the federal dollar during 1861 and 1862; it fell from 6:1 to 14:1 after the battles of Gettysburg and Vicksburg in July 1863, fell to 26:1 after the fall of Atlanta in September 1864, and declined to 100:1 at the close of the war, after which time it of course became worthless. For Southerners who owed (or were owed) money based on wartime transactions, the question of whether such transactions could legally be enforced—and if so, what amount should be paid in federal currency—was of fundamental economic and political importance. To repudiate Confederate money transactions would seriously disturb the South's economy, but it would also strike a sharp blow at the legitimacy of the Confederacy and at Southerners who still cherished a lingering affection for the prewar order. The Supreme Court took a middle path, holding that Confederate money transactions were valid unless they directly aided the Confederate war effort. Practical considerations were important: Chase explained that "While the war lasted . . . [Confederate notes] were used as money in nearly all the business transactions of many millions of people. They must be regarded, therefore, as a currency, imposed on the community by irresistible force."[8]

Many Southern courts followed *White* and *Thorington*, but some did not. The courts' differing reactions and the language they used provide valuable insight into the postwar reconciliation process at the state level. Two general patterns emerged. Several states consistently took a centrist path: they legitimated Confederate governmental acts unrelated to the war effort but made clear that they did so for practical, not ideological, reasons. In a second, larger group of states, views of federalism fluctuated as Restoration, Reconstruction, and Redemption courts succeeded each other.

THE CENTRIST STATES

There was no clear geographic or political divide between the centrist and fluctuating states. North Carolina was the most influential of the centrist states, largely because of Chief Justice Pearson's prestige. Pearson made clear in two 1867 cases, *In Matter of Hughes* and *Phillips v. Hooker*, that his pragmatic bent in matters such as amnesty for wartime acts also extended to federalism. In *Hughes*, Pearson upheld the federal government's 1865 directive to the conquered states to call constitutional conventions, stating emphatically that only federal approval was needed in order to hold the conventions and that a convention was necessary to save North Carolina from the "horrors of anarchy." Pearson also made clear that prewar states' rights doctrine would not receive a sympathetic hearing in his court: "[O]ur state is not an independent nation, but is a member of the Union. . . . That question [the right to secede] we must suppose to have been settled by the result of the war."

Phillips involved a challenge to North Carolina's "scaling" law, one of many such laws enacted in the South immediately after the war in order to settle the legality of wartime financial transactions. The scaling laws steered a middle course in their treatment of such transactions: they affirmed that the transactions were enforceable, but recalculated or "scaled" debts based on the value of Confederate currency in federal dollars either at the time the debt was incurred or at the time it fell due. In *Phillips*, the debtor argued he should not have to pay because Confederate money transactions helped sustain the rebellion and therefore could not be condoned. Pearson declined to use the case to either praise or denounce the Confederacy. Instead, he suggested the Confederacy was simply irrelevant to the postwar period: the scaling law must be upheld because it was the only practical solution to a dilemma which, if not addressed, could destroy the postwar Southern economy. Pearson worried that to strike down Confederate currency transactions would mean that "encouragement is to be given to dishonesty, justice is not to be administered, and the people of the country are to be involved in utter perplexity and confusion, in order to make a useless show of zeal on the part of the courts 'to punish rebels.'" *Phillips* became one of the most important court decisions of the Reconstruction era: it was widely cited and followed in other Southern states.[9]

Pearson and his colleagues also served notice that there were other limits to the respect they would accord Confederate memory. Their concept of "acts in furtherance of the rebellion" encompassed a broad variety of transactions that came before them during Reconstruction. Some cases presented hard choices: for example, the court refused to allow a Confederate officer injured in a train accident to recover damages from the railroad because he had been traveling to join his unit at the time. Salt, which was vital for meat preservation and general public health, was in chronically short supply during the war and many local governments throughout the South borrowed money to purchase salt for their residents. Southern courts divided as to whether salt purchases were related to the war effort, but Pearson and his colleagues held that they were and that loans made to finance the purchases were uncollectible. The fact that health concerns were implicated did not matter: "The laws of war," said Pearson, "are paramount to motives of charity and humanity. Starving the citizens was resorted to [by the Union], in order to compel the authorities to surrender."[10]

The Mississippi supreme court's centrism is more surprising than North Carolina's. Unlike North Carolina, Mississippi had no significant Unionist element before the Civil War and the judges on its Restoration court had supported secession enthusiastically. But like Pearson, they rejected *ab initio* in words more pragmatic than defiant. To accept the doctrine, said Judge William Harris, would mean that "the citizens of this State were in a state of anarchy among themselves, without laws, constitution, or government, for the regulation of their private, internal, local affairs, during the progress of the war." Harris could not resist a direct swipe at *ab initio*, commenting that "because the government of the United States detained Mississippi in the Union by coercion of arms, it does not follow that Mississippi thereby became extinct as a state," but in the end he agreed that wartime state laws conflicting with federal law should be abrogated.[11]

Curiously, Mississippi's Reconstruction court also rejected *ab initio* and made little attempt to indoctrinate Mississippians in the new federalism. Reconstruction Chief Justice Ephraim Peyton agreed with Harris that *ab initio* "would lead to consequences productive of incalculable mischief."[12] The Reconstruction court upheld Confederate money transactions for pragmatic reasons, and after *Thorington* was decided, the court went out of its way to affirm that it considered *Thorington* binding. In 1876, a year after Reconstruction ended in Mississippi, the court denounced *ab initio* in ideological rather than pragmatic terms and in the process pronounced an epitaph on judicial Reconstruction in Mississippi. "Immediately succeeding the close of the war," said Judge Simrall, " . . . various and incongruous theories were put forward by jurists and judges. The times were not then propitious for calm and unimpassioned juridical discussions." Mississippi had never accepted those theories, and Simrall made clear that it never would.[13]

Virginia's supreme court also took a centrist path but was more ambivalent than its North Carolina and Mississippi counterparts. In 1872, the court acquiesced in the federal government's primacy, but only grudgingly. "It seems now to be generally conceded that the decisions of the Supreme Court are binding upon the State courts," said Judge Francis Anderson. "But I hold that this court is also supreme in its sphere, and is not bound to follow with 'blind submission' any court on earth." Anderson's colleague Waller Staples regretfully noted that Judge Roane's states' rights crusade 50 years earlier represented "old fashioned doctrines and ha[s] now but few avowed supporters"; he gloomily predicted the federal government would "in the end, absorb every vestige of the rights of the states." But the court generally agreed with other centrist courts on *ab initio*, Confederate currency, and the invalidity of acts in aid of the rebellion, although it disagreed with North Carolina and held that government purchases of salt during the war must be paid for because they were an "act of charity, humanity and self-preservation" rather than a war-related measure.[14]

South Carolina and Florida also adhered to a centrist path: both states' Reconstruction courts supported scaling and rejected appeals to invalidate Confederate currency transactions.[15] The only case of real note in either state involving federalism concerned the estate of John C. Calhoun, the leading prewar defender of interposition and states' rights. Following Calhoun's death his widow, Floride, sold the family plantation and slaves to relatives; after losing the slaves to emancipation, the relatives argued they need not pay the balance due to Floride because South Carolina's Reconstruction constitution outlawed slave sale contracts. Floride argued that the state constitution could not override a clause in the United States Constitution prohibiting states from impairing contracts, and the South Carolina court agreed. Floride perhaps did not appreciate the irony that she had won by taking a federalist position, but the court did, commenting with amusement: "It is probably not a matter of wonder or surprise that the consequences of the war, which has wrought so many changes, should have worked so material an alteration in the political sentiments of the South."[16]

THE GREAT DEBATE: GEORGIA AND ALABAMA

Among the states whose views of federalism fluctuated during Reconstruction, Georgia and Alabama are of particular interest because their courts engaged in a vigorous intramural debate about the nature of the new federalism. The Georgia and Alabama Restoration courts upheld their states' scaling laws and firmly rejected *ab initio*. In Georgia, Hiram Warner, who joined the Restoration court shortly before its demise, rejected *ab initio* in uniquely Unionist terms. He agreed that Georgia citizens owed paramount allegiance to the federal government, but he rejected Hamilton's theory of federalism, reasoning that Georgians owed allegiance to the federal government only "[b]ecause the State, acting in her sovereign capacity, has commended them to do so." Warner's colleague Iverson Harris protested that Georgia had both the right to secede and the right to have its wartime government treated as a legitimate government by postwar courts.[17]

The Restoration courts set the stage for debates over federalism within the Alabama and Georgia Reconstruction courts. In late 1868 and 1869, Warner and Joseph Brown took opposite sides in a series of cases addressing Georgia's scaling law and portions of its new Reconstruction constitution. For Warner, sanctity of contract trumped all other considerations, and he viewed *ab initio* as a subterfuge to evade the federal Constitution's ban on impairment of contracts. "Where there is a will to nullify [the federal contracts clause]," he warned, "some way will be found to do it, and that way, on the present occasion, is to assume that Georgia was not a state in the Union at the time of the adoption of the Constitution of 1868." Warner argued that because Georgia's scaling law gave juries power to set whatever compensation seemed fair, it impermissibly interfered with the parties' right to contract as they saw fit. He also argued that Georgia's Reconstruction convention could not invalidate slave sale contracts made before emancipation and that the constitution's expanded homestead exemption could not be applied to contracts made before its enactment.

Brown, on the other hand, adopted the very argument Warner rejected: because Georgia had not been readmitted to Congress at the time it adopted its Reconstruction constitution, it was not a state subject to the limits the federal Constitution placed on the states. It was subject only to the will of Congress, which had approved the new constitution and Georgia's Reconstruction laws. Brown believed the need for relief measures trumped constitutional niceties, including sanctity of contract, and he did not apologize for his use of *ab initio* to sustain relief measures. Despite his recent history as a states' rights firebrand, Brown in his Republican incarnation rejected Warner's solicitude for Georgia's prerogatives as a state. In Brown's view, "the conqueror had the right to dictate the terms of settlement" and the idea that Georgia retained its state rights intact was "not only a practical absurdity, but . . . contrary to equity and common sense." If the authors of the federal Constitution had seen the effects of the war, in which "two thirds of the whole property of the state . . . had been destroyed," they would have put the impairment of contract doctrine aside and supported Georgia's effort to "save something of the wreck" and to "compel an equitable distribution of the losses among debtors and creditors." Brown persuaded Henry McCay, the swing judge, to side with him on all issues except Confederate money transactions, which McCay voted to uphold. As one Redemption judge later recognized, Brown effectively committed Georgia to *ab initio* by a very indirect path. The Redemption court did not overturn the Reconstruction court's rulings even though it protested that federalism, "at first a compact of compromises and concessions, was rewritten by a mailed hand" during Reconstruction.[18]

The debate in Alabama was similar but sharper. In 1869 Alabama's Reconstruction court adopted *ab initio*. Judges Elisha Peck and Thomas Peters, both firm Republicans, agreed with Hamilton that the national government derived its power directly from the people, not the states, and thus Congress had plenary power to dictate the terms on which Alabama would be allowed to resume its former rights as a state. This was too much for Judge Benjamin Saffold, a Pearsonian pragmatist, who argued that "when an illegal government has existed for a considerable time, it is better to acquiesce in what has been done, than to still further convulse and demoralize society, by vainly seeking to run a thread of legality through the mode of its doing." Peters rejoined that any "presumption that sets these insurrectionary [acts] on the basis of legal authority, by reason of their necessity, will change the republic into an empire and a tyranny for a like reason." The Reconstruction court also took a hard line against Confederate money transactions and upheld an ordinance of Alabama's 1868 constitutional convention decreeing that such transactions were invalid. Although using Confederate money was not a crime, "the circulation of these notes ... was necessary to their use by the Confederate government in aid of the war" and was thus "efficient and indispensable aid to the rebellion, though involuntary." The Redemption court quickly reversed this holding after taking office, relying on *Phillips* and *Thorington*, which it praised as embodying "humane and enlarged ideas."[19]

LINGERING BITTERNESS: TEXAS, ARKANSAS, AND LOUISIANA

Farther west in Texas, Arkansas, and Louisiana, *ab initio* and the new federalism were equally controversial but prompted little judicial debate. Feelings were too strong, and as Restoration, Reconstruction, and Redemption courts succeeded one another, they simply overruled each other with little comment. In 1868, Texas's Military Court suggested that no acts of Confederate governments could be recognized under any circumstances. The next year, when the court refused to enforce the state's scaling law, Jack Hamilton used the occasion to lecture Texans about the new federalism, explaining that the scaling law "is in conflict with the constitution ... because it seeks to give value to the promises of a confederation of states entered into in hostility to the national authority and for its final overthrow, which promises were illegal and treasonable in their character, and are not susceptible of being validated by any power in the government." Texas's Semicolon Court[20] refused to validate Confederate money transactions even after *Thorington* was decided, declaring in 1872 that "no contract was ever made to be executed in Confederate money that does not come within the rule" of being in aid of the Confederate war effort. The Redemption court summarily overturned its predecessors' currency decisions soon after it took office. The court declined to criticize its predecessors directly, but Judge John Ireland could not resist a gibe at the Semicolon Court's refusal to follow *Thorington:* he noted that although the Reconstruction government's view "was originally supposed to be in harmony with the views of those public servants controlling the affairs of the United States [,] [s]uch, however, is not the view taken of these contracts by the judiciary department of that government."[21]

The gulf between Arkansas's Restoration, Reconstruction, and Redemption courts was, if anything, deeper than the gulf in Texas. Arkansas's Restoration court rejected *ab initio* with a mixture of Pearsonian practicality and defiance. Judge David Walker, who had served on the court before the war and had supported secession, reviewed the history of federalism and unsurprisingly reached a conclusion the exact opposite of Alexander Hamilton's: the American people, acting through the states, had exercised their paramount power to create a federal government of limited powers. Walker declined to address the question of whether Arkansas had the right to secede, but he unhesitatingly denounced *ab initio:* "However much this may be indulged in, by wild theorists in politics, it can never be sanctioned by the judiciary." Four years later, the Reconstruction court, led by John McClure, reversed Walker. McClure made his own review of the history of federalism and concluded that Hamilton's theory of federalism was correct. He adopted *ab initio* in terms as strong as those in which Walker had rejected it: the idea that the Arkansas Confederate government's acts, "during the period it has been incubating treason, are legal, valid or binding, is a heresy that should not emanate from the highest judicial tribunal of a State."[22]

McClure and his colleagues were equally adamant in refusing to enforce Confederate money transactions. They rejected any suggestion that the practical hardships of such a ruling should influence their thinking. All persons using Confederate money, said McClure, "became stockholders in the rebellious and treasonable conspiracy of the insurgents . . . and [the] use of such pretended money, by the rebellious conspirators . . . must share the fate of the rebellion." The Reconstruction court explicitly refused to follow *White* and *Thorington,* relying, ironically, on state sovereignty as its main reason for doing so. As in Texas, McClure's Redemption successors promptly adopted the rules laid down in *White* and *Thorington* and denounced *ab initio* as "a proposition so monstrous and mischievous in its consequences as to shock the sense of judgment of any reasonable and dispassionate mind."[23]

Louisiana was unusual in that both its Restoration and Reconstruction courts refused to enforce Confederate currency transactions. Louisiana incorporated a proscription against Confederate currency into its Reconstruction constitution and its supreme court upheld the proscription until 1873, when the United States Supreme Court instructed Louisiana to follow the *Thorington* rule. Both the Restoration and Reconstruction courts took a broad view of what constituted transactions in aid of the rebellion, holding with North Carolina (and contrary to Virginia) that wartime salt purchases fell in that category.[24] In the one case where the Reconstruction court had an opportunity to address the new federalism directly, the court held that *ab initio* was at bottom a political question but indicated its sympathy for the doctrine. Judge James Taliaferro, with memories of his wartime imprisonment by the Confederacy still fresh, commented that the Confederacy "had, no doubt, the good wishes of the few who yet remain hostile to the march of liberal sentiment, and who cling to the idea of the idea of the divine right of kings. But on which side in the fearful strife were the sympathies of the masses of mankind?"[25]

"SPORT TO YOU BUT DEATH TO US": TENNESSEE AND WEST VIRGINIA

Ab initio found its most fervent support in Tennessee and West Virginia, where the political balance between Unionists and ex-Confederates was closest. Unionists in each state viewed the Confederacy's defeat as an opportunity to take permanent political control and feared the consequences if they did not succeed. Unreconstructed Confederates and other conservatives in each state were equally apprehensive about how they would fare if the Unionists succeeded.[26]

In 1865, Tennessee's Unionist constitutional convention prohibited enforcement of all Confederate-era governmental acts and laws. The new supreme court promptly endorsed this sentiment, holding flatly that "the courts of the country are bound to treat [Confederate laws] as if they had never been promulgated." Judge James Shackelford contended that the war put an end to any need to treat the Richmond government as legitimate for any purpose.[27] In West Virginia Judge James Brown expressed the same sentiment (and Unionist fears of the threat posed by postwar conservatives) more bluntly, stating that opposition to *ab initio* "reminds one of the language of the frogs to the boys in the fable: 'It may be sport to you, but it is death to us.'"[28] Both states' courts were equally prompt to condemn Confederate money transactions and after *Thorington* was decided, both joined the Alabama, Texas, and Louisiana Reconstruction courts in refusing to follow that decision. In Tennessee, Judge George Andrews, echoing McClure, stated that "the intended and the actual effect of . . . [Confederate] currency, was to make every noteholder a stockholder in the Confederacy, and directly interested to the extent of his investment to secure the ultimate success of the Rebel cause." In West Virginia, Judge Brown explained that such currency "was the life blood of the rebellion . . . and appealed directly to the interest of every holder to aid in its accomplishment."[29]

When conservatives regained control of Tennessee and West Virginia in the early 1870s, they promptly enacted new constitutions, repealed laws favoring *ab initio*, and created new supreme courts. The Redemption courts in each state quickly overturned Reconstruction court decisions as to *ab initio* and Confederate currency. The Tennessee court criticized its Reconstruction predecessors openly, in pointed contrast to most other Southern Redemption courts, explaining that a change in the law was necessary because the Reconstruction court's work was "ill-considered," "palpably wrong," and the product of "a time of great civil commotion . . . calculated to disturb and sway the course of thought and reason." Although the court freely condemned the perceived excesses of the new federalism, it refrained from commending the lost Confederate cause, going only so far as to say that the Confederacy should be treated as a *de facto* government because of its "irresistible force and power." West Virginia's Redemption court relied heavily on Tennessee Redemption decisions in reversing its predecessors' course, but it used more circumspect language. The court explained that "the questions arising and growing out of the complications of the war in this state are exceedingly difficult . . . and we are compelled, in a great degree, to look to the attainment of justice" as to Confederate governmental acts unrelated to the war effort.[30]

CONSERVATIVE FEDERALISM ON THE BORDER: THE CASE OF KENTUCKY

Border state courts had little occasion to squarely address the new federalism except for Kentucky, which had long had a complicated relationship with the federal government. Kentuckians took deep pride in their state's heritage as the first American outpost west of the Allegheny Mountains; this pride manifested itself as "a complex of fierce love for the Union [and] violent opposition to any infringement of the state's constitutional rights or interference in the state's affairs." During the war, Kentucky experienced the new federalism more intimately than any other loyal state: the Union army thwarted two major Confederate invasions of the state, but it also took many harsh measures to maintain control of the state and suppress civilian opposition to the war effort.[31] Kentucky's highest court was concerned about the shift: after the war, it consistently searched for ways to preserve the traditional balance between state and federal power, and in the process, it voiced some unique perspectives on the new federalism.

The court made its first major pronouncement shortly after the close of the war, when it was asked to overturn wartime federal laws that encouraged recruitment of slaves for the Union armies by promising emancipation to them and their families. The laws were deeply unpopular in Kentucky, and the court openly voiced its constituents' unhappiness with federal intrusion into slavery. The court also objected that the 1866 Civil Rights Act's provision allowing blacks who could not testify under Kentucky law to remove their lawsuits to federal courts was an infringement of the state's "unquestionable right to regulate her own domestic concerns, and prescribe remedies, including rules of evidence, in cases in her own courts." But in another case, Chief Justice George Robertson acknowledged that the United States

Chief Justice George Robertson, Kentucky. Courtesy of the Filson Historical Society, Louisville, Ky.

Supreme Court had the final say on all issues involving the federal Constitution, and he then delivered a lengthy mediation on the nature of the new federalism. Robertson likened the states to planets orbiting a federal sun and stated with a certain air of fatalism that "This new and beautiful organism is yet in the course of practical development" and that time would tell whether there was more danger "from the centrifugal tendencies of the States, or the centripetal attractions of the central government."[32]

One Kentucky judge, Rufus Williams, consistently defended the new federalism. Williams agreed with Alexander Hamilton that the "[federal] government is not sovereign, but it is supreme, and designed to be perpetual." Williams also echoed Abraham Lincoln's vision of the federal Union, arguing that if Kentucky and other states were to unduly second-guess the federal government's wartime actions, the United States "must vanish from the world as a thing of the past, and with its downfall must go the last brightest evidence of man's capability for self-government." His colleagues rejoined that the war "did not essentially change the fundamental relations of the citizens of those revolting states to the federal government."[33]

REMOVAL LAWS AND THE FINAL TRIUMPH OF THE NEW FEDERALISM

A final issue that prompted debate over the new federalism, and which led to its ultimate triumph, was the validity of federal laws permitting the removal of certain types of lawsuits from state courts to federal courts. During the Civil War and Reconstruction, Congress expanded the scope of removal dramatically. In 1863, it allowed federal officers to remove lawsuits brought against them in state courts, and two of the cornerstone federal Reconstruction laws expanded removal further: the 1866 Civil Rights Act allowed defendants not accorded basic civil rights in state courts to remove their cases to federal court, and the 1867 Reconstruction Acts allowed out-of-state litigants to remove their cases by filing an affidavit stating a belief that "from prejudice or local influence, [they] will not be able to obtain justice in such State court."[34]

Removal laws were intimately connected with federalism because they represented an effort to ensure that cases falling within the jurisdiction of both the federal and state courts would end up in hands of federal authorities.

The removal provisions of the 1866 Act and 1867 Reconstruction Acts were an all but open statement by Congress that it did not trust Southern courts to give justice to blacks and Unionists. Yet apart from Kentucky, Southern reaction to the acts was mild. Wisconsin, far to the north, mounted the most serious challenge to the laws: in a series of cases in the late 1860s and early 1870s Wisconsin's supreme court challenged federal removal laws as impermissibly infringing on states' rights.[35] In *In re Tarble* (1870), the Wisconsin court held that states had the right to issue writs of *habeas corpus* releasing prisoners held in federal custody, and in *Morse v. Home Insurance Co. of New York* (1872), it held that states had a right to prohibit corporations from invoking federal removal laws as a condition of being allowed to do business in the state. The United States Supreme Court reversed both decisions. Justice Stephen Field made clear that the High Court had the final word in all cases of conflicting constitutional interpretation: "The two governments in each State," said Field, "stand in their respective spheres of action in the same independent relation to each other, except . . . in the supremacy of the authority of the United States when any conflict arises between the two governments."[36]

Postwar Southern courts refrained from joining Wisconsin's crusade. On one occasion, Virginia warned against construing removal laws so as to "confer upon the federal courts the extensive, all-pervading and dangerous jurisdiction, which would constitute the federal courts appellate tribunals to the state courts." But other state courts enforced the removal laws with little comment and in Georgia, Judge McCay went so far as to remind his constituents that federal courts were not necessarily enemies. Both federal and state courts, said McCay, "are Courts of our own creation, and each is intended for the public good—the good of the State and the people of the State, as well as the people of other States. It [Georgia's federal district court] is not a foreign Court, but a Court sitting under a Constitution and laws made by and for the State and people of Georgia."[37]

Several common themes emerge from the reactions of postwar Southern courts to the demise of the Confederacy and the rise of a newly powerful federal government. First, all courts acknowledged that the Union's victory completely delegitimated the Confederate war effort and that persons who had directly risked money or property on the success of the Confederacy would have to bear the loss. This unanimity played an important part in reinforcing Southerners' acceptance of the military result of the war.

Second, it is surprising that so many Southern courts followed a consistently centrist path throughout Reconstruction, deferring modestly to their constituents' enduring emotional ties to the Confederacy by refusing to adopt *ab initio* but taking every opportunity to urge acceptance of federal supremacy for practical reasons and conspicuously refraining from honoring the Lost Cause. Such behavior confirmed that the nationalistic strain in prewar Southern judicial culture had survived the war largely unscathed, and judicial nationalism played an important role in helping the South adjust to the realities of the new federalism. Even in states where the political tides shifted repeatedly during Reconstruction, deeply ingrained legal tradition required courts to show proper respect for precedent and overturn precedent by force of judicial reasoning rather than judicial fiat. Even the most ideological Southern judges were forced to cabin their opinions within a logical framework, and in Georgia and Alabama, this produced a genuine contribution to the *ab initio* debate.

Four years after the end of Reconstruction, John Forrest Dillon, author of the nation's leading treatise on removal law, cited the *Tarble* and *Morse* decisions as marking the final extinction of the prewar concept of states' rights. Judge Dillon took a sanguine view of the evolution of federalism, concluding that "serious conflicts between the State and Federal Courts have been almost wholly avoided" and that the rule of federal primacy in deciding federal constitutional issues "remains, after the lapse of nearly a century, almost intact and [thus] the admiration with which it has been regarded by statesmen, lawyers and judges, is not undeserved."[38] Dillon's view contains a grain of truth as to Southern courts, but it is too simplistic. Although some courts actively promoted the new federalism, most merely accepted it as a practical reality rather than an ideal. After the end of Reconstruction, Redemption courts continued to accept this reality but also showed a continuing desire to protect their states' prerogatives where possible. Dillon also overlooked a final irony. By definition, Southern state courts exercised *state* power to reconcile their constituents to the new federalism, and the fact that each state court chose its own method of reconciliation confirms that the Civil War transformed states' rights but did not come close to killing them.

CHAPTER 6

The Constitutional Legacy of Reconstruction

> I do desire we shall use the opportunities we now have to our best advantage, as we may not ever have a more propitious time. We know when the old aristocracy and ruling power of this State get into power, as they undoubtedly will . . . they will never pass such a law as this.
> —Francis Cardozo (South Carolina), 1868[1]

Constitutions have long been viewed by lawmakers and legal scholars as the cornerstone of the American governmental system. A constitution sets forth the fundamental, "organic" law of the state: all laws and other acts of the state must conform to its dictates. Ideally, constitutions are confined to general, immutable principles and ideals, and the task of filling in the details necessary to implement those principles is left to the branches of government created by the constitution. Concomitantly, because constitutions embody fundamental principles, they should be amended sparingly and should be replaced with new constitutions only in the most extreme circumstances.[2]

The reality of state constitution-making has fallen short of these ideals. From the American Revolution on, many states concluded that solutions to the leading controversies of the day—for example, the proper extent of suffrage in the late eighteenth and early nineteenth centuries and the proper extent of state support for corporations and internal improvements in the mid-nineteenth century—should be fixed in their constitutions rather than left to legislatures and shifting political tides. In the words of one scholar, nineteenth-century state lawmakers "came to view constitution-making as a progressive enterprise, requiring the constant readjustment of past practices and institutional arrangements in light of changes in circumstance and political thought."[3]

But even in states that changed their constitutions frequently, constitutions were always viewed as being above mere statutes. State laws generally made the process of calling and holding a constitutional convention cumbersome, and it was never done lightly. Thus when Congress required the ex-Confederate states to create new constitutions, Southern Republicans and other supporters of reform saw an opportunity not only to implement desired changes in their states' legal systems but to put a stamp of permanence on those changes. Some conservatives predicted the changes would "last just as long as the bayonets which ushered them into being . . . and not one day longer," but to a surprising degree, this proved not to be true. Many such reforms, most notably common schools, homestead exemptions, and expanded property rights for married women, had gained acceptance in the North and even parts of the South before the Civil War; Reconstruction conventions completed the reform process. Redemption constitutions retained most such reform measures and also preserved a number of basic civil rights provisions found in Reconstruction constitutions. These constitutional reforms represent one of the major legal legacies of Reconstruction.[4]

SOUTHERN CONSTITUTIONS PRIOR TO RECONSTRUCTION

Southern constitutions on the eve of the Civil War were highly diverse: they had been enacted in several different eras and reflected the concerns of those eras. The pre-Jacksonian constitutions of South Carolina (1790), Georgia (1798), Alabama (1819), and Missouri (1820), like other constitutions of that period, were short and focused mainly on basic powers of government: they did not address issues of concern to conventions held in the mid-nineteenth century. Constitutions enacted after 1830 addressed the cycle of state support for private enterprise followed by default, debt, and reaction that had begun in the 1820s. State and local governments tried to promote new industries and forms of transportation by enacting corporate charters conferring special benefits on railroads and other companies willing to undertake such tasks, and sometimes also subsidizing the companies through stock purchases and land and cash grants. The ventures had a high failure rate, particularly during the depressions of 1837–40 and 1857–58, leaving many state and local governments saddled with crushing debt. As a result, with the exception of North Carolina, every Southern state that enacted a new constitution between 1830 and 1861 imposed permanent restrictions on government aid to private enterprise. Most states limited the amount of aid and credit the legislature could give to corporations. Tennessee (1834), Texas (1845), Louisiana (1845), and Kentucky (1850) also prohibited their legislatures from enacting special charters for individual corporations; and Kentucky, Maryland, and Virginia, which enacted the last Southern prewar constitutions in 1850–51, placed limits on the total debt the legislature could incur.[5]

When the Confederate states enacted secession constitutions in 1860–61, they did not repudiate the basic forms of government they had developed under the Union. Most contented themselves with amendments to their existing constitutions affirming secession, state sovereignty, and the sanctity of slavery. Likewise, in 1865, most Restoration constitutional conventions did little more than repudiate secession and abolish slavery. But strikingly, most of the conventions also declined to renew prewar limits on aid to private enterprise. Most likely, the delegates, mindful of the severe damage the war had inflicted on their states' economies, did not want to close any possible avenues to recovery; they also knew that as a practical matter, their states would be unable to provide aid for some time.[6]

RECONSTRUCTION CONSTITUTIONS AND CIVIL RIGHTS

The Reconstruction constitutions are the only American constitutions that arose from externally imposed forces rather than internal state forces. The federal Reconstruction Acts of 1867 placed all ex-Confederate states except Tennessee under military rule; as a condition of ending such rule and gaining readmission to Congress, the acts required the states to call new conventions and provide for black suffrage. This background meant that the constitutions carried the potential for revolutionary change but also for complete failure.

Although Congress made clear that constitutional reform was necessary, it did not specify any details of reform other than black suffrage. Republicans hoped that an electorate composed largely of Unionists would elect convention delegates who would instinctively gravitate to appropriate reform measures. Native white Unionists, blacks, and carpetbaggers collectively dominated the Reconstruction conventions, but the comparative strengths of each group varied widely in each convention and the groups did not always see eye to eye. Blacks won a plurality of seats in Louisiana, South Carolina, and Florida, where they composed a large portion of the population. Native Unionists obtained a plurality in all other states; carpetbaggers had a significant presence only in Virginia, Florida, Alabama, Mississippi, and Arkansas. The Reconstruction conventions gave black Americans their first opportunity to participate directly in the shaping of American law. A number of black delegates took leading roles in the convention debates; the records of the four states that published their full convention debates (Louisiana, Virginia, Arkansas, and South Carolina) provide valuable insight into the hopes and concerns Southern blacks had for their role in the new postwar order.[7]

In the Louisiana convention, which produced perhaps the most radical of the Reconstruction constitutions, leaders of New Orleans' long-established free black community dominated the black delegation. Two delegates, Robert Cromwell and E. D. Tinchant, quickly made clear that they would insist on broad guarantees of social as well as political rights, including equal access to public accommodations and integrated schools. Black delegates also paid close attention to suffrage issues but divided as to whether a loyalty oath should be imposed as a condition of suffrage. Cromwell and the majority favored an ironclad oath, but Tinchant rejoined that he had been "taught to look upon the men of my race as fully equal to the white men, and able to fight their way through without the help of any partial proscriptive measure directed against their opponents." Many white delegates expressed dismay at the lengths to which blacks insisted on going: John Ludeling, who was soon to join the state's Reconstruction court, refused to sign the constitution because "social equality is attempted to be enforced, and the right of citizens to control their own property is attempted to be taken from them for the benefit of the colored race." But the black delegation obtained most of what it wanted.[8]

Black delegates in Virginia and Arkansas also tried to enshrine as many guarantees of rights as possible in their constitutions. The most prominent member of the black contingent at Virginia's convention was Thomas Bayne, who had escaped from slavery in 1855, had established a dental practice in Massachusetts, and had returned to his native state after the war. Bayne's primary objective was to secure black suffrage and ensure that it could not be limited in future; he was supported by several influential white Republicans, including convention chair John Underwood. Underwood, a native New Yorker, had moved to Virginia before the war and had established an experimental integrated colony despite fierce opposition; he was forced to leave Virginia at the beginning of the war but was appointed a federal district judge in 1863 and returned to the portion of the state controlled by Union troops. Underwood continued to pursue social reform while a federal judge, and he remained a

Judge John Underwood, Virginia. Courtesy of the Library of Congress.

highly controversial figure. At the convention, he went beyond Bayne, emphasizing that "the poor and ignorant have been denied all means of education by our laws, and are in the greatest need of the protection of the ballot"; he also urged that suffrage be extended to women.

Bayne, Underwood, and their allies met with only limited success. When a motion early in the convention to place a universal male suffrage provision in the state's bill of rights failed, Bayne bitterly commented that "we must [now] sit down, just as we did in old master's day, and wait for old master to tell us who our friends are. . . . I take my ground that you are living just under the shadow of the cowhide and the whipping post, and that our remembrance of it is too recent for any such talk" of compromise. The convention eventually inserted a suffrage provision allowing black males to vote and hold office but excluding Virginians who had supported the Confederacy or who were unable to take a loyalty oath. The exclusionary clauses proved highly controversial. General John Schofield, the military commander of the Virginia district, was concerned that it would not be possible to govern the state if ex-Confederates could not hold office, and he delayed a vote on the constitution until Congress agreed that the clauses could be voted on separately from the rest of the constitution. In late 1869, the voters ratified the constitution but rejected the exclusionary clauses.[9]

In Arkansas, delegates devoted the majority of their time to civil rights issues, particularly suffrage and whether the constitution should prohibit miscegenation. William Grey, the leading black voice in the debate, had a background that was unusual even for an era in which many blacks had taken extraordinary personal journeys to arrive at their places as Reconstruction lawmakers. Grey was born into slavery about 1830 on the Virginia plantation of Henry S. Wise, a prominent politician who served in Congress and as Virginia's governor before the war. Grey was rumored to be Wise's son; Wise emancipated Grey, saw to it that he received a basic education, and employed Grey as his secretary during his service in Congress. Grey was perhaps the only slave in the South who had such intimate access to the inner workings of state and federal government. At the end of the war, Grey, now free, moved to Arkansas: he quickly became a successful merchant and began a career in local politics that lasted until his death in 1890.

At the Arkansas convention, white Radicals were willing to support basic civil and political rights for Arkansas blacks but, unlike their Virginia counterparts, they could not stomach any measures that appeared to promote social equality. John McClure, who like his Louisiana colleague Ludeling would soon be promoted to chief justice of his state's supreme court, shared Ludeling's distaste for such measures: he explained that "in legislating upon the heels of a revolution, it is not safe to disturb the ancient and fixed landmarks of society . . . we begin to create a revolution the moment we attempt to establish the line." Grey

William Grey, Arkansas. Courtesy, Arkansas History Commission. All Rights Reserved.

realized he and his black colleagues could not overcome this wall of opposition; they therefore decided to bear witness for future generations, a role that would become familiar to American blacks in many contexts during the century to follow. The debate over a proposed antimiscegenation clause provided the chief opportunity for witness. Grey pointed out that miscegenation between whites and slaves had been common before the war and suggested that if interracial marriage was to be penalized, so should interracial cohabitation. He also pointed out that miscegenation laws, like all race-based laws, would require lawmakers to define how much black ancestry was sufficient to make a person "black" in the eyes of the law and would create a genealogical quagmire. In the end, Grey and his colleagues accepted a compromise that left the issue to the legislature, but Grey warned that any future antimiscegenation laws must treat the races alike: "I want the bill [for past discrimination] paid in full."[10]

South Carolina's was the only convention in which black delegates enjoyed an absolute majority, yet the convention devoted as much attention to economic issues as to civil rights and produced a relatively moderate constitution. In his opening address to the delegates, Restoration Governor James Orr, a moderate Unionist, warned that no constitution could endure that ignored white conservative opinion completely. Orr assured the delegates that many whites would accept reforms that increased economic opportunity for both races, such as homestead exemptions, debt relief measures, and common schools: reforms such as these, he argued, could become permanent if they were detached from racial issues. Orr displayed genuine sympathy for the trials the delegates faced:

You have a great problem to solve, such an one as has rarely been given to man; you are to undertake an experiment which has not thus far in the experience of mankind been successful. That experience shows that, when placed upon terms of equality, the races have not harmonized. It is for you to demonstrate to the contrary.[11]

Orr's remarks perhaps contributed to the convention's moderation, but the main cause was the nature and size of the black delegation. Majority status meant there was less need to present a united front than there was in conventions with small black delegations, and the delegation's leadership included independent-minded politicians such as Francis Cardozo, Robert Elliott, Robert DeLarge, Jonathan Wright, Richard Cain, and William Whipper. Some of these leaders had been born to free parents in Northern states and had come to South Carolina during or shortly after the war as soldiers or relief workers; others were native-born. All went on to higher office after the convention: Cain, DeLarge, and Elliott served in Congress, Cardozo served as South Carolina's secretary of state and treasurer, Wright served on the state's supreme court, and Whipper served in the legislature.[12]

The South Carolina convention began with an extended debate whether debtor relief measures should be incorporated in the new constitution. Cain pointed out that the vast majority of the state's debt was owed by planters and other wealthy whites and opposed any measures to stay collection of debts, but Cardozo objected and eventually prevailed, warning that lack of relief would lead to repudiation of debts and that South Carolina would suffer if it gained a reputation as a repudiator state. The convention then moved to the issue of whether prewar slave sales contracts should be enforced or repudiated. Elliott, supported by Wright, argued for repudiation as matter of morality: parties to such contracts "were guilty of the enormous crime of slavery." Slave buyers had already been penalized by the loss of their slaves, and "we are now to pass sentence upon the seller . . . [who] shall be punished by the loss of his money." Cardozo, again concerned about the state's image of fiscal responsibility, argued against the proposed provision precisely because it discriminated against sellers, but this time he did not prevail. Roles changed when education was discussed. Unlike their Louisiana colleagues, South Carolina's black delegates did not insist on integrated schools, but Cardozo argued strenuously that a common school system should be created and that integration should be permitted if not required. Cardozo believed a strong school system was indispensable to preservation of blacks' civil rights: he warned that whites' prewar power over blacks was "built on and sustained by ignorance" and that when whites returned to power in the future, "they [would] take precious good care that the colored people shall never be enlightened" unless a right to education were secured in the constitution. Cardozo's colleagues agreed on the necessity of a school system but disagreed as to many of the operational details. DeLarge and Cain feared that allowing integration would completely undermine any white support for a common school system. Wright joined Cardozo in supporting a poll tax to fund the schools but Elliott and DeLarge warned that if conservatives regained power in future, they could use the tax as an effective weapon to limit black suffrage. Cardozo eventually prevailed: the new constitution provided for both compulsory attendance and a poll tax.[13]

RECONSTRUCTION CONSTITUTIONS AND THE COMPLETION OF PREWAR REFORMS

The Reconstruction constitutions provided a means by which several major mid-nineteenth century reforms that had taken hold in most of the North and parts of the South before the war could complete their progress through the South. Three reforms in particular were taken up by the Reconstruction conventions: statewide public school systems, homestead exemptions, and married women's property rights. Redemption conventions in most states preserved these reforms.

Common School Systems

From the colonial era onward, there was a distinct regional variation in American attitudes toward education. The Southern colonies, settled primarily by Anglicans, adhered to the church's position that families and the church, not the state, were responsible for education. This was reinforced by a general belief among the Southern elite that widespread education was at best an extravagance for most workers and at worst a threat to the social order. By contrast, the Puritan dissenters who settled New England believed that in order to thwart the "chief project of that old deluder, Satan, to keep men from the knowledge of the Scriptures," it was vital to make education and literacy accessible to all. Between 1789 and 1830, many northeastern states developed public school systems, but Southern states were slow to embrace such changes. Movements for state common school systems, free to all white children, began in North Carolina and Georgia in the 1830s and in Alabama and Tennessee in the 1850s, but only North Carolina and Georgia provided meaningful financial support for such schools before the Civil War. Calls for educational reform arose sporadically in other Southern states but as of 1861, most states provided free schooling only for the poor; this created a stigma, and many poor families shunned the schools out of pride.[14]

Reconstruction lawmakers largely completed the work of the common schools movement in the South and laid the groundwork for permanent school financing systems. Support for such reform was not confined to white Republicans and blacks. Jabez L. M. Curry, an Alabama conservative, became a leading national spokesman for educational reform and at least two states, Florida and Arkansas, enacted important educational reform measures during the Restoration period.[15] But Reconstruction legislatures and constitutional conventions performed the bulk of the work: every ex-Confederate state except Alabama, Texas, and Tennessee provided for common schools in its Reconstruction constitution. War-related destruction in the South also surely played a role: Republicans and conservatives alike realized the South would need every available tool, including public education, to regain the road to prosperity. The only real controversy was over school integration. Conservatives and white Republican delegates feared that even a compulsory school attendance requirement would raise the specter of forced integration and would undermine white support for public schools, but where compulsory attendance provisions were passed, they reluctantly acceded to them in order to ensure there would be some educational opportunity for poor whites unable to afford private schools. Redemption conventions uniformly preserved common schools provisions after the end of Reconstruction.[16]

Homestead Exemptions

Another reform completed in the South during Reconstruction was the movement for homestead exemptions. Debtor relief laws, including laws exempting essential personal items from seizure by creditors, had existed throughout the United States since the colonial era, but the movement to extend such exemptions to homesteads was fueled largely by the high value that early Mississippi Valley settlers placed on land ownership and by the severe depression of the late 1830s. Two southwestern states, Texas and Mississippi, were the first to enact homestead exemption statutes. Most Northern and Southern states enacted similar laws prior to the Civil War, but only a handful of states viewed the homestead exemption principle as one of constitutional magnitude. Texas was the first state to enshrine the homestead exemption in its constitution (1845), but in the South only Maryland (1851) followed suit before the war.

Like common schools, homestead exemptions gained increasing favor after the war as Southern lawmakers looked for ways to hasten economic recovery. Most Southern states expanded their statutory exemptions after the war and five states (Virginia, North Carolina, Georgia, Alabama, and Arkansas) elevated the exemptions to constitutional status, despite the expostulations of some conservatives that such measures were "an act of direct robbery." The only serious concern was whether such exemptions could be applied retroactively to debts incurred before their enactment. Redemption conventions uniformly preserved Reconstruction-era exemption provisions and one state, West Virginia, created a constitutional homestead provision for the first time during the Redemption era. It is possible that constitutional homestead exemptions would have become universal in the South even if Reconstruction had never occurred, but Reconstruction conventions provided the occasion to complete such change and the reformist bent of most Reconstruction convention delegates increased the odds that such change would take place. Tellingly, Kentucky and Delaware, the only two states that did not enact constitutions during Reconstruction, did not incorporate homestead provisions in their first post-Reconstruction constitutions.[17]

Married Women's Property Rights

Confirmation of married women's rights in their separate property was another reform that gained a foothold in the South before the war and was completed during Reconstruction. During the colonial era and the early years of the nineteenth century, most states adhered to the marital unity doctrine of British common law, which gave husbands nearly absolute power over property their wives brought to the marriage, although courts in many states sanctioned devices for sheltering such assets from husbandly control. In the 1830s, a movement arose to allow married women direct control over their property. Its supporters were motivated more by a desire to protect families from spendthrift husbands than by any real desire to empower wives; nevertheless, the new laws were regarded as a genuine political and economic advance for women. Like homestead exemptions, married women's property laws appeared first in the southwest: Mississippi enacted the first such law in 1839, and most other southwestern states followed suit before the war. The movement also spread through the North in the 1840s and 1850s, spurred heavily by New York's decision to enact a married women's property rights law in 1848. Texas was the first Southern state to insert married women's provisions in its constitution (1845), but the Texas provisions merely reflected the state's longstanding community property system for married couples, a carryover from the state's time as a Spanish colony and Mexican province. The only other Southern state to insert a married women's clause in its constitution before the war was Maryland (1851).[18]

Reconstruction conventions in eight states added married women's property rights clauses to their constitutions. In five states (Florida, Alabama, Mississippi, Louisiana, and Arkansas), this was a less dramatic change than might at first appear: all five states had enacted married women's property statutes before the war, and their Reconstruction conventions merely confirmed that such rights would not be disturbed lightly. But in three states (North Carolina, South Carolina, and Georgia), the new constitutional provisions represented the first enactment of married women's rights. Reconstruction lawmakers, like their predecessors, acted primarily out of a desire to protect families from the creditors of impecunious husbands rather than to empower wives, but they recognized their actions would have a direct impact on women's rights. For example, James Allen of South Carolina appealed to his fellow convention delegates "who have . . . seen women suffer from the hands of the fortune hunters; the plausible villains . . . who are still going about the country boasting that they intend to marry a plantation, and take the woman as an incumbrance." As with homestead exemptions, married women's property clauses might have become universal in the South even if the Civil War and Reconstruction had never occurred, but the Reconstruction conventions provided a powerful catalyst and, at a minimum, hastened such reform in many states. The Redemption conventions of all states except Louisiana preserved married women's property rights clauses in their constitutions, and West Virginia's Redemption convention added such a clause for the first time.[19]

REDEMPTION AND THE CONSTITUTIONAL LEGACY OF RECONSTRUCTION

Indications that Reconstruction constitutions might leave a significant legacy appeared soon after Reconstruction ended. Most Southern states promptly enacted new constitutions but several, including the Deep South states of Mississippi, South Carolina, and Florida, did not. This fact did not go unremarked by conservatives: when South Carolina finally held a Redemption convention in 1895, delegate Alfred Aldrich complained that the 1868 constitution "was designed to degrade our State, insult our people and overturn our civilization" and lamented: "It is a stain upon the reputation of South Carolina that she has voluntarily lived for eighteen years under that instrument after she had acquired full control of every department of her government." The exact reasons for delay varied. In several states, internal feuds among Democrats had to be resolved before constitutional change could proceed, and in other states such as North Carolina where Republicans remained relatively strong, they blocked major constitutional alterations. But the legacy of Reconstruction also played a role. The controversy that surrounded the universal suffrage provisions of many Reconstruction constitutions was mooted by the 15th Amendment in 1870, and many nonracial reforms of the Reconstruction era were popular and quickly ceased to be controversial; thus conservatives in many states saw little practical need to enact new constitutions immediately. States that did enact new constitutions did so more as a symbolic than as a practical repudiation of Reconstruction: "despite all the Bourbons could do, the stamp of the carpetbagger still remained."[20]

Redemption conventions made significant changes in two areas. First, they placed checks on some of the racial reforms of Reconstruction, albeit modest ones. Ten Redemption constitutions added an explicit requirement that schools be segregated; the only Reconstruction constitution that had included such a clause was Missouri's. Two states, South Carolina and Florida, eliminated Reconstruction clauses acknowledging the primacy of the federal government, but three states (North Carolina, Georgia, and Mississippi) retained such clauses. All prohibitions against enforcement of slave contracts were eliminated, although this was more of a housekeeping measure than a policy statement because virtually all such contracts had expired by the time Reconstruction ended. Redemption constitutions enacted during the "straight-out" era (1890–1915) contained a variety of suffrage qualifications that in practice rendered many blacks and poor whites ineligible to vote, but the early Redemption constitutions (enacted between 1870 and 1885) retained the universal male suffrage provisions incorporated in the Reconstruction constitutions they replaced. The conservatives who dominated the early conventions were no more solicitous of blacks' voting rights than their straight-out era colleagues, but they were mindful of the 15th Amendment and were more concerned than their successors that constitutional suffrage restrictions would attract unfavorable attention from Congress and result in a new wave of federal interference.

Many Redemption conventions also reduced the powers Reconstruction conventions had conferred on state and local governments. Reconstruction saw a reversal of the prewar tendency to limit state subsidy of improvement companies: Reconstruction conventions generally did not enact limits on the amount of debt that state and local governments could incur or on governmental power to grant subsidies. Most Redemption conventions, reacting to scandals and debt that had arisen in the wake of Reconstruction-era railroad subsidies, went in the other direction. Missouri's 1875 Redemption constitution, which served as a model for several other states, went to great lengths to discourage government subsidies: it placed a ceiling of $250,000 on all state debt, prohibited state and local support of development companies, and established detailed railroad regulations that would have been more aptly left to the legislature. Similarly, delegates to Georgia's 1877 convention quoted with approval Amos Akerman's characterization of subsidies as "the signal vice of the age . . . an ingenious contrivance of public plunderers to lull the vigilance of the people by a way of raising money that is not immediately felt in taxation." The delegates then prohibited the legislature and all municipalities from subsidizing private companies in any way and laid the groundwork for sale of the state's remaining ownership interest in railroads. Texas's Redemption convention enacted similar measures despite complaints from some business promoters that "such retrenchment is not economy [but] essentially the worst kind of wastefulness." Ultimately, the number of states with constitutional prohibitions on state and municipal aid to corporations increased dramatically during Redemption and constitutional limits on special corporate charters, which had existed in only a few Southern states during Reconstruction, expanded to most states.[21]

The hardiness of Reconstruction constitutions also stemmed from the fact that they were part of a broader continuum. Reconstruction constitutions were not created from scratch: in most states, they preserved many basic rights their predecessor constitutions had created and many of the basic features of the executive, legislative, and judicial branches of state government, and most Redemption constitutions did likewise. But the Redemption conventions also chose to preserve many of the important reforms their Reconstruction predecessors had initiated. Many reformers, such as Francis Cardozo, had viewed the Reconstruction constitutional conventions as an opportunity not only to implement desired social changes both racial and nonracial, but to increase the chances that the changes would endure. They were not altogether wrong: the constitutional changes that survived form one of the major legacies of the Reconstruction era.

CHAPTER 7

A Republic of Paupers: Shaping the Individual's Role in the Postwar Economy

North Carolina, like several of her Southern sisters, had passed a stay law, which threatened a serious injury to her interests. By preventing the collection of debts, it destroyed credit, of which the people, in their present condition, stand so much in need. Although unconstitutional and impolitic, so great was the popularity of this law, that the ablest politicians feared to make an effort for its repeal.

—John T. Trowbridge, 1865

[R]ebellion changes the ordinary channels of law . . . In 1865, this land was one wilderness of desolation, covered with a people ruined, who had not been the authors of the misfortunes around them. To have administered naked law by the old standard, would have levied and sold the lands for a song, and turned out the women to go in rags, and caused their children to be beggars. It was a necessity that invoked the highest statesmanship of the State.

—Judge O. A. Lochrane (Georgia), 1871[1]

The Civil War brought economic disaster to the South. By the spring of 1865, more than 250,000 men, the core of the prewar Southern work force, had died in the war. Large swaths of the Confederate and border states had been destroyed by advancing and retreating armies and raiders. Slave property, which accounted for a substantial portion of Southern assets in 1860, was gone, as was the Confederate currency system that had formed the basis of internal commerce during the war. Southern whites of all classes were reduced to near destitution: those who owned land saw it reduced to a fraction of its prewar value, and most Southerners who did not own land had little else. The newly freed slaves had no assets other than their ability to work. Occupying Union forces and the Freedmen's Bureau provided emergency food rations and prevented outright starvation, but the American concept of government would not expand to include economic recovery programs for another half century, and Southerners were expected to provide their own economic salvation. As a result, Southern lawmakers of all political views devoted much attention to short-term relief and long-term recovery measures during the Reconstruction era.

The second great postwar economic problem the South faced was the creation of a free labor system that could successfully absorb millions of former slaves. The most profound and enduring changes in the Southern labor system arose out of experiments at the personal level, in "interactions . . . in which victories were often tentative and outcomes subject to challenge and revision." Three distinct groups participated in these experiments. White planters needed black labor but wanted to obtain it on terms that maximized their profits and control over the details of the work; conversely, black workers wanted to maximize their independence and their control of the fruits of their labor. Both groups often depended on merchants to supply on credit tools, seed, and other supplies necessary to make the crop, and merchants wanted access to crops as security for repayment. The struggle between these competing interests played out largely through the enactment of crop lien laws: such laws gave different priorities to each group, and as each group's political strength changed, the laws were frequently amended to change the order of lien priority.[2]

DEBTOR RELIEF: STAY LAWS AND THE END OF IMPRISONMENT FOR DEBT

Lawmakers were acutely aware of the dilemma observed by John Trowbridge during his travels in the South immediately after the war. Many Southerners were deeply in debt and were near destitution; any effort to collect such debts would drive them to ruin and would greatly increase the charitable burden of states unable to meet the burden they already faced. But the South desperately needed capital to rebuild its economy, and lenders were unlikely to advance capital if they could not collect debts owed them. Furthermore, jurists had serious concerns whether new laws sheltering debtors' assets from collection could constitutionally be applied to debts incurred before the laws were enacted. The ex-Confederate states struck a wide range of balances between these competing interests.

During the war, most Southern states adopted laws that stayed (i.e., suspended) efforts to collect debts from persons in military service. These laws attracted little opposition: most people felt it would be unfair to penalize soldiers who, because they were serving the Confederacy, could not return home to defend themselves. At the end of the war, many states concluded it would be equally unfair to penalize persons unable to pay their debts because of the ruin of war, and they created a variety of stay laws to tilt the balance at least temporarily in favor of debtors. North Carolina was particularly active: its 1865 constitutional convention enacted conditional stay laws allowing debtors extensions of time to respond to collection lawsuits if they made regular payments on their debts, and subsequent legislatures and the 1868 convention went further, temporarily staying all collection lawsuits. South Carolina, Georgia, Texas, West Virginia, and Maryland also enacted conditional stay laws.[3] Alabama and Mississippi enacted direct stay laws, which either flatly prohibited collection lawsuits for defined periods of time or allowed suits but gave debtors extensions of time to respond and delayed collection of judgments. Along the border, Missouri, Arkansas, and West Virginia added a twist: their stay laws applied only to Union loyalists and not to persons who had aided the Confederacy.[4]

The stay laws were enacted at the end of a period of intense judicial scrutiny of debtor relief measures throughout the United States. Many states had enacted stay laws and other relief laws following the depressions of 1837–40 and 1857–58, and creditors regularly challenged the laws as an unconstitutional impairment of their contract rights. Several of the challenges made their way to the United States Supreme Court, and in *Bronson v. Kinzie* (1843) and a series of related cases, the Court drew a wavering line between relief measures that were unconstitutional and those that were not. Legal remedies that existed at the time a contract was made became part of the contract, and subsequent debtor relief measures would not be deemed to impair the contract unless they amounted to a "material" change of remedy. During the decades following *Bronson*, federal and state courts had great difficulty drawing a clear distinction between material and immaterial changes of remedy; one Virginia judge complained in frustration that the *Bronson* rule was "vague, uncertain and calculated to confuse and mislead." The most the courts could say was that modest deferrals of a debtor's day of reckoning would be upheld, but if a law went too far in postponing or thwarting creditors, it would be struck down.[5]

Postwar Southern courts had no more luck with this riddle than had their predecessors. Several courts changed their views as the Reconstruction era progressed. North Carolina's supreme court initially upheld the state's postwar stay laws, reasoning that creditors still had substantial remedies available. But in 1869, Governor Holden urged the legislature to eliminate such laws, arguing that "the 'evil day' of payment is postponed in most cases to be felt with added force by the debtor" and that while "we may lament [the debtor's] misfortunes and sympathize with him, . . . the fact remains that he is still in possession of property which justly belongs to his creditors, some of whom may have been reduced to his condition by his failure to meet his obligations." Shortly after Holden's speech, the court reversed itself and struck down the postwar stay laws, concluding that they had done more harm than good. Tennessee followed a similar course: in 1865 its Reconstruction court upheld a conditional stay law, concluding that such laws were a reasonable response to postwar economic hardship, but in 1871, the state's Redemption court reversed course, holding that such laws substantially impaired creditors' rights.[6]

Other states reacted to stay laws in different ways. There were no clear divisions on this subject by region or between Republicans and conservatives. The Arkansas and South Carolina supreme courts followed a pattern opposite to that of their counterparts in North Carolina and Tennessee. In one of its last decisions, Arkansas's Reconstruction court struck down the state's broad stay law, but soon afterward, the Redemption court by a 3–2 vote overruled the decision and upheld the law. Alabama's Restoration court and the Reconstruction courts of South Carolina and Texas approved stay laws, although the Alabama court criticized its state law for preventing Alabamians from obtaining needed credit. A few states rejected stay laws altogether for reasons of pride or caution. The Virginia legislature enacted a series of stay laws between 1863 and 1866, but in the latter year, Virginia's supreme court struck down all such laws, concluding that the federal Constitution "interdict[ed] to the States all legislative interference with contracts, such as had so disastrously relaxed the morals, interrupted the commerce, and disturbed the harmony of the States." This split triggered a long-term battle over efforts to scale down the state's debts that dominated Virginia politics into the 1880s.[7]

The war and Reconstruction also provided the catalyst for the final demise of imprisonment for debt in the South. Debtors' prison was a relic of the preindustrial age, an age when creditors and debtors were usually members of the same small community: it was believed the social stigma of prison would induce debtors to pay their obligations timely and that if they did not, family and friends might pay for them. Although the institution prevailed throughout the American colonies, it was never as effective as creditors hoped. Beginning in the late eighteenth century, as banks and other impersonal institutions began to dominate lending, imprisonment was gradually abandoned and replaced with more modern security devices such as collateral and systems for discounting the value of promissory notes. The South Atlantic states were the last to retain imprisonment for debt, although it was seldom used. North Carolina and South Carolina formally abolished the institution in 1867 and 1868, respectively; South Carolina's supreme court, perhaps wishing to emphasize its disapproval of the old system, held that the change applied to past as well as future debts.[8]

HOMESTEAD LAWS

The first debtor relief measures in American history were colonial laws exempting some items of debtors' personal property from collection by those to whom they owed money. These laws reflected the "instincts of natural justice and humanity" cited by West Virginia's legislature as a force behind stay laws, but they reflected more practical considerations as well. Many lawmakers believed that if debtors were allowed to retain farming implements or other tools of their trade, together with other basic possessions necessary to sustain life, they would have a better chance to remain productive members of society and would not become a burden on taxpayers. Most states enacted personal property exemption laws after independence; because of the constant tension between the beliefs just described and creditors' desire to collect as much of their debts as possible, the exemption laws varied widely in their details.

In 1839 Texas broke new ground, extending the exemption concept from personal to real property. The homestead exemption was a product partly of the deep-seated Jeffersonian and Jacksonian belief that farmers and other small-scale entrepreneurs should be preserved as the core of American society, partly of frontier conditions that made ownership of land essential for long-term economic survival and partly of the depression of 1837–40. When Texas joined the Union in 1845, it enacted a liberal constitutional provision sheltering all homesteads, however valuable, from creditors. The homestead concept spread rapidly: virtually every state that enacted a new constitution between 1845 and the outbreak of the Civil War included either a detailed homestead exemption or a requirement that the legislature enact such an exemption, and other states created homestead exemptions by statute. Postwar poverty in the South gave new impetus to homestead exemptions, and during Reconstruction, the exemption movement completed its work in the South. Every southern state that had not previously enacted a homestead exemption did so, and many states expanded their prewar exemptions.[9]

The general concept of exempting property essential to survival from debt collection was never seriously challenged; the main issue with which courts wrestled was whether Reconstruction-era exemptions could be applied to debts incurred before they were enacted. Creditors argued that they made contracts expecting to be able to reach all of the debtor's property except that which the law sheltered at the time of the contract, and that to impose new limitations later on would impair their contract rights. During Reconstruction, Southern courts that addressed the issue gave a variety of responses. The Virginia and Kentucky supreme courts rejected retroactive exemptions and Virginia's court stopped just short of voiding the state's 1868 homestead law as a whole, criticizing it as "partial and class legislation" in favor of the poor, legislation that would "relieve nine-tenths of the citizens of the State from the payment of their debts, while the remaining

Chief Justice Joseph Brown, Georgia. Courtesy of the Kenan Research Center Atlanta History Center.

Judge Hiram Warner, Georgia. Courtesy of the Library of Congress.

tenth must pay to the last dollar every debt they ever contracted."[10]

States farther south were more sympathetic to retroactive exemptions. In Georgia, Joseph Brown and Henry McCay upheld the state's Reconstruction homestead law over a vigorous dissent by Hiram Warner. Brown characteristically defended retroactive exemptions in blunt, practical terms, stating that it was desirable to free debtors' homes from "old liens which were expected by both debtor and creditor to have been satisfied by property which was swept away by the deluge of destruction," and that retroactive laws were necessary to "prevent . . . the reduction of a large majority of her [Georgia's] population to a condition of bankruptcy and vassalage." Warner replied that both creditors and debtors had suffered in the war's aftermath.[11]

Georgia also enacted two controversial relief laws that arguably made it the most debtor-friendly state in the Reconstruction South. The Relief Act of 1868 authorized juries to reduce the amounts of wartime debts according to the "equities of each case." The Relief Act of 1870 prohibited creditors from obtaining judgments unless they certified that they had paid all taxes they owed, and it allowed debtors to reduce their debts by asserting countervailing "setoff" claims for other war-related losses. The 1868 Act held seeds of anarchy: it could be interpreted to allow juries unlimited discretion to favor debtors over creditors or vice versa, and Georgia's supreme court hastened to eliminate this possibility by ruling that equitable adjustments must be based on proven wrongdoing by one of the parties related to the contract, not on jury sympathies or one party's general misfortunes. The 1870 Act, however, proved too much for the court to stomach: all of the judges concluded the act's setoff provisions impermissibly "confound[ed] the principles of equity and mercy," and only Henry McCay believed the tax affidavit provision was a legitimate means to enforce tax collections.[12] An exasperated Warner charged that the Relief Acts had "culminated in the wholesale plunder of the public funds and public property of the State. . . . The sooner this putrid carcass . . . shall be buried out of sight by the constitutional judgment of the courts, the better it will be . . . for the honor and credit of the State." He soon got his wish: the federal Supreme Court held both relief acts unconstitutional in 1873. Brown and McCay left the court before these decisions were handed down, and their successors accepted the decisions with little protest. Several other Southern and border states considered the validity of retroactive stay laws only after the federal Supreme Court had spoken, and they also deferred to the High Court's antiretroactivity rule.[13]

North Carolina also enacted retroactive homestead exemptions but did not yield as readily as Georgia when the United States Supreme Court decided against retroactivity. In *Hill v. Kessler* (1869), Judge Edwin Reade, speaking for North Carolina's supreme court, reasoned that homestead laws could be applied retroactively because contracts "are made, not only with reference to the remedy existing, but also to such reasonable changes, as the interest of society require, and the State may think proper to make." This was sweeping language, and it drew an alarmed dissent from Chief Justice Pearson, who pointed out that it had no logical stopping point: it would allow the legislature to destroy contract rights and remedies for any purpose the legislature deemed remedial or beneficial. If the majority was acting in the name of progress, said Pearson, it was "a progress in this particular, I fear, of dishonesty and fraud." North Carolina adhered to Reade's position until 1878, when the federal Supreme Court forced the state to follow a no-retroactivity rule.[14] Louisiana was also resistant: in *Robert v. Coco* (1873), its supreme court flatly refused to acknowledge that remedies were in any way a part of contract obligations. A creditor's "security for the payment of the debt may have been impaired by the law, with reference to a certain piece of property," said Judge P. H. Morgan, "but his rights under the obligations he holds have not been interfered with." The Alabama and Mississippi supreme courts also allowed retroactive application of their state's Reconstruction homestead laws initially, but eventually bowed to the federal Supreme Court.[15]

CROP LIEN LAWS AND THE RISE OF THE SHARECROPPING SYSTEM

The sharecropper has long been one of the iconic images of the South, as portrayed, for example, in James Agee's and Walker Evans's portraits of eroded farms and gaunt farm families in the 1930s, and in more recent histories of the black exodus from the rural South during the early twentieth century. For many Americans, the image of the sharecropper instantly evokes the enduring problems of poverty and race in Southern history. But the origins of the sharecropping system demonstrate that the image and the reality are far apart. Although white planters experimented with sharecropping after the war as a means of controlling black labor and deviating from the prewar order as little as possible, many black workers viewed the system as their best hope for true freedom and economic independence. In the end, the system was "a shifting conflict on a terrain where victories and defeats remained provisional, and trial and error altered each group's perceptions of its own self-interest."[16]

In order to understand the sharecropping system, it is necessary to define its terms and the roles of its participants precisely. Tenant farming existed in the South for decades before the Civil War. Tenants agreed to pay a fixed rent to the landlord, typically in the form of produce. Most landlords wished to supervise their tenants closely, in order to make sure that their property was well treated and that the tenant did not abscond with the crop or its sale proceeds without paying his rent. Conversely, tenants wanted as little interference as possible. If they were to be paid in cash or a portion of the crop, they wanted to ensure that the landlord would not appropriate the crop without paying them first. The common law struck a balance: it gave tenants the legal right to control use of the land during the tenancy but gave landlords limited rights of entry. The landlord owned the crop up to the time of harvest and the tenant owned it thereafter. Tenants usually obtained their tools, seed, and other supplies on credit to be paid for at harvest; the supplies sometimes came from their landlords and sometimes from independent merchants who also had an incentive to obtain a security interest in the crop. Beginning in the late 1820s, several Southern states enacted lien laws giving landlords a limited security interest in the crops, but the issue was not urgent: slave labor and small landowning farmers, not tenants, dominated agriculture in most parts of the South.[17]

The picture changed dramatically at the end of the war when millions of slaves became free workers. There was little prospect of their becoming landowners in the short term: planters refused to sell them land, they had little or no capital with which to buy it in any case, and the federal government did not seriously consider helping them acquire land. Most former slaves would have to continue as agricultural laborers. Because of postwar poverty, many planters could not pay their workers in cash, and compensation in the form of a share of the crop quickly became common. Both planters and workers perceived advantages in the sharecropping system. It enabled planters to free up what little cash they had for other purposes, and it gave landlords greater rights of supervision over sharecroppers than over tenants. But the system also gave black workers the prospect of compensation directly proportional to the work they did—a prospect far different from that of slavery and one that many workers regarded as a fundamental badge of freedom.[18]

The question remained: in years when crops were poor and did not cover the costs of rent, supplies, and a reasonable return to the worker, how would the crops be apportioned and who would bear the shortfall? The basic nature of sharecropping gave the landlord an inherent advantage. As the Georgia supreme court explained, "The possession of the land is with the owner as against the cropper. This is not so of the tenant."[19] But workers and merchants naturally opposed landlord primacy, and after emancipation Southern lawmakers pursued an often erratic, often improvisational, quest to strike a workable balance between these competing interests.

There was no clear difference between Restoration and Reconstruction governments as to lien priorities, but Redemption governments generally favored landlords more than their predecessors. Restoration legislatures created a variety of liens: Georgia and Mississippi, for example, allowed landlords liens for both rent and supplies advanced and allowed merchants a lien for supplies but said nothing about the relative priority of the liens. The Mississippi supreme court eventually ruled that supply liens took priority. Several states, including the Carolinas, Alabama, and Louisiana authorized supply liens but not rent liens; to confuse matters further, the North Carolina legislature provided that supply liens were "superior to all other liens" but also that the portion of the crop due to a landlord "shall be deemed [his] property . . . as fully as if vested in him." South Carolina's court also ruled that supply liens took priority, commenting that such liens tended to "encourage[ ] the cultivation of lands, which would otherwise be unproductive for the want of supplies to support the labor which could be readily furnished."[20]

Restoration legislatures did not entirely neglect the interests of agricultural workers: in order to protect competing creditors, many legislatures provided that statutory liens would not be valid unless put in writing and recorded. Like the black code provisions requiring labor contracts to be in writing, these provisions were facially neutral as between landlords and workers but they conferred a real, if incidental, benefit upon workers. Likewise, Reconstruction legislatures concentrated on increasing protection for agricultural workers but did not entirely neglect the interest of landlords. For example, North Carolina added a worker lien in 1868 but did not repeal its prewar lien laws. Florida's Reconstruction legislature specified that the state's new worker's lien had only "equal and undivided application with the landlord's lien"; Alabama gave agricultural workers a lien subordinate to the landlord's rent lien but not to supply liens. In Louisiana, merchants played a particularly powerful role in commerce because of the state's position as the main shipping point for the Mississippi Valley; as a result, both Louisiana's Restoration and Reconstruction legislatures continued the state's prewar policy of priority for merchant liens. South Carolina, Mississippi, and Arkansas were the only states to enact laws unequivocally giving workers a crop lien superior to all others.[21]

At the end of Reconstruction, Redemption legislatures in most states moved quickly to recalibrate the statutory balance in favor of landlords. In the late 1870s, the North Carolina, Mississippi, Alabama, and Arkansas legislatures explicitly declared that rent liens would be superior to supply and worker liens; Florida, Texas, and Louisiana later followed suit. North Carolina and Alabama eliminated the requirement that liens be in writing and recorded, and North Carolina abolished the distinction between tenants and sharecroppers by giving landlords the right of possession of crops in both situations.[22]

Upper South and border states that were not subject to the Reconstruction Acts had favored landlord liens before the war and continued to do so during Reconstruction. Tennessee, Kentucky, Maryland, and Missouri all gave rent liens priority over other liens before the war. Tennessee's Reconstruction legislature gave supply liens second priority to rent liens, and soon afterward, the state's Redemption legislature countered by specifying that landlord supply liens took priority over merchant supply liens. Maryland's Redemption legislature took the same course. Kentucky's 1858 rent lien law continued unchanged throughout the war and Reconstruction, and the Kentucky supreme court consistently affirmed that "it is the policy of the law to prefer landlords." Missouri qualified its rent lien laws by putting an eight-month limit on such liens.[23]

State supreme courts played little or no role in shaping lien policy, and there were few differences of opinion between Restoration, Reconstruction, and Redemption courts as to lien laws. Notwithstanding the laws, landlords, merchants, and agricultural workers frequently customized their lien and payment relationships through individual contracts. When such contracts led to lien disputes, courts invariably applied the terms of the contract as centuries of legal custom and precedent required them to do. Opportunities to make sweeping holdings affecting all agricultural relationships were rare. Only two judicial rules of widespread application emerged, and both were products of inherent judicial conservatism rather than political impulse. First, Restoration, Reconstruction, and Redemption courts alike tended to interpret lien laws narrowly: for example, they were reluctant to alter the established common-law rule of tenant ownership of crops unless the legislature had explicitly done so. Conversely, the courts rejected worker attempts to apply homestead laws and other property exemption laws broadly in order to shelter crops from landlords' rent liens. They reasoned that because the crops at issue were the direct product of land and of supplies provided by the landlord, it would be fundamentally unfair to prevent the landlord from obtaining his return on investment.[24]

Second, the courts consistently rejected workers' efforts to characterize agricultural relationships as partnerships: they emphasized that tenant and cropper contracts "simply establishe[d] a rule whereby . . . labor is to be compensated." The workers' argument had the potential to revolutionize agricultural and social relationships in the South. Landlords and croppers clearly shared risk and agreed to divide the profits of a joint venture, which are hallmarks of a legal partnership, and partnership law would have given workers much more extensive control over the details of their work and the disposition of the crop. But adoption of the partnership theory would have required the courts to stretch contract law well beyond its existing boundaries and to ignore the reality that landlords wanted to maximize their control over land and crops, not enter into shared governance arrangements. Not even Radical judges were willing to go as far as the workers wanted.[25]

The legal history of economic relief measures in the postwar South can be summarized as a clash between legislators' strong desire to take extraordinary measures to help their constituents in a time of extraordinary poverty, and Southern judges' deep sense of obligation to defend contract and property rights. Legislators experimented with a variety of relief measures including absolute and conditional stays of collection efforts, expansion of homestead exemptions, and adjustment of agricultural lien priorities in ways that they believed would promote the postwar economy without unduly disturbing traditional landowner, merchant, and worker relationships. With a few exceptions, most notably Brown of Georgia and Reade of North Carolina, Southern judges firmly declined requests to jettison traditional contract principles in order to boost the South's postwar economy. Courts were willing to uphold debtor relief laws that could reasonably be viewed as merely postponing creditors' rights to recover debts owed or as merely modifying the procedures for recovery; but if the laws at issue were retroactive or the judges sensed that the laws went beyond the line they had drawn, they did not hesitate to overturn the laws.

The courts' course seemed contrarian and perverse to many Southerners at the time it was pursued, but in fact it was another example of the unifying role Southern judges and American judicial tradition played during Reconstruction. The judiciary facilitated long-term economic and legal stability by adhering to traditional contract principles even in difficult times. But the rule was different for corporations. Corporations played a crucial role in the South's economy for the first time after the war, but unlike individuals, they were creatures of the states, and accordingly, their right to make and enforce contracts was more qualified. The legal treatment of Southern corporations after the war is the subject of the next chapter.

CHAPTER 8

The South Confronts Corporations

It is idle to lament at this late day the rampant spirit of speculation which a few years ago busied itself with preying upon credulity of the people everywhere; painting glowing pictures of the golden flood of prosperity that was promised as sure to follow the speedy construction of railroads throughout the country. . . . The fact that the calculations of the benefits to be derived from the subscription were delusive, that the experiment was unfortunate, that the enthusiastic hopes cherished by the citizens as to the advantages contemplated have been blasted, may excite the sympathy of the country in their behalf, but they can constitute no excuse for a court of justice in refusing to administer the law alike to all persons, and at all times. No individual can be excused from the payment of his debt because the business in which he embarked has proved a failure.
—Judge Edwin Randall (Florida), 1871[1]

The rise of corporations as a device for doing business was one of the most important developments in nineteenth-century American law. Corporations both contributed to and reflected the nation's transition from a predominantly rural, agricultural economy to a diversified commercial and industrial economy reliant on towns and cities linked by a modern transportation network. The massive scale of production and trade fostered by the industrial revolution could be carried on efficiently only through business entities governed by uniform rules, not through the personal relationships between producers and consumers on which the preindustrial era had depended. Legal limits on owners' personal liability for debts of failed businesses were needed to encourage entrepreneurs to take the risks necessary to advance the economy. The corporate form of doing business satisfied both needs.

By the mid-nineteenth century, some corporations, particularly the larger railroad companies, had acquired wealth and power on a scale never before conceived for private businesses. Americans regarded such corporations with ambivalence. In the words of one Midwestern judge, they believed that such companies "are the most marvelous invention of modern times" and "have done more to develop the wealth and resources . . . [and to] promote the general comfort and prosperity of the country, than any other and perhaps all other mere physical causes combined"; but like one of the judge's colleagues, they also saw corporations as "a new power . . . practically too strong for [the law's] ordinary private remedies . . . [which if] outside of public control are dangerous to public and private right." The struggle between these hopes and fears expressed itself in three legal controversies that began before the Civil War and continued through the Reconstruction era: whether state and local governments should assist private companies in building railroads and other internal improvements; the extent to which government should directly regulate such enterprises; and whether legislatures should create corporations through individual charters or general laws applicable to all corporations. These controversies bedeviled Southern and Northern states equally, and they provided a point of commonality between the newly reunited sections that has seldom been examined by historians but made an important contribution to the process of reunion.[2]

RECONSTRUCTION AND PUBLIC ASSISTANCE TO PRIVATE ENTERPRISE

The concept of state aid to corporations originated in the South. Virginia began subsidizing canals to connect its major rivers to its trans-Appalachian region as early as 1785, and in 1832, it became the first state to guarantee payment of loans made to internal improvement companies. During the early nineteenth century, most other states concluded that railroads and other internal improvements were vital to their growth and prosperity, and they followed Virginia's lead. American states went through three phases between 1800 and 1875: an initial, "wide-open" phase, in which they freely subsidized improvement enterprises, sometimes more than their means permitted; a second, "reactive" phase, in which they responded to fiscal problems of the wide-open era by restricting aid to corporations; and a third phase, in which restrictions on state aid remained in place but counties, cities, and other municipalities were allowed to fill the gap, with limits.

In the South, some states created variations of the Virginia model. Georgia and North Carolina constructed and directly operated railroads within their borders, and Alabama, Mississippi, and Texas experimented with use of public land grants to finance railroad construction. Starting in the 1830s, Maryland, Virginia, the Carolinas, Georgia, and Tennessee all passed through their "wide-open" eras and provided substantial state subsidies for railroad construction. Kentucky took a conservative position as to state aid but encouraged its counties and other local governments to provide aid. The wide-open era came to an end in many states with the depression of 1837–40, as internal improvement enterprises failed and left state and municipal investors with heavy losses. In Maryland, one legislator noted that "so large a portion of the State's capital and credit ha[d] been embarked on the construction of Rail Roads and Canals, that these works now constitute[d] the leading feature of the fiscal policy of the State." After the depression, Maryland was forced to suspend interest payments for seven years and tried without success to sell its stock in the Baltimore & Ohio Railroad. Virginia, North Carolina, and Tennessee experienced similar vicissitudes; South Carolina and Georgia weathered the hard times better because they were more cautious about over-extension than their sister states.[3]

The reactive era began in some parts of the South after 1837. All Southern states that enacted new constitutions between 1837 and 1860 (Texas, Kentucky, Maryland, and Virginia) placed limits on state and local subsidies of railroads and other corporations. A delegate to Kentucky's 1849 convention observed that "there [was] no one subject, on which the people are so universally agreed, as the propriety of limiting the debt-contracting power of the legislature," and his observation was equally applicable to other states. The Kentucky convention prohibited the legislature from providing any kind of aid to corporations, placed a $500,000 cap on state debt, and prohibited the legislature from exceeding that figure, except to meet temporary tax collection shortfalls or unless approved by referendum. After voicing uncharacteristically Jacksonian concerns that "debt renders capital the ally of tyranny," Maryland's 1851 convention enacted similar limits. Other Southern states continued to subsidize railroads freely in the 1850s. Some did so because they were just beginning construction of their rail systems; others felt that the potential gains to be realized from new rail lines still outweighed the risks. Even the states entering their reactive eras did not close the door completely to subsidies by counties, cities, and other municipalities. Hundreds of municipalities throughout the South took advantage of the opportunity, and some incurred debt out of all proportion to their ability to pay.[4]

Starting in the late 1830s, state and local subsidies were regularly challenged, mostly in states entering their reactive eras. Challengers relied chiefly on two arguments: first, that subsidies to private enterprise did not serve a public purpose; second, because municipalities were created by state legislatures, constitutional prohibitions on state subsidies also applied to municipalities. Most courts rejected these arguments. A few courts expressed regret that their states had not restricted municipal subsidies, but antebellum Southern courts presented with the issue had no such qualms: they rhapsodized that railroads, "the most magnificent discovery of the age," had brought "blessings innumerable [and] prosperity unexampled." Southern courts also emphasized that freedom of contract and local autonomy should be respected: as Judge Thomas Ruffin of North Carolina explained, "The ability of the people, according to their own judgment, is to govern. The law does not force them to subscribe, but allows them to take what stock they will."[5]

The subsidy issue did not come to a head in most Southern states until after the war. At that time, they were faced with a dilemma: the war had dealt a double blow to internal improvements in the South by leaving widespread damage in its wake and decimating the ability of state and local governments to repair existing improvements, let alone pay for new ones. There was deep concern that state legislatures and municipal governments could not be relied on to keep support of private enterprise within reasonable bounds, but there was also a strong feeling among both Republicans and conservatives that if support were not given, the South might never recover. Accordingly, during Reconstruction a new cycle of wide-open subsidies followed by reaction and a shift in emphasis to municipal subsidies took place in many parts of the South.[6]

The leading scholar of nineteenth-century subsidy policies has suggested that in most ex-Confederate states Restoration and Reconstruction governments promoted "wide-open" subsidy policies and that Redemption governments led a reaction, pointing to Reconstruction-era waste and failed projects and promising retrenchment and economy. But a closer survey of subsidy laws indicates that in most states, the reaction against subsidies began in the late 1860s, regardless of which government was in power at the time. That is not surprising: by that time, public concern was rising throughout the United States over discriminatory freight and passenger rates and other perceived evils associated with postwar railroad consolidation. Between 1868 and 1875, Reconstruction governments in Virginia, Georgia, Arkansas, and Tennessee prohibited all state subsidies of corporations; Redemption governments in Mississippi and Alabama did the same, and Redemption governments in North Carolina and Georgia explicitly reaffirmed prohibitions initiated by their predecessors.[7]

Municipal subsidies became the preferred form of government railroad aid after 1870, but state governments in all regions frequently tried to limit such subsidies. In 1865, Missouri became the first Southern state to impose postwar limits on municipal subsidies when it inserted a provision in its Reconstruction constitution allowing subsidies only if approved by two-thirds of municipal voters. During the late 1860s and early 1870s, Reconstruction governments in Florida, Mississippi, and Tennessee also prohibited or limited municipal subsidies; Redemption governments in Georgia and Arkansas later did likewise. In Texas, the 1874 Redemption legislature repealed municipal restrictions but the 1876 Redemption constitutional convention reinstated them. Only Mississippi diverged from this pattern: the 1874 Redemption legislature repealed limits on aid enacted by its Reconstruction predecessors in 1871.[8]

Several states tried more innovative methods of limiting railroad subsidies. Missouri, which arguably devoted more attention to subsidy issues during the Reconstruction era than any other Southern state, provides a particularly instructive example. Despite the 1865 constitution's prohibition of state subsidies and imposition of limits on municipal subsidies, there was "a mass hysteria in communities throughout Missouri to get on the railroad bandwagon" in the late 1860s. The legislature then concentrated on improving the state's position in other ways: to facilitate sale of its railroad stock and give the railroads a chance to regain solvency, it released many state liens on railroad assets, notwithstanding a constitutional prohibition on doing so. In 1871, the legislature, now controlled by conservatives, enacted the first municipal debt ceiling in the South: a municipality's debt for railroads and other internal improvements could not exceed 10 percent of the total assessed value of its property. In 1875, Missouri's Redemption constitution flatly prohibited direct municipal subsidies and reduced the debt ceiling to 5 percent.[9]

Missouri's supreme court followed a policy of restraint in dealing with railroad subsidy issues, commenting that "the legislature has authorized companies to make [municipal] subscriptions . . . [and] they must themselves bear the burdens which they put it in the power of knaves to pile upon them." In 1873, the court rejected an attempt by municipalities to escape liability on their bonds based on the argument that they lacked power to issue the bonds. "This court," warned Judge William Napton, "has acquiesced in the general and prevalent doctrine. Millions of dollars have been invested on the faith of such decisions, and it would be a bold and hazardous experiment to undertake a new investigation of the subject." Other Redemption courts agreed.[10] Texas's Restoration, Reconstruction, and Redemption courts displayed striking unanimity in the face of repeated efforts by the city of San Antonio to escape its obligation to pay for railroad stock the legislature had authorized it to purchase in 1850. The Restoration court rejected the city's initial attempt in 1866, concluding that it should follow the majority of other states and allow subsidies. In 1869, the Military Court agreed, and two years later, the Semicolon Court refused to revisit the issue. In the late 1870s, San Antonio mounted a final wave of challenges, perhaps hoping the Redemption court would repudiate all Reconstruction-era decisions. But the court rebuked the city for assuming it was "practicable, on a doubtful question, to easily procure a change of decision with every change in the members, who might, from time to time, compose the Supreme Court." The court also expressed hope that new limits on municipal subsidies recently placed in the 1876 constitution would put an end to the controversy, and it made clear that it would uphold future subsidies only if they complied strictly with the new constitutional limits.[11]

In Kentucky, Judge Mordecai Hardin added a new perspective in a case challenging subsidies that Mercer County had provided for improvements along the Kentucky River, arguing that the court should scrutinize such subsidies to ensure that they benefited the entire county and not just the riverside portion. But Hardin failed to persuade his colleagues: they presumed that municipal subsidies were in the general public interest even if they did not benefit all parts of the municipality equally. In North Carolina, the 1868 Reconstruction convention extended the referendum requirement for municipal subsidies to state subsidies, but the legislature frequently ignored the new provision. The North Carolina supreme court repeatedly urged the legislature to be more circumspect about subsidies, but with only limited success.[12]

THE DARTMOUTH COLLEGE DOCTRINE
AND CORPORATE REGULATION

After the Civil War, railroads throughout the United States moved into a new phase of development in which most local lines were consolidated into a few large, centrally controlled networks. Consolidation was often viewed in the late nineteenth century as an unmitigated evil, but it was in large part a response to the economic necessities of the times. Railroads cost huge sums to build and they incurred heavy operational expenses that could not easily be reduced in hard times. As railroads extended throughout the United States after the war, interstate and interregional traffic became increasingly important sources of revenue. In order to gain access to this source of business and reduce costs through economies of scale, railroads were forced to consolidate and share traffic. They also made joint agreements as to freight and passenger rates, partly out of desire to increase profit and partly because unrestricted competition could (and often did) drive revenues below the level needed to survive. Bitter public memories of the losses caused by prewar railroad failures lingered, however, and postwar consolidation and rate cartels triggered calls for government intervention. During the late 1860s and 1870s, many American states enacted laws limiting the rates railroads could charge for freight and passengers. Some states also created railroad commissions, which represented a milestone in administrative law as the first important state regulatory agencies.[13]

The South was squarely in the mainstream of this trend. Upper South and border states were among the first to enact postwar regulatory laws, which enjoyed support from Republicans and conservatives alike. Missouri did not wait for the end of the war: the Radical-dominated 1863 legislature imposed a detailed railroad rate schedule, and in the early 1870s, the state's Redemption legislatures enacted additional rate laws. Virginia and West Virginia, concerned about the Baltimore & Ohio's influence over their economies, enacted their first rate laws in 1866. West Virginia's Redemption legislatures placed additional limits on railroad consolidation, and at the end of Reconstruction era, Virginia became one of the first states in the nation to create a railroad commission.

Other Southern states joined the regulatory movement as it crested in the 1870s. Alabama, Arkansas, Kentucky, Tennessee, and Delaware all passed rate laws between 1872 and 1877. North Carolina enacted a unique rate law: the legislature reserved the right to set rate ceilings and prohibited railroads from raising rates after consolidating with each other, but it also assured railroads that rate laws would not be enforced if the effect was to reduce annual prof-its to less than 10 percent of capital.[14] Only a few states, mostly in the Deep South, waited until after Reconstruction to enact rate laws. The strength of regulatory sentiment by the mid-1870s was such that whereas no Southern state had sought to enshrine the principle of regulation in its Reconstruc-tion constitution, many states did so in their Redemption constitutions. Some states, most notably Missouri, inserted detailed regulations more suitable for statutory enactment than for a constitution.[15]

Railroads throughout the United States mounted vigorous constitutional challenges to the new regulatory laws. They relied chiefly on the Contracts Clause of the United States Constitution, which prohibits states from impair-ing existing contract obligations, and on the federal Supreme Court's decision in *Trustees of Dartmouth College v. Woodward* (1819), holding that because a corporate charter is a contract between the legislature and the corporation, the state may not apply subsequently enacted regulatory laws to the corpo-ration: to do so would impair the contract rights embedded in the charter. Railroads argued that recent regulatory laws constituted an impermissible modification of their charters and deprived them of profits and other prop-erty without due process of law. In most cases, the states responded that large corporations affected the public interest so deeply that the new regulations were justifiable as part of the states' police power—that is, their general power to promote the public good.[16]

In the South as elsewhere, courts gave these arguments a mixed reception. They uniformly applied the *Dartmouth* doctrine to laws restricting freight and passenger rates, holding that such laws could not be applied to railroads char-tered before the laws went into effect. The Missouri supreme court, however, suggested that railroads had a separate obligation as common carriers not to charge "exorbitant" rates, and it all but invited unhappy customers to chal-lenge rate schedules under this theory. Southern courts were more reluctant to apply the *Dartmouth* doctrine to the many tax breaks legislatures had writ-ten into prewar railroad charters, although most courts reluctantly concluded the doctrine applied even to taxation. In Georgia, Judge McCay complained that under the *Dartmouth* doctrine "it now often happens that in a thoughtless hour the state, with but a nominal consideration, is shorn of its most important prerogatives"; in Florida, Chief Justice Edwin Randall agreed that "the essen-tial elements of sovereignty necessary for the perpetuation of governments [should] not be made the subject of a permanent grant by the legislature." Only North Carolina rejected the *Dartmouth* doctrine in tax cases. Chief Jus-tice Pearson explained that the state must "preserve its own existence by equal taxation," which is always "subject to the change of circumstances that future events may develop." He also hinted with bemusement that the court felt it had a duty to save the North Carolina legislature from itself:

A matter of this kind, instead of being, in its strict sense, a contract, is more like the act of an indulgent head of a family dispensing favors to its different members, and yielding to importunity. So the Courts, to save the old gentleman from being stripped of the very means of existence, by sharp practice have been forced to reverse the rule of construction, and to adopt the meaning most favorable to the grantor.[17]

Other states made more modest efforts to limit the reach of the *Dartmouth* doctrine. In Mississippi, the Reconstruction court refused to apply the doctrine to shield existing lottery companies from the 1869 legislature's decision to ban all lotteries, reasoning that lottery charters cannot be "dignified with the name of contract." Even courts that applied the *Dartmouth* doctrine in tax cases made clear they would give the doctrine as narrow a scope as possible. For example, the Missouri supreme court warned it would apply the *Dartmouth* doctrine to new tax laws only where the legislature had "expressly" limited its taxing power in the corporate charter and the railroad had specifically negotiated for the tax breaks at issue, and Georgia's supreme court held that consolidating railroads would be deemed to subject themselves to all laws in effect at the time of consolidation, even if those laws contravened the original charters of the consolidating railroads.[18]

Ultimately, anti-*Dartmouth* constitutional clauses, providing that new corporate charters would be granted only on condition that the corporation agree to submit to all future laws enacted by the legislature, proved to be the most effective means of protecting regulatory laws. In the South, only Maryland and Kentucky enacted anti-*Dartmouth* clauses before the war, but such clauses proliferated after the war. Only Maryland and Virginia placed such clauses in their Reconstruction constitutions, but after antisubsidy sentiment rose in the early 1870s, six additional states placed anti-*Dartmouth* clauses in their Redemption constitutions. Courts routinely upheld such clauses, holding that newly incorporated companies must accept them as a condition of incorporation.[19]

GENERAL INCORPORATION LAWS

At the start of the nineteenth century, virtually all corporations were created by individual charter. The American industrial age, which would make the corporation the leading form of industrial and commercial enterprise, had not yet begun: corporations were perceived as individual and unique, and legislators dealt with new companies accordingly. Many persons forming companies believed they could use the legislative process to gain special provisions giving them an advantage over potential competitors—an attitude vividly illustrated by the furor attending the United States Supreme Court's decision in the *Charles River Bridge Case* (1837) that state legislatures could grant a particular privilege to more than one company.[20]

Countervailing pressures soon arose. As the industrial revolution progressed, legislatures were forced to devote an increasing amount of their time to corporate charters. Suspicion of corporations, particularly banks, as potential threats to popular democracy and individual opportunity became an important tenet of Jacksonian philosophy. As a result, between 1810 and 1850, many states attempted to enact statutory and constitutional restrictions on bank corporations. These efforts yielded little: eventually, all but the most devout Jacksonians grudgingly conceded that banks were essential to a modern commercial economy. But resentment against corporate privilege lingered, and as a result, the concept of replacing individual charters with general incorporation laws equally applicable to all companies (or at least all companies in a particular economic sector) "seems to have appeared rather suddenly" in the mid-1840s. In 1845, Louisiana became the first state in the Union to include a general incorporation law requirement in its constitution; Tennessee (1834), Texas (1845), and Maryland (1851) placed some limits on individual corporate charters in their prewar constitutions, and Kentucky and Missouri enacted statutory limits.[21]

After the Civil War, the general incorporation movement spread to the newer Western states and revived in the South. Many states began by experimenting with incorporation laws applicable to companies in defined economic sectors such as transportation, mining, and manufacturing; similar laws were later enacted for other sectors, and eventually omnibus incorporation laws appeared. North Carolina provides a good example. Its Reconstruction constitution required corporations to be created through general laws except "in cases where, in the judgment of the legislature, the object of the corporations cannot be attained under general laws." In 1871, the legislature enacted a general incorporation law for railroads that regulated rates, consolidation, and many other details of operation; a few months later, it enacted an equally detailed law applying to virtually all other types of corporations.

General incorporation laws and limits on special charters were equally popular with Reconstruction and Redemption governments. General incorporation and limiting laws were enacted in South Carolina and Arkansas during Reconstruction and retained after Redemption; were initiated in Georgia, Texas, Tennessee, and West Virginia during the Redemption period; and were enacted during both periods in Alabama and Missouri. The increasing legislative burden imposed by individual charters was the main force behind reform in many states, but lingering Jacksonian sentiments played an important role in spurring postwar reform in the South. For example, when Alabama's supreme court struck down a law creating a private lottery as violative of the state's constitutional mandate for general incorporation laws, Judge Benjamin Saffold suggested that the mandate was enacted because popular sentiment against "exclusive privileges" "had not been sufficiently observed by the legislature and the courts." Saffold also suggested the clause was closely linked to another clause in the Alabama constitution prohibiting special privileges and titles of nobility of any sort.[22]

Legal responses to economic issues such as debtor relief and the growth of corporations provided a point of common ground between the postwar South and the rest of the United States—and, in many cases, between Republican reformers and their Redemptionist successors. Support of debtor relief measures and the desire to balance encouragement of corporations as the best vehicle for the South's entry into the industrial age against fears of corporate overreaching cut across racial and political lines. Southern lawmakers looked for guidance to Northern laws and court decisions generated during Northern states' wide-open and reactive eras, and Northerners could easily sympathize with Southern efforts to address problems characteristic of each era. These issues played a subtle but crucial role in the South's legal and political reassimilation as part of the United States.

CHAPTER 9

Reconstruction and Women's Rights

The old and barbarous common law doctrine of the absolute civil nonentity of the femme covert . . . has been gradually but surely dissolving, under the more liberalizing tendencies of the courts of equity, which have been disposed to regard wives as human beings, with personal rights, and free thoughts, endowed with discretion, and as, socially, the equal of their barons. . . . [But] in each State the law regarding married women has its own peculiar phase, made up of its own legislation and the disjecta membra of the old cast-iron common law structure—the latter often seriously disturbing the spirit and purpose of the former.
                                        —Judge John Eakin (Arkansas), 1882

Those only who have lived where the negro equals or outnumbers the white population can understand his character, and the grave problem now confronting this nation. The danger in enfranchising a large class uninstructed in the duties of citizenship and totally ignorant of any principles of government . . . should serve to emphasize the unwisdom and injustice of denying the ballot because of sex to one-half of its American-born citizens who, by education and patriotism, are qualified for the highest citizenship.
                                        —Caroline Merrick (Louisiana), 1898[1]

Reconstruction is identified with the struggle to establish basic civil rights for black Americans. But the years between 1863 and 1877 were also an important period in the history of American women's rights. Congressional debates over the 14th and 15th Amendments prompted Susan B. Anthony and other early leaders of the women's movement to demand that

women be protected under the amendments, and prompted the forma-
tion of women's rights associations in many states the movement had not
previously reached. Efforts to increase married women's right to control
property they brought to their marriages, which had begun in the 1830s
but had slowed in the decade before the Civil War, revived. During the
Reconstruction era, married women's property laws were enacted in several Southern states that had resisted the movement before the war, and a
slow extension of new rights began that continued into the early twentieth
century. Like the postwar corporate regulatory movement, the postwar
women's rights movement was national in scope and the South was very
much in the movement's mainstream. The women's rights movement provided another area of commonality that helped facilitate the South's rein-
tegration into the Union.

MARRIED WOMEN'S RIGHTS IN THE ANTEBELLUM SOUTH

Prior to 1835, married women's property rights in all Southern states
except Louisiana were derived from English common law. The cornerstone
of the common law's approach to married women was the marital unity doctrine, which made the husband the legal master of the marriage and gave him
complete control over all property that his wife brought to the marriage. Sir
William Blackstone explained the doctrine in his influential *Commentaries on
the Law of England* (1765–69): "By marriage, the husband and wife are one
person in law: that is, the very being or legal existence of the woman is suspended during the marriage, or at least is incorporated and consolidated into
that of the husband: under whose wing, protection, and cover, she performs
every thing."[2]

But from colonial times on, British and American courts used contract
law and equity rules to give wives a measure of control over property they
brought to the marriage or acquired during the marriage. The courts did so
not out of any particular desire to empower women, but to preserve stable
property ownership and social order. In the South, daughters of the planter
class remained a part of their original families after they married and reten-
tion of family land holdings was a key to preserving family wealth and power.
Accordingly, premarital agreements under which a husband allowed his wife,
a member of her family, or a family-designated trustee to control her property for her benefit were common and were routinely enforced.[3]

British courts eliminated the requirement of an independent trustee and
allowed married women to manage their separate property directly beginning
in 1769; in the early nineteenth century, American judges, led by Chancellor
James Kent of New York, began to follow suit. This more relaxed attitude
reflected a recognition that separate estates for women provided an "opportunity to protect a portion of [the couple's] assets from some of the risks of
the marketplace" in an age when marriage was often "an integral part of
the acquisitive scramble" in an industrializing society. Separate estates were

commonly used as a device to shelter wives' property from the creditors of impecunious husbands.[4]

In the mid-1830s, a new tool for protecting separate estates appeared: the married women's property act. Early "debt-free" married women's acts typically provided that the wife's separate property could not be reached by her husband's creditors to pay his debts, but went no further. Later "separate estate" acts allowed married women to manage and dispose of their separate property without their husbands' consent. But small differences in wording often were crucial, and in close cases, both prewar and postwar Southern courts tended to interpret such laws conservatively. For example, Florida's 1845 married women's property act appeared at first blush to be a separate-estate law: it provided that property brought by a woman to her marriage "shall continue separate, independent, and beyond the control of her husband," although it allowed husbands to retain "care and management" of such property. But in 1860, Florida's antebellum supreme court indicated that "care and management" meant husbands retained their traditional right to unfettered use of such property, and in 1877, the state's Reconstruction court agreed, holding that "there does not appear to have been any language used in the act with a design to remove the disabilities imposed by the common law upon a feme covert."[5]

Married women's property laws first arose in the newer Southern states. In 1835, Arkansas's territorial legislature enacted the first American debt-free law, and in 1839, Mississippi followed suit, stating in broad terms that a married woman "may become possessed of property in her own name and as of her own property." Mississippi's supreme court quickly made clear that the new law was limited in scope: the court stated that it was "designed to guard the specific property from any liability for the debts and contracts of the husband" but "reaches no further," and emphasized that under the marital unity doctrine, husbands still had the right to control all income and proceeds derived from their wives' separate property. Married women's property acts spread rapidly in the 1840s, particularly after New York considered incorporating a debt-free provision in its 1846 constitution and enacted an influential debt-free law in 1848. Many southwest and border states, including Maryland (1841, 1851), Kentucky (1842), Florida (1845), Alabama (1845, 1847), and Missouri (1849) enacted debt-free laws and constitutional provisions before the Civil War; but the older Southern states, apparently satisfied that their existing common-law and equity rules were working well, did not.[6]

A combination of economic, humanitarian, and practical legal concerns gave rise to the married women's acts. In the early nineteenth century, popular views of married women's role in society changed in several important ways not entirely consistent with each other. As the Jacksonian concept of popular democracy took hold, many Jacksonians began to ask whether their democracy should be extended to women as well; but at the same time, a "cult of true womanhood" developed that would shape women's role in American society for much of the nineteenth century. The concept of "true womanhood" held that women were more virtuous and more inherently noble than men but that because of such traits, they must be sheltered and protected from the world of men, including business and politics. The concept meshed nicely with the view that sheltering a wife's separate property was desirable because it would encourage men to take greater risks with their own assets and further the economic growth essential to the nation's future.[7]

The events surrounding the enactment of Mississippi's debt-free law exemplify these forces. Many members of the state's 1839 legislature stayed at a boarding house in Jackson operated by Piety Smith Hadley. Mrs. Hadley's husband, a state senator, was deeply in debt and thus had strong incentive to sponsor a debt-free law. Mrs. Hadley made a good profit from her boarding house, and it is said that she persuaded many of her legislative boarders to vote for the law by persistently raising the issue while they ate their meals. If so, Mrs. Hadley deserves recognition as an important figure in American women's history. Debate records show that several legislators supported the law because it advanced women's rights, but a larger group supported the law mainly as a means of protecting wives from husbandly improvidence, as was true in most other states that enacted married women's laws. Debt-free laws did not always work an immediate change in women's rights: traditional equitable devices such as marital trusts had often been equally effective in sheltering wives' separate property and giving wives real control over their property. But the new laws were the first explicit affirmation in common-law states that married women should have some control of their separate property, and that affirmation had real importance for women.[8]

Alabama and Maryland came closest to granting wives fully separate estates before the war. An 1847 Alabama law provided that "no husband shall by his marriage acquire a right" to his wife's separate property, but the state's Reconstruction court held that the law, though "an important statute . . . intended to enlarge [married women's] powers," was really a debt-free law and was not intended to give married women the same powers as femes soles (single women). In 1860, the Maryland legislature revised its 1842 debt-free law to state that married women could hold "all of their property of every description for their separate use, as fully as if they were unmarried." Maryland's supreme court, unlike Alabama's, indicated the amendment *did* give a married woman "the power of devising [separate property] the same as if she were a feme sole," thus giving Maryland the distinction of being the first Southern state to enact a separate estate law.[9]

Louisiana and Texas presented a special case because of their civil law heritage. Louisiana was a colony of both France (1718–62, 1801–3) and Spain (1762–1801) before its purchase by the United States; both colonial powers administered a civil law system that had its origins in Roman law rather than British common law and applied a community property doctrine to marriage. The doctrine, which was preserved in Louisiana's 1808 Civil Code, gave husband and wife a joint interest in all property brought to the marriage or acquired during the marriage. In other respects, however, Louisiana law had much in common with Anglo-American law: it gave husbands the exclusive right to manage community property, and it allowed wives and their families to carve out separate property, known as paraphernal property, prior to marriage.

As a Spanish colony and a Mexican province, Texas also operated under a community property system. After gaining independence from Mexico in 1836, American settlers divided over whether to retain the Mexican civil law system or convert to the common law; in 1840, they compromised by adopting a hybrid system similar to Louisiana's. When Texas joined the Union in 1845, its constitutional convention rejected efforts to return to a pure community property system but incorporated some community law principles into the constitution and directed the legislature to provide additional protection for wives against husbandly improvidence. Led by Chief Justice John Hemphill, who was an expert on Hispanic civil law and supportive of civil law principles, the Texas supreme court interpreted the constitution broadly to give women the right to manage their separate property independent of their husbands and held that husbands' creditors could reach such property only if no community property was available to satisfy debts.[10]

RECONSTRUCTION AND MARRIED WOMEN'S PROPERTY RIGHTS

Historians have differed as to the role the Civil War and Reconstruction played in changing the social and legal position of Southern women. Some scholars have suggested that the many male deaths and widespread destruction caused by the war impelled women to take a more prominent role in postwar society and even that "the South became a matriarchy during the war." More recent scholarship suggests that although the war allowed (and in some cases forced) Southern women to work outside the home and take a more active role in management of family businesses, it did not result in a significant shift in their cultural role. Many wives believed preservation of traditional family roles was necessary to soften the psychological trauma the war had inflicted on their husbands and perhaps also to salve their own sense of loss. A contemporary journalist observed that "it was as though the 'mighty oak' was hit by lightning and only the 'clinging vine' kept it erect." In the words of Lee Ann Whites, "rather than agitating for a general structural change in the dependent position of all white women, [Southern women] . . . demand[ed] that men be more responsive to the needs of the women and children that they at least in theory were committed to protect and provide for. They demanded, in other words, a more paternalistic patriarchy."[11]

Legal historians have debated whether Reconstruction produced major advances in women's rights or simply solidified prewar reforms. A systematic examination of prewar married women's property laws suggests the truth lies somewhere in the middle. Reconstruction gave birth to modern women's property rights in only three Southern states, namely the Carolinas and Georgia, and most Southern states did not give married women full control over their separate property, earnings, and businesses for several decades after the end of Reconstruction; but Reconstruction ushered in a period of active reform and real advances in women's rights in virtually every Southern state.[12]

The states that came into the married women's property rights fold during Reconstruction enacted debt-free laws. The time for fully separate estates had not yet come. In South Carolina's Reconstruction convention, James Allen suggested that because "we have passed page after page of enactments explaining the rights of man," it was appropriate to extend married women's property rights as well, but he devoted most of his argument to the economic advantages of such laws. Another delegate emphasized that "all this section does is to protect the woman against the bad debts of her husband." Georgia's convention essentially reaffirmed a Restoration-era debt-free law enacted in 1866; delegates justified it in terms of protecting married women rather than increasing their rights. There is no reason to believe the motivation of the North Carolina convention was different.[13]

Reconstruction further solidified the place of married women's property acts in Southern law: most states that had enacted such laws before the war now elevated them to constitutional status.[14] Redemption constitutional conventions later renewed Reconstruction married women's provisions with little debate.[15] Only Virginia and the border states of Tennessee, Kentucky, Missouri, and Delaware declined to enshrine married women's property rights in their constitutions, but each state enacted laws advancing married women's property rights. Kentucky took an important step toward full separate estate status in 1868 when the legislature passed a law explicitly giving wives full rights to dispose of their separate property without their husbands' consent; Tennessee followed suit a year later. Virginia was the last Southern state to adopt a married women's law; the delay probably resulted from the state's unique antipathy to debt repudiation and debtor relief. Nevertheless, in the mid-1870s, a debt readjustment movement gathered strength in Virginia, and perhaps as an offshoot of this changing sentiment, the legislature finally enacted a debt-free law in 1877. Missouri lawmakers paid surprisingly little attention to women's rights during Reconstruction, but the 1875 Redemption legislature enacted one of the earliest separate estate laws, providing that a wife's separate property was "under her sole control."[16] Most states did not provide for fully separate estates until the last years of the nineteenth century and the early twentieth century.[17]

Some Southern states also moved into a new phase of married women's rights during Reconstruction, enacting laws giving wives the right to retain their wages, operate businesses, bequeath property, and file lawsuits independent of their husbands' control. The traditional rule that wives' wages belonged to their husbands became a particularly sore point for Southern women during Reconstruction: at least eight Southern states enacted laws giving married women exclusive control over their wages and prohibiting husbands' creditors from reaching the wages.[18] Southern women had enjoyed limited rights to operate businesses as "free traders" since colonial times, but such rights were subject to extensive restrictions. Typically, a married woman could not operate her own business without permission from her husband or a court, and the law generally gave the husband the right to use and control her business earnings and profits. North Carolina, Florida, and Arkansas eliminated all restrictions on free trading and gave wives sole control over their business earnings (as well as sole liability for their business debts) during Reconstruction; Louisiana, Tennessee, and West Virginia followed suit in the 1890s.[19] Texas was the only Southern state to eliminate restrictions on wives' ability to make wills before the war; it was followed by Georgia, Mississippi, West Virginia, and Delaware during Reconstruction and by Arkansas and Maryland during the Redemption era. South Carolina, Alabama, Arkansas, and Delaware eliminated restrictions on the right of married women to appear in court during Reconstruction, and Missouri joined them in 1889.[20]

Reconstruction and Redemption judges differed little in their approaches to the new postwar laws. Their inclination, like that of their antebellum predecessors, was to interpret married women's laws narrowly. In North Carolina, Chief Justice Pearson and his colleagues recognized that under the married women's rights clause in the state's Reconstruction constitution, they were "called upon to make a new departure, leaving old ideas behind," but they did so grudgingly. In *Baker v. Jordan* (1875), the court concluded that husbands were still "overseers" of their wives' separate property: because husbands still had a legal obligation to support their families, reasoned Pearson, they were "entitled to [their wives'] services, and to contribution from the profits of her estate." The next year the court announced it would limit wives' powers over their separate property to those explicitly enumerated in the constitution, although it repeatedly emphasized that if such rules threatened hardship to wives in future cases, those wives could still resort to traditional equitable remedies.[21]

Courts in other states followed a similar pattern. Mississippi's Restoration and Reconstruction courts limited wives' rights to contract independently, holding that "the feme covert is still subject to her common law disabilities, except as to the class and subjects of contracts therein enumerated." The protective impulses of the "cult of true womanhood" also surfaced occasionally, as when the court praised a prewar law prohibiting wives from mortgaging their separate property as "a wise provision intended to secure . . . the wife . . . against any possible contingency of loss through the fraud, force or undue influence of her husband." However, the Mississippi court took a more liberal view of the state's limited free trader laws and disclaimed any intent to "exercise a sort of guardianship over [wives'] transactions." Florida's Reconstruction court also made clear it would interpret the postwar laws narrowly.[22] Alabama's Reconstruction court agreed, but its reasoning was more subtle. The court concluded that Alabama law enlarged married women's powers only "to a certain limit" and that such powers were "all that can be wisely bestowed upon her," but the court drew a striking equation between women's rights and civil rights.

"'All men are created equal,' and the word 'man' includes persons of both sexes," reasoned Judge Thomas Peters. "Then, the wife is the peer and equal of the husband in all her great rights of life, liberty and the pursuit of happiness. And to protect her in these important rights, the statute under discussion was enacted."[23]

During Reconstruction, a few courts showed signs of breaking from this pattern and foreshadowed the transition to full separate-estate laws that would take place over the next half century. In *Barton v. Barton* (1870), the Maryland supreme court indicated it would not interpret the state's pioneering separate-estate law restrictively. No other Southern state enacted a full separate-estate law during Reconstruction but the courts of two states, South Carolina and Georgia, joined Maryland in declining to interpret postwar laws restrictively. In *Witsell v. Charleston* (1876), Judge Ammiel Willard explained that the married women's property movement had arisen because the common law created "an anomaly in the deprivation of the power to do right, unaccompanied by the deprivation of the power to do wrong"—that is, it neither barred husbands from using the marital unity doctrine to oppress women nor allowed women to act to protect themselves. Unlike Peters, Willard and his colleagues viewed women's rights in terms of eliminating restrictions rather than providing protections, and they firmly laid down a rule of liberal interpretation: "Now that the Constitution has reversed the rule of the common law, and substituted general competence for the former rule of incompetence . . . it is not for the Courts, on nice readings of its text, to restore a state of things from which the Courts of equity have long striven to be released." Somewhat surprisingly, when a similar case reached the state's Redemption court in 1881, that court also adopted a liberal interpretation rule and spoke approvingly of the *Witsell* decision.[24]

Georgia's supreme court also opted for liberality, ruling that the state's Reconstruction constitution "lays down an entirely new rule for the future. . . . Husband and wife . . . are, in law, so far as property is concerned, two distinct persons, with distinct and separate rights." In *Urquhart v. Oliver* (1876), the Redemption court reaffirmed that "women remain, after marriage, as effectually separated from men as they were before marriage." Even Judge Logan Bleckley, who expressed doubt that the constitution went as far as his colleagues thought, concurred in their holding: "To abide by the letter of the Code . . . is turning round and looking toward the past. . . . I doubt, but do not dissent." Many other states eventually enacted separate-estate statutes, mainly between 1890 and 1910.[25]

RACE AND WOMEN'S SUFFRAGE IN THE POSTWAR SOUTH

When freedoms and rights are expanded, the expansion can move in unanticipated directions. This proved true during the American Revolution, when the Declaration of Independence not only gave rise to a new nation founded on the "self-evident truth . . . that all men are created equal," but unexpectedly moved many slaveowners to conclude that the creed should be extended to black Americans, thus triggering a wave of manumissions throughout the North and Upper South. Likewise, the new birth of freedom for blacks that came out of the Civil War prompted many women, and a surprisingly large number of male lawmakers, to ask why that freedom should not also be extended to women. Rebecca Hazard, a Missouri feminist, explained:

I think the cruel war had much to do in educating . . . women . . . into a sense of their responsibilities and duties as citizens; at least all who first took part in the suffrage movement had been active on the Union side during the war, and that having ended in the preservation of the government, they naturally began to inquire as to their new rights and privileges in the restored Union.[26]

The years immediately after the war witnessed the birth of the National Woman Suffrage Association (1869) and of separate suffrage movements in many states, including Virginia, South Carolina, Texas, Kentucky, Maryland, and Missouri. Debates in Congress and the states over black suffrage were intertwined with debates over women's suffrage. Although women's suffrage leaders did not have a realistic chance of success, they presented their case vigorously to Congress. Charles Sumner and many of his fellow Radicals actively supported extension of suffrage to both blacks and women, but most moderate Republicans opposed women's suffrage for pragmatic reasons, believing that suffrage did not enjoy sufficient popular support and that accordingly, it was better to conserve political energies for the battle over black suffrage and defer the battle over women's suffrage to another day. Black leaders were likewise divided: Frederick Douglass supported women's suffrage but others believed that rights for blacks should be secured first.[27]

Some prominent Reconstruction-era lawmakers in the South publicly supported women's suffrage. In Virginia, Judge John Underwood linked the Unionist and feminist perspectives on freedom: as president of Virginia's Reconstruction constitutional convention, he advocated elimination of suffrage restrictions based on both race and gender, and in 1870, he sponsored the first meeting of the Virginia women's suffrage association in his courtroom. Underwood retained the idealized view of women fostered by the "cult of true womanhood" and in fact employed the concept as a tool for his cause, arguing that admission of women to suffrage would elevate and civilize male electors. William Whipper, a leading black delegate in South Carolina's Reconstruction convention and husband of Frances Rollin, a leading South Carolina suffragist, sounded the same theme and also linked Unionism and feminism. "Sooner or later," proclaimed Whipper, "everything in the shape of tyranny must yield; and, however derisively we may treat these noble women who are struggling for their sex, we shall yet see them successful in the assertion of their rights."[28]

In the end, suffragists failed because they could not get conservatives and moderates to take them seriously. Underwood's and Whipper's efforts were rejected by wide margins in the Virginia and South Carolina conventions.

Feminists also made strong efforts to obtain suffrage in the Louisiana and Texas Reconstruction and Redemption conventions; they received a serious hearing, but they too failed. They renewed their efforts in several Redemption conventions held in the 1890s, arguing that enfranchisement of white women could help offset the threat posed by black suffrage. Convention delegates again gave them a respectful hearing but decided to reduce Southern blacks' political power by limiting rather than expanding suffrage. Many Southern women resisted suffrage because they feared that extension of suffrage and other new rights would cause them to lose the special legal protections they enjoyed as women. Mary Clarke, a North Carolina suffragist, lamented that "until the Southern women can be made to feel the pecuniary advantages to them of suffrage, they will not lift a finger or speak a word to attain it."[29]

The final suffrage effort of importance during Reconstruction took place in Missouri. The state was not a leader in the enactment of married women's property laws, but it was unusually receptive to women's participation in the professions and the public arena. Elizabeth Cady Stanton and her colleagues were surprised but pleased that Missouri, "a slave state, was the first to open her medical and law schools to women, and [that] the suffrage movement from the beginning . . . enlisted so large a number of men and women of wealth and position, who promptly took an active interest in the inauguration of the work." Virginia Minor and her husband Francis Minor, a prominent St. Louis lawyer, were members of that group. In 1869, frustrated by Congress's failure to extend the vote to women, they decided to take action. The Minors accepted the generally recognized principle that states had the right to regulate and limit suffrage—given the extensive efforts of Missouri radicals to preclude ex-Confederates from voting in the late 1860s, they could hardly have done otherwise—but they took the position that the 14th Amendment did not allow states to discriminate based on *any* characteristic that was immutable and not controllable by the individual, including gender as well as race.

In 1872, Virginia attempted to vote in the presidential election and was turned away from the polls. Francis, assisted by U.S. Senator John Henderson, then challenged his wife's exclusion in Missouri's supreme court. The court refused to adopt his expansionist view of the 14th Amendment and was not ready to take women's suffrage any more seriously than most of its constituents: it politely but firmly held that the amendment was intended to protect blacks only, and when the Minors appealed to the United States Supreme Court, the High Court agreed. Thus, the *Minor* case did not break new legal ground, but it nonetheless became an important political milestone in women's history. Between 1890 and 1918, 20 states enacted women's suffrage by statute or constitutional amendment, and the remaining states followed suit when the women's suffrage amendment to the United States Constitution was ratified in 1919.[30]

Like debtor relief and regulation of corporations, women's rights evolved in the Southern states in much the same manner as the rest of the nation both before and after the Civil War. During Reconstruction, the married women's property act movement completed its course in Northern and Southern states alike, and states in both regions wrestled with the implications the 14th Amendment had for women's suffrage and other rights sought by women. These commonalities provided another channel through which the process of reassimilating the South into the stream of American postwar political and social change took place.

CHAPTER 10

Southern Law during the Bourbon Era (1877–1890)

> With this volume we pass to another era in the judicial history of Texas. Those who have before construed the laws of this state, and who have assisted in the effort to preserve constitutional freedom for its citizens, again constitute the court of last resort.
>
> —Alex W. Terrell and Alex S. Walker (Reporters, Texas Supreme Court), 1874[1]

The Reconstruction era ended in 1877 after conservatives defeated the last remaining Republican governments in the South and after President Rutherford Hayes withdrew most federal troops from the South as part of a tacit bargain that had enabled him to prevail by a single electoral vote in the 1876 election despite losing the popular vote. But Reconstruction ended at different times in different states. On the border, conservatives controlled Kentucky and Delaware throughout the Reconstruction era. They regained control of Maryland as early as 1867, and in 1870, after the enactment of the 15th Amendment and the reenfranchising of many ex-Confederates, they also regained Virginia, Tennessee, Missouri, and Georgia. Georgia Republicans had controlled state government for barely a year, and in Virginia, they never really gained control: a coalition of moderate conservatives and Republicans defeated the Radical candidate for governor in the election at which the state's Reconstruction constitution was ratified. Conservatives gained control of West Virginia in 1872, Texas in 1873, and Mississippi and Arkansas in 1874; after brief periods of divided government, they took control of Alabama in 1874 and North Carolina in 1875. The last Republican governments fell after the 1876 elections in Louisiana, South Carolina, and Florida.

In some states, the transition was peaceful, but in others, it was marked by fraud and violence. Extreme conservatives openly proclaimed their intent to return as closely as possible to the prewar racial order by any means necessary. The elections that restored conservatives to control in Mississippi and South Carolina were blighted by voter intimidation, antiblack riots, and killings. Arkansas, Texas, and Louisiana also witnessed armed confrontations between conservative and Republican forces before the latter, recognizing that they could not prolong their power without federal support that was no longer forthcoming, ceded the contest. But Hayes and Congressional Republicans made clear that although they accepted the end of Reconstruction, they would not tolerate repeal of the basic civil and political rights conferred on Southern blacks, and that states that tried to revert to the prewar social order might face renewed federal intervention. Awareness of this risk, together with many conservatives' uneasiness about the violence surrounding the end of Reconstruction, enabled moderate conservatives to prevail over extremists in most states in the struggle for control of post-Reconstruction governments.[2]

Hailed as "Redeemers" by their constituents and later denominated "Bourbons" as time passed and their place in Southern history became clear,[3] moderate conservatives promised to clear away the legal and social changes Reconstruction had brought to their states. The belief that Redemption washed away the sins of Reconstruction long formed an essential part of the South's self-image. But the reality was different. Redeemer lawmakers generally supported a middle racial ground: they tacitly agreed to protect property rights, other basic civil rights, and personal security for blacks if blacks would refrain from interfering with white political control and pressing for social equality. Redeemer lawmakers did not favor any restructuring of the prewar social order among whites, and in many states, they eliminated Reconstruction-era measures that modified that order, most notably crop lien laws. But some Reconstruction-era measures such as debt relief laws, married women's property rights, and public school systems proved to have enduring popular appeal and were left intact. In many respects, the legal legacy of Reconstruction proved surprisingly hardy.[4]

THE REDEMPTION COURTS

Most Southern states replaced their Reconstruction judges as soon as circumstances allowed, either by enacting new constitutions that created new supreme courts or by replacing the judges when their terms expired. In a few cases, Redeemers pressured sitting judges to resign, most notably Jonathan Wright of South Carolina. Like most black lawmakers of the Reconstruction era, the chances of war led Wright from humble beginnings to a meteoric rise and an equally meteoric fall. Born into a free black family in Pennsylvania in 1840, he attended college in the North and then read law in his native state. At the end of the war, he volunteered for service with the American Missionary Society and was sent to Beaufort, South Carolina, to aid in the Society's effort to educate newly freed slaves. He was quickly marked as a man of ability and was elected to the

Judge Jonathan Wright, South Carolina. Courtesy of *Harper's Weekly* Magazine, March 5, 1870.

state senate. In 1870, when he was only 30 years old, his colleagues elected him to fill a vacancy on the supreme court. Black lawmakers, who composed a majority of the legislature, insisted that a black justice should occupy at least one seat on the court and white legislators viewed Wright, a moderate by temperament, as more acceptable than his rivals William Whipper and Robert Elliott. Wright's judicial career was uneventful until late 1876 when, after an election marred by wholesale violence against black voters, he joined his colleagues in deciding an election challenge in favor of Wade Hampton, the Redeemer candidate for governor. Rumors circulated that Wright had been pressured by his judicial colleagues to vote in Hampton's favor and that he had feared for his safety if he did not. Wright later attempted to reverse his opinion, but his colleagues blocked him from doing so. The following year, with Hampton in office, Wright resigned under threat of impeachment; he died a few years later in obscurity.[5]

Not all Southern states reconstituted their supreme courts at the end of Reconstruction. All three of Florida's Reconstruction judges remained in office until the state enacted a new constitution in 1885; there was little pressure to remove them because they were generally regarded as "men not easily corrupted." Georgia's Reconstruction judges were replaced piecemeal: Joseph Brown and Henry McCay were not forced out of office but resigned in 1870 and 1875, respectively, to pursue business opportunities, and Hiram Warner remained on the court until his death in 1881. Missouri's Reconstruction judges also retired at times of their own choosing. In states that replaced their judges at the end of Reconstruction, the new judges often had much in common with their predecessors. Redemption courts, like Reconstruction courts, were heavily stocked with prewar Unionists who had elected to stay with their states after secession. Conservative Unionists such as Thomas Ashe and William Smith of North Carolina, David Walker of Arkansas, and Thomas A. R. Nelson of Tennessee had supported Andrew Johnson's vision of a program of quick readmission to the Union with minimal social and political changes and had opposed Congressional Reconstruction: this cast them into political exile during Reconstruction but made them candidates for the Redemption courts.

Nelson provides a particularly striking example. A leading Tennessee Unionist before the war, he actively opposed secession and was arrested by Confederate forces when he attempted to travel to Washington to take his seat in Congress in 1861. Nelson stoutly supported Johnson in the latter's struggle with Congress over Reconstruction and represented the president at his impeachment trial; he was skeptical of efforts to make blacks the full civil and political equals of whites, but he occasionally represented individual blacks without charge in cases where he felt injustice was being done to them.[6]

Very few Redemption judges were firebrands. Several, most notably David Walker and Elbert English of Arkansas and Oran Roberts of Texas, had served on their courts before the war; their reappearance had value as a symbol of the return to traditional ways desired by the Redeemers. Others such as Josiah A. P. Campbell of Mississippi and George Moore of Texas had served as judges during the Restoration period. But even judges such as Roberts who had been thoroughgoing secessionists conspicuously declined to vilify their Reconstruction predecessors or to encourage the resurrection of prewar social values. A few frontal attacks were made on Reconstruction-era decisions: Virginia's 1870 legislature authorized the state's new supreme court to accept or reject decisions of the state's Reconstruction court as it saw fit, and Texas's Redemption court refused to treat any decisions of the state's Military Court as binding because the Military Court judges had been appointed by federal authorities rather than under the Texas constitution. But in the main, Redemption judges upheld actions of Reconstruction officials because, as Judge Amos Manning of Alabama explained in 1875, "this is required by the necessities of society." Respect for precedent was essential to social stability and was therefore paramount.[7]

LEGACIES OF RECONSTRUCTION: CIVIL RIGHTS AND EDUCATION

The distinction drawn during Reconstruction between civil, political, and social rights remained firmly in place during the Redemption era. The 14th and 15th Amendments made clear that blacks' basic civil and political rights could not be directly restricted. Redemption lawmakers accepted this fact and devoted most of their energies in the civil rights arena to preserving social distinctions between the races. North Carolina's 1877 legislature summarized the prevailing attitude in a resolution enacted to allay Northern fears:

[W]e recognize the duty of the stronger race to uphold the weaker, and that upon it rests the responsibility of an honest and faithful endeavor to raise the weaker race to the level of intelligent citizenship. . . . [W]hile we regard with repugnance the absurd attempts, by means of "civil rights" bills, to eradicate certain race distinctions, implanted by nature and sustained by the habits of forty centuries . . . we do, nevertheless, heartily accord alike to every citizen, without distinction of race or color, equality before the law.[8]

Because Redemption lawmakers elected not to interfere with black Southerners' basic civil rights and because most blacks had resigned themselves to an indefinite postponement of social equality and of any chance for real political power, there was little civil rights litigation at the state level during the Redemption era. In the rare cases that arose between 1877 and 1890, Southern supreme courts enforced blacks' rights under existing laws but showed no inclination to expand such rights. For example, in *Britton v. Atlanta & Charlotte Air-Line Railway Co.* (1883), a train conductor allowed Elsie Britton, a black passenger, to sit in a smoking car usually reserved for whites but warned her he could not control the conduct of whites in the car. A group of whites later entered the car and ejected Britton; she then sued the railroad for failing to protect her safety and security as a passenger. The North Carolina supreme court could easily have rejected Britton's claim on the ground that she failed to heed custom and the conductor's warning, but instead it concluded that once the conductor allowed Britton in the car, she was entitled to stay. Britton, said Judge Thomas Ruffin, Jr., had "acquired an established right to the seat which she occupied upon entering the defendant's train. She held it by the same tenure that every other passenger upon the train held his seat . . . and upon being notified that her ejection had taken place, the first duty of the officer was to see her restored to it."[9]

Other Redemption courts readily upheld laws enforcing social segregation but scrutinized such laws closely to ensure that they afforded blacks the same legal rights as whites. In 1874, Texas federal judge Thomas Duval struck down the state's prewar antimiscegenation law because it penalized only whites for racial intermarriage; the legislature then enacted a new law that penalized whites and blacks equally, and the state's newly created intermediate appeals court held in 1877 that because the new law applied to both races equally, it did not violate the 14th Amendment or federal civil rights.[10]

Redemption legislatures worked hard at shoring up the color line in public schools and revising Reconstruction-era educational reforms. Most Northern states created systems of free common schools between 1789 and 1830, but Southern states lagged behind. Some created free schools for indigent white children prior to 1830; several southwestern states including Mississippi, Louisiana, Tennessee, and Kentucky enacted common school laws in the 1830s and 1840s, but the laws became moribund because of lack of state funding and local support. The common school movement made gains throughout the South in the 1850s, but the gains were largely wiped out in the war.

Reconstruction governments revived the common school ideal. Many Reconstruction constitutional conventions, influenced by Northern views on education and awareness of blacks' intense desire for education, required their states to establish statewide common school systems. Reconstruction legislatures departed from their prewar predecessors by providing substantial state education funding and creating central controls over education for the first time. This turned out to be an enduring legacy of Reconstruction. As in other regions, most details of day-to-day operation were left to local school districts but funding was overseen by state government.[11]

The thought of black and white children mixing in the schools was deeply disturbing to most white Southerners, almost as much as miscegenation.

Nevertheless, most Reconstruction governments took care to specify that black and white children should have equal educational opportunities and that such opportunities should be provided out of a unitary school fund, not one divided by race. During Redemption, a few states experimented with systems under which taxes collected from each race were used exclusively for schools attended by that race; others authorized local districts, which were usually all-white or all-black, to supplement state school funding with bond issues. The practical effect of such measures was to deny black pupils access to the much higher revenues that could be collected from white taxpayers; this, in turn, made such measures vulnerable to challenge under the equal protection clause of the 14th Amendment and similar clauses in many state constitutions. Accordingly, most states avoided such measures and maintained a unity school fund for all pupils.[12]

Redemption courts soon proved that such caution was justified. In the early 1880s, Kentucky state and federal courts struck down that state's segregated school fund law, and several years later, North Carolina's supreme court followed suit. Kentucky's supreme court made clear that under the 14th Amendment, education taxes must "be provided for by general laws applicable to all classes and races alike." The North Carolina court reached the same conclusion and went on to defend the right of black pupils to at least a minimally fair share in terms that Reconstruction judges would have applauded:

[I]s it not obvious [that segregated fund laws] would be subversive of the equality and uniformity recognized in the system of public schools, which looks to a fair participation of all its citizens in the advantages of free education? . . .

Nor can we shut our eyes to the fact, that the vast bulk of property, yielding the fruits of taxation, belongs to the white people of the State, and very little is held by the emancipated race; and yet the needs of the latter for free tuition, in proportion to its numbers, are as great or greater than the needs of the former. The act, then, in directing an appropriation of what taxes are collected from each class, to the improved education of the children of that class, does necessarily discriminate "in favor of the one and to the prejudice" of the other race.[13]

When a new wave of resistance to black political and social equality arose in the 1890s, several Southern states again created segregated school funds. These efforts ended on an ambiguous note in 1899 when the United States Supreme Court decided *Cumming v. Georgia*. The *Cumming* case was curious in several ways. The city of Augusta maintained segregated school funds; because of financial constraints, it closed the black high school in order to keep black elementary schools fully open. The Georgia supreme court rejected the argument of black parents that the city's decision violated their children's right to an equal education, reasoning that the 14th Amendment extended only to elementary schools. Justice John Marshall Harlan, speaking for the federal Supreme Court, agreed. He made clear that education was primarily a state concern and that accordingly, federal courts would interfere as little as possible, particularly where decisions were motivated by economics; but Harlan was careful to note that if the black parents had been able to show the high school closing was based purely on race, "different questions might have arisen." *Cumming* thus hinted—but did not decide—that even though overt racial discrimination in school funding was unconstitutional and black and white pupils must have equal educational opportunity through the elementary level, segregated funds might be acceptable.[14]

LEGACIES OF RECONSTRUCTION: THE NEW FEDERALISM

The legal disputes in the South over the proper postwar balance between state and federal power came to an apparent end in the mid-1870s when the federal Supreme Court held that state courts could not interfere with proceedings in the federal courts and that in cases of conflict between state and federal courts over constitutional issues, the Supreme Court had the final word. The Court's decisions brought to the fore two types of statutes that became increasingly popular after Reconstruction as a modest means of containing federal power: antiremoval license laws that required corporations to agree not to remove lawsuits to federal court as a condition of obtaining a license to do business in the state, and antiremoval revocation laws that required state officials to revoke the licenses of corporations that removed lawsuits.[15] In one of its decisions, *Morse v. Home Insurance Company* (1874), the Supreme Court held that license laws impermissibly encroached on federal sovereignty but two years later, in *Doyle v. Continental Insurance Company* (1876), a divided Court upheld Wisconsin's revocation law. Three dissenters argued that revocation laws, like license laws, were "derogatory to the jurisdiction and sovereignty of the United States [and were] mischievous and productive of hostility and disloyalty to the general government."[16]

This small pocket of state primacy was a continuing subject of debate among Southern lawmakers. Ultimately, it revealed the persistence of judicial nationalism among Redemption judges. In the late 1880s, West Virginia and North Carolina tried to attack federal removal laws indirectly by enacting local-registration laws requiring foreign corporations (that is, corporations chartered in other states) to register as local corporations before doing business in their states. Under federal law, foreign corporations sued by local residents usually could remove their cases to federal court, but local corporations could not. A closely divided North Carolina supreme court upheld its state's local-registration law, but West Virginia's court held that its law could not be used to circumvent federal removal laws. In 1895, Kentucky's supreme court struck down the state's license law, stating in broad terms that "any legislation . . . by which it is proposed or designed to take away [the removal] privilege, even under the power of the state to fix the terms upon which the corporation may enter that state for the purpose of doing business, is unconstitutional and void." But nine years later, in *Prewitt v. Security Mutual Life Insurance Company* (1904), a closely divided court upheld the state's revocation law. Two dissenters, concerned that *Prewitt* would be interpreted as a new call to arms for states' rights, defended federalism in terms reminiscent of several Reconstruction courts, arguing that "it is a narrow and provincial view to regard these national laws as a harsh and severe edicts imposed by a foreign suzerain, instead of benignant laws imposed by ourselves in the interest of a broad and national justice." In 1910, Mississippi's supreme court followed *Prewitt*, but four years later, the court concluded that even revocation laws encroached impermissibly on removal laws. In 1922, the federal Supreme Court effectively ended the new round of controversy it had created in *Doyle* when it tacitly overruled that case and concluded that revocation laws infringed on federal sovereignty.[17]

LEGACIES OF RECONSTRUCTION: CORPORATE SUBSIDIES AND CORPORATE REGULATION

The American industrial revolution first gained a real foothold in the South during the Redemption era. In the 1880s and 1890s, the textile and tobacco industries of central North Carolina expanded dramatically and transformed the state's economy; the hill regions of northwest Georgia and north Alabama, with active encouragement from their state governments, used local coal and iron deposits to create large-scale ironworks and metal industries. Redemption lawmakers were caught between modernizing economic forces and the strong desire of many of their constituents to restore the social order as closely as possible to its antebellum state. Thus it is not surprising that the approaches Redemption lawmakers took toward corporations often were obscure or seemingly contradictory.[18]

The Redemption constitutions provided one of the most important expressions of this conflict. Redemption conventions in about half of the Southern states substantially cut back government powers, including taxing powers, state and local governments' ability to create and subsidize railroads and other internal improvement, and sometimes the very size of state government itself. But other states conspicuously refused to enact new constitutions: they retained for a time their Reconstruction constitutions that put relatively few restraints on governmental aid to enterprise.[19]

The picture was further complicated by the varying reactions of Redemption governments as sentiment for greater government control and regulation of corporations crested during the 1870s. As previously noted, most American states passed through an initial "wide-open" era, in which they freely assisted railroads and other enterprises promising public benefit; a subsequent "reactive" period in which they responded to the debt such assistance had generated by restricting state subsidies of enterprise; and a final "municipal" period, in which municipalities were allowed to aid enterprise on a limited basis. Southern states in the forefront of the early internal improvements movement, most notably Virginia, Maryland, and Kentucky, passed through their wide-open and reactive periods before the Civil War, thus corporate regulation was not a topic of controversy in these states during either Reconstruction or the Redemption era. The wide-open era did not come to other Southern states, particularly the later-settled southwestern states, until the 1850s; as a result, they entered their reactive periods after the war. There was no clear divide between Reconstruction and Redemption governments' approaches to corporations in such states. In a few states, most notably Georgia, Reconstruction legislatures maintained a wide-open policy which their Redemption successors deliberately ended. But in some cases conservatives as well as Republicans supported generous state and local subsidies. In other states including the Carolinas, Florida, and Tennessee, Reconstruction legislatures began restricting state aid to internal improvement companies in the early 1870s but declined to restrict municipalities from providing such aid, and Redemption legislatures continued this mixed policy with little change.[20]

LEGACIES OF RECONSTRUCTION: CONTROL OF THE LAND

Redemption lawmakers drew a clearer line between themselves and their predecessors when they addressed postwar use of farmland and forests. This was particularly true for agricultural lien laws. As earlier noted, emancipation and wartime devastation forced landowners, merchants, and agricultural workers to compete for first rights to crops grown by the workers. In most states, there was a distinct tilt toward landowners and away from tenants and merchants during Redemption. North Carolina provided perhaps the most dramatic example: its 1877 legislature repealed a Reconstruction lien law that had given preference to agricultural workers and replaced it with a law giving priority to landowners. Other states, including Mississippi, Alabama, and Arkansas, enacted changes striking a balance between workers, landowners, and merchants shortly after the end of Reconstruction. In Louisiana, proposals to follow suit met with strong resistance from merchants, and ultimately, compromises were reached in the early 1880s, giving merchants protection against competing claims of tenants and landowners. In Mississippi, tenant farmers were unusually numerous and were able to use their power to limit increases in landlords' rights and preserve some protection for themselves. In the end, the increased protection Reconstruction legislatures had given tenants was reduced but did not entirely vanish.[21]

Fencing and enclosure laws for land use control received substantial attention from Reconstruction and Redemption lawmakers. Under British common law, forests and other lands not enclosed by fences or hedges were open to all persons for grazing stock and for hunting. The common law rule was gradually discarded in England but it persisted in America; Southern states clung to the rule with particular tenacity. For example, when the advent of railroads resulted in frequent accidental killings of stock that wandered from unenclosed farms onto railroad tracks, many states enacted laws requiring stock owners to erect fences, but such laws were rare in the South. When stock accident cases came before antebellum southern courts, the courts generally held that the stock owners had no obligation to prevent their animals from roaming freely and could not be held responsible for failing to keep the animals off the railroads' lines.[22]

The state of fencing law changed dramatically in the South during the early years of Redemption. In 1872, Georgia and North Carolina enacted local-option stock laws authorizing certain counties to require animal owners to confine their animals and making owners automatically liable for damage if they did not. Mississippi, Alabama, and South Carolina all enacted similar laws between 1876 and 1880. Several states quickly extended their local-option laws to cover most of the state, and South Carolina enacted a statewide compulsory fencing law in 1881.[23] The fencing laws were controversial: small farmers, who relied heavily on common land for grazing, often resisted implementation of local-option laws. In Texas, antifencing forces ultimately prevailed, largely because livestock played a larger role in agriculture in Texas than elsewhere in the South and because water was scarce in the livestock belt of central and west Texas. The "range wars" between farmers who favored fencing and cattlemen who did not—later to become an important part of the state's image in literature and film—began in the early 1880s when drought conditions impelled desperate cattlemen to cut fences in order to give their animals access to water. The 1881 legislature devoted much of its time to considering the problem and ultimately enacted a compromise: fencing of public lands was prohibited, but use of such lands for water and grazing was only allowed on a limited basis. The compromise ended the active phase of the war, but many parts of the state continued actively to resist any limitations on land use.[24]

Did the fencing laws represent a continuation of or a reaction to Reconstruction-era policies? At least one scholar has argued that Redemption-era fencing laws represented an effort by large landowners to consolidate their political and economic power and also had a racial component in that Southern blacks relied heavily on hunting and fishing in unenclosed areas for their food. This may read too much into the laws. Fencing laws were enacted in some states before the Civil War, primarily because those states were filling up and lawmakers believed such laws would promote better order between landowners and land users. There is no reason to believe the impulses behind postwar Southern fencing laws were different. Texas's experience confirms that the controversy over the laws was driven more by desire for order than social power and had no particular racial component. The laws, then, were not a reaction to Reconstruction but rather were a sign that the South's agricultural economy was entering a mature stage.

At the end of the 1880s, it appeared that the South's postwar legal system had stabilized. White moderates had created a racial system that had rolled back many Reconstruction-era reforms but preserved a small core of basic civil and political rights to blacks and gave them some protection from the violence that had marred the later stages of Reconstruction. State courts had indicated that although they would not expand black rights, they would enforce existing statutory rights strictly. The South had joined the North in addressing problems of debtor relief, corporate regulation, and accommodating the new postwar balance of power between federal and state governments. In short, to all appearances, the South had rejoined the mainstream of American law. However, the region was about to embark on a new era in its legal history that would dispel any notion that the South's legal distinctiveness or the controversy over Reconstruction's legal legacy had come to an end.

CHAPTER 11

The Impassable Chasm: Southern Law during the Straight-Out Era (1890–1915)

[There is an] impassable chasm that separates [the races]. In the home, the school, the church, the public place—in truth, everywhere—it exists. These observations are not set down in any spirit of unkindness or hostility to the colored race, or with a view to create or encourage discrimination or repression that will place obstacles in the way of their improvement or advancement, but rather to note an irremovable and remediless condition that must be acknowledged and that will be steadfastly adhered to.
—Judge John Carroll (Kentucky), 1907

It is also claimed that the negro is an inferior race. I grant it. It would be a high compliment to slavery and oppression that with only thirty years of freedom the negro is the equal of the white man, who has had the advantage of two hundred years of American civilization. . . . School houses open to them [whites] everywhere, . . . while all the avenues to learning and education have been closed against the negro, and are only yielding now to his indomitable perseverance and unyielding will.
—William J. Whipper (South Carolina), 1895[1]

Beginning in the late 1880s, the tacit bargain that Redemption leaders had struck with Southern blacks and Northern public opinion a decade earlier—namely, a promise to protect a core of basic civil rights for blacks and shield them from violence in return for subservience—began to erode, as did the relative racial calm that had prevailed during the Redemption era. Between 1887 and 1902, a movement to disfranchise black voters swept the South, resulting in the enactment of new "straight-out" constitutions and statutes that dramatically reduced black voter turnout in most states. Many Southern whites felt that *de facto* segregation of the races in public places was no longer sufficient: legal ratification of segregation was necessary. As a result, most states enacted Jim Crow laws, mandating segregation in places where black and white Southerners were likely to cross paths. Exclusion of blacks from juries became endemic, peonage laws were enacted that bore disturbing resemblances to the 1865–66 black codes, and near the end of the straight-out era, the movement to isolate blacks reached its peak when several Southern cities enacted ordinances requiring residential segregation.

Why did the Redemption-era bargain erode, and why did white attitudes toward blacks change? Historians have offered several explanations. Tension between Southern elites and working-class whites was a major force behind the straight-out era. Reconstruction had ended in large part because whites of all classes had shared a common perception of black political power as a threat that must be eliminated. During the post-Reconstruction years, this bond weakened as blacks' political power faded and economic conflicts among whites came to the fore. The threat of white disunity galvanized a new generation of Democratic leaders such as Benjamin Tillman of South Carolina; eventually, they were able to restore white unity by exploiting working-class whites' fears that blacks would match or surpass them economically and socially.

At a deeper level, the fears that surfaced in the 1890s were not new. As the historian George Fredrickson has argued, they "had [their] origins in the proslavery imagination, which had conceived of the black man as having a dual nature—he was docile and amiable when enslaved, ferocious and murderous when free." Blacks could not be reenslaved, but they could be controlled and cabined by legal and extralegal means. Lynchings and other incidents of violence against blacks increased; eventually, even liberal Southerners came to view segregation as the only viable means of forestalling such violence.[2]

Conservatives made their most aggressive attempt to roll back Reconstruction's legal legacy during the straight-out era. Their effort was successful in many respects, but its limits were more interesting and more important than its successes. Southern states decimated black suffrage, restricted the freedom of black workers, and enforced racial separation in many areas of life, but in order to avoid running afoul of the 14th and 15th Amendments, they had to enact laws racially neutral on their face, and they were compelled to concede as the price of segregation that blacks were legally entitled to accommodations equal to those of whites. This concession was seldom honored in practice, but it created a small opening through which lawmakers of a later time might convert nominal equality of rights into a more genuine equality.

EARLY DISFRANCHISEMENT: THE MISSISSIPPI AND SOUTH CAROLINA CONSTITUTIONS

Efforts to limit black voting in the South began shortly after the end of Reconstruction. Bourbon leaders quickly learned how to use fraud, intimidation, and ballot box manipulation to produce heavy Democratic margins and neutralize Republicans, who still had pockets of strength in hill regions throughout the South. Georgia's 1877 Redemption convention established a cumulative poll tax: voters had to pay an annual tax in order to vote, and if they did not pay, the tax carried over from year to year, making it ever more difficult to vote as the tax mounted. The tax drastically curtailed voting among both blacks and poor whites. South Carolina adopted a more elaborate "eight-box" law in 1882, which required voters to fill out separate ballots for separate offices and place them in separate boxes; if a ballot was mistakenly placed in the wrong box, it was not counted. Illiterate voters of both races found it difficult to comply with the law, which several other states copied during the 1880s.[3]

A more systematic disfranchising movement began in the late 1880s. In 1889, Tennessee required voting to be by secret ballot and the following year, it enacted an annual (but noncumulative) poll tax. Arkansas adopted virtually identical measures in 1890–91. Secret ballot laws had a dual nature: they were favored by progressives, who viewed them as a means of reducing election fraud and freeing urban voters from domination by party bosses, but in the South, they also proved to be an effective disfranchising tool. Illiterate black and white voters were now effectively denied help in filling out their ballots, and as a result, they often filled out ballots incorrectly and lost their vote.[4]

"Straight-out" leaders, joined by some Bourbon lawmakers, continued to seek more effective ways of disfranchising black voters. In the early 1890s, Mississippi and South Carolina held long-delayed Redemption constitutional conventions that became important laboratories for these experiments. The success Mississippi Bourbons had had in suppressing the black vote was reflected in the fact that only two Republicans were elected to the state's 1890 constitutional convention: Isaiah Montgomery and Horatio Simrall, the former Reconstruction supreme court justice who now added a final turn to his long and winding legal career.

Montgomery, the convention's only black delegate, quickly resigned himself to the fact that disfranchisement was inevitable, and he supported a literacy test for suffrage in the hope it would allow at least some blacks to continue to vote. Simrall had been a lifelong moderate Unionist, but the political tempests of the age had led him to express his moderation in odd ways. After the war, he had actively opposed the black codes and other efforts to defy national authority, but he had also opposed the 14th Amendment as an infringement on his state's sovereignty. Despite his conservative temperament, as a judge, Simrall had no difficulty accepting major civil rights reforms such as Mississippi's 1873 public accommodations law. At the 1890 convention, his mixed views on federalism returned to the fore. Congress had readmitted Mississippi to representation in 1870 on condition that the state would never modify its constitution to impose new limits on suffrage, and the 1890 convention was concerned that Congress would view new limits as an act of defiance. Simrall helped prepare an opinion that Mississippi had never legitimately left the Union, therefore Congress had no power to impose conditions on its readmission and Mississippi was free to limit suffrage as it wished.[5]

Simrall's opinion opened the door to an extensive debate over the best means of limiting suffrage. In addition to a simple literacy test, the convention seriously considered a property ownership qualification. Both tests were unacceptable to a majority of delegates, who feared they would eliminate working-class whites as well as blacks from the polls. An "understanding" clause, which would allow local registrars to exclude voters who could not explain a section of the state constitution presented to them, seemed more promising: it gave local officials broad discretion to determine what explanation would be adequate, thus allowing them to exclude blacks and include working-class whites virtually at will. Despite concerns that an understanding clause would encourage continuation of the voting fraud that had become endemic during the Bourbon era, the convention ultimately incorporated an understanding clause into the new constitution along with a poll tax.[6]

South Carolina's 1895 convention followed a pattern similar to Mississippi's but attracted more attention, mainly because it featured an unusually frank discussion of the racial motives behind disfranchisement. After Benjamin Tillman won the governorship in 1890, he called for and eventually obtained a new convention to set suffrage limits, which he viewed as "a fitting capstone to the triumphal arch which the common people have erected to liberty, progress and Anglo-Saxon civilization since 1890." Tillman's efforts were temporarily checked when black voters challenged the voting laws for convention delegates as racially discriminatory. Federal judge Nathan Goff, a West Virginia Republican who had recently replaced the deceased Hugh Bond, agreed. Goff was offended by the frankness with which the state's attorney defended the racially exclusionary nature of the laws, and noted accurately that the laws were designed "to so legislate as to apparently respect constitutional requirements, but at the same time to stab to the death the rights and immunities guaranteed by them." However, an appeals court reversed Goff's decision on the ground that the complaining voters had not claimed actual discrimination at the polls and that the issue ultimately was a political one in which the courts could not interfere.[7]

Tillman denounced Goff as a puppet, "brought from his home in West Virginia . . . to overthrow the rule of the people in our State," and the convention election proceeded, but opposition to Tillman also continued. Unlike Mississippi, South Carolina blacks had preserved small pockets of power, most notably in Georgetown and Beaufort counties. Beaufort had been a center of black political activity since the Civil War, when it was occupied by Union troops and served as the location for experiments in black economic empowerment. In 1895, Beaufort sent six black delegates to the convention, led by Robert Smalls and William Whipper. Smalls had become a leading black hero of the Civil War in 1863 when, in order to escape to freedom, he captured a Confederate launch in Charleston harbor and took it into the Union lines. During Reconstruction, he served several terms in Congress, and after Reconstruction, he remained a power in county politics. Whipper, a flamboyant man, was one of the state's leading Radicals. Born into a prosperous free black family in Pennsylvania, he first came to South Carolina as a Union soldier; after the war, he married Frances Rollin, a member of a prominent Charleston free black family, who became a leading advocate for women's suffrage during Reconstruction. Perhaps influenced by Frances, Whipper advocated universal suffrage as a delegate to the 1868 Reconstruction convention. He also served in the legislature during Reconstruction; in the early 1880s, he left the state but after three years decided to return and do what he could to preserve the legacy of Reconstruction.[8] At the 1895 convention, Smalls, Whipper, and their colleagues agreed that any effort to preserve meaningful black suffrage would be hopeless and that the most they could do was bear witness to the wrongs inflicted upon them. They did so with skill and spirit.

The black delegation managed to interest Joseph Pulitzer's *New York World* in their plight, and during the convention, the *World* regularly reported to its large Northern readership on the efforts of Tillman, "the one eyed master of South Carolina," to disfranchise more than half a million black voters. Whipper and Smalls engaged Tillmanites in a prolonged debate over suffrage at the same time Tillmanites and Bourbon delegates were debating the best means of black disfranchisement. Whipper proposed a broad suffrage measure similar to the one he had advocated in 1868; white delegates ultimately rejected it by a lopsided margin, but they gave Whipper a hearing, and Tillman responded by admitting the convention's purpose with a degree of frankness unusual even for the straight-out era:

[W]e are met in convention openly, boldly, without any pretense of secrecy, to announce that it is our purpose, as far as we may, without coming in conflict with the United States Constitution, to put such safeguards around this ballot in future, to so restrict the suffrage and circumscribe it, that this infamy can never come about again. . . . [We must] reduce [blacks'] voting strength so that there will never be enough of them to do more than to put either one white faction or the other in control of the government.[9]

Like their Mississippi counterparts, white delegates to the South Carolina convention had difficulty agreeing on the best means of disfranchisement. Bourbon delegates were comfortable with literacy or property-owning qualifications, but Tillmanites objected that such criteria would disfranchise as many poor whites as blacks. Both factions were sensitive to the possibility of federal intervention: "How," asked Tillman, "do you propose to get around the Chinese wall, the impassable bulwark which the Fifteenth Amendment throws around the negroes, except by an educational or property qualification?" Ultimately, the white factions agreed on a Mississippi-like mix of property and educational qualifications together with an "understanding" clause that would give local registrars broad discretion to include whites but exclude blacks from the voter list. Several delegates worried that the "understanding" clause would open the door to a renewal of the voting fraud on which Bourbons had often depended in the past, but Tillman rejoined that the benefits of racial control would outweigh the risk of fraud: "Some poisons in small doses are very salutary and valuable medicines."

The black delegates were able to secure a few concessions. The 1895 constitution preserved many of the nonracial reforms incorporated in the Reconstruction constitution; segregation in the schools was now officially mandated, but the convention also provided for construction of a black teacher training school and required counties to pay damages to relatives of lynching victims. When inclusion of a miscegenation clause was discussed, Smalls challenged white delegates by proposing an amendment whereby any white man cohabiting with a black woman would be disqualified from holding office. The measure was quickly tabled but drew a grudging public concession from Tillman that both races contributed to miscegenation. The black delegates closed the convention with a final act of witness, formally asking for (and receiving) permission to be excused from signing the new constitution. Robert Anderson of Georgetown sadly concluded: "We are told the law of injustice will roll on until it reaches its climax, and then a reaction is bound to come."[10]

LATER DISFRANCHISING MEASURES

The Mississippi and South Carolina conventions set the parameters for disfranchisement debates in other states. During the decade after 1895, most of the remaining states in the Deep South enacted disfranchising constitutions or laws; they did not copy Mississippi and South Carolina to the letter, but they found that those states had devised virtually all of the possible disfranchising devices that might pass constitutional muster. In addition to a poll tax and an understanding clause, Louisiana's 1898 convention considered a "grandfather clause," which would automatically allow descendants of Civil War veterans to vote. Mississippi had rejected such a clause for fear that the courts would find it overtly discriminatory against blacks, and many Louisiana leaders raised the same concerns. Ultimately, the convention decided to rely on a combination of understanding and grandfather clauses and a poll tax to achieve the goal of excluding blacks from suffrage while including as many poor whites as possible.[11]

In 1900, North Carolina conservatives procured an amendment to the state constitution adding a grandfather clause, and in 1901, Alabama enacted a new constitution that incorporated a poll tax, a grandfather clause, and a "good character clause." The latter clause, which was similar to understanding clauses, left much discretion to local registrars to admit or exclude whites who did not qualify for suffrage under other provisions. Alabama Bourbons like their South Carolina counterparts succeeded in placing an antilynching provision in the constitution as well as a clause prohibiting division of state school funds based directly on race. Virginia in its 1902 constitutional convention relied more heavily on an understanding clause than other states. Carter Glass, a delegate who later in life would play an important part in shaping the New Deal as a United States senator, reassured the convention that the understanding clause would likely survive a constitutional challenge. "[W]e have accomplished our purpose strictly within the limitations of the Federal Constitution," explained Glass, "by legislating against the characteristics of the black race and not against the 'race, color or previous condition' of the people themselves. It is a fine distinction indeed."[12]

Texas and Georgia were the last states to enact disfranchising measures. Their efforts were more perfunctory than those of other Deep South states. Georgia's cumulative poll tax had proven very effective in suppressing the black vote, and the state contented itself with enacting a series of election laws in 1907 modeled on Alabama's constitutional provisions. White lawmakers in Texas concluded that a poll tax would be the simplest and most effective means of ensuring that the black vote remained low, and voters amended the state constitution in 1902 to provide such a tax.

The border states proved mostly immune to the disfranchisement movement. When conservatives gained control of the Maryland legislature in 1904, they enacted a poll tax and an understanding clause, but the new laws attracted widespread opposition and were repealed a few years after their enactment. Missouri, Kentucky, West Virginia, and Delaware enacted no new election laws of importance during the straight-out era. Several factors may account for this lack of reaction. Unlike the Deep South states, each border state had a competitive Republican Party; each had a lower percentage of blacks in its population than the Deep South states, thus making blacks less of a political presence and threat; and commercial and cultural ties to the North may have softened border whites' hostility to black suffrage. In the end, the border states concluded that existing laws had created an acceptable political balance between the races and there was no need to change.[13]

Concerns about the constitutionality of the new disfranchisement measures died quickly. In *Ratliff v. State* (1896), Mississippi's supreme court rejected a challenge to the 1890 constitution's suffrage provisions and held that the only test of constitutionality was whether the measures were facially discriminatory, that is, whether they were worded to discriminate against black voters. The court recognized the disfranchising purpose of the suffrage measures—given the nature of the debates at the convention, it could hardly do otherwise—but it adamantly refused to look at either the intent behind the measures or their practical effect. Two years later, the federal Supreme Court endorsed this approach in *Williams v. Mississippi* (1898), reasoning that "it has not been shown that [the suffrage provisions'] actual administration was evil, only that evil was possible under them." In *Giles v. Harris* (1903), the Court considered Alabama's disfranchising laws and again rejected any suggestion that it should actively examine the effect as well as the letter of such laws. There was a hint of frustration in the Court's decision: it noted that Alabama's grandfather clause came very close to outright discrimination against blacks and noted the potential for discrimination inherent in the understanding clause, but it tacitly conceded there was little it could do even if it wanted to take a more active role. There would be no point in forcing state officials to register voters under a fundamentally flawed system, and ultimately, only Congress had the power to enact and enforce antidiscrimination measures.[14]

THE RISE OF JIM CROW

Jim Crow laws put an official stamp on the dividing lines between civil, political, and social equality that had first appeared during Reconstruction. Relatively few segregation laws were enacted during Reconstruction, and after the federal Supreme Court ruled in *Hall v. DeCuir* (1878) that state accommodations laws could not be applied to interstate transportation, it appeared that a balance had been achieved: segregation would be a matter for private decision by business owners based on the demands of the marketplace. But in the 1880s and 1890s, a new generation of Southern blacks began to press transport companies and operators of segregated hotels, theaters, and other public places for genuinely equal accommodations. Many operators desegregated rather than pay the cost of separate but equal facilities. In reaction to this trend and perhaps also encouraged by the *Civil Rights Cases* (1883), a series of decisions in which the United States Supreme Court struck down the 1875 Civil Rights Act's restrictions on racial discrimination in public places,[15] Southern legislatures mandated segregation in a wide variety of settings.

School segregation came first. Most Reconstruction constitutions and statute books were silent on the subject, but during the first years of Redemption, several Deep South states together with Virginia, Kentucky, Tennessee, and Delaware codified school segregation in their statutes and constitutions. Laws mandating segregated railroad cars were enacted in two waves, the first between 1887 and 1892 and the second between 1899 and 1904. Streetcar segregation laws, which were enacted in about half the Southern states, soon followed. Few legislatures extended segregation laws to hotels and theaters, probably because such facilities were considered more private than transportation facilities and because segregation in such places had long been the custom.[16]

Initially, there was some doubt as to whether the Jim Crow laws were constitutional. It was generally accepted that railroads and other companies could impose segregation as a matter of choice, but it was not certain whether state legislatures could require them to do so. This question was laid to rest in *Plessy v. Ferguson* (1896). The *Plessy* case became famous when the federal Supreme Court overruled it 60 years later in *Brown v. Board of Education of Topeka* (1954), thus inaugurating the modern civil rights era and rendering *Plessy* a discredited symbol of a bygone age, but *Plessy's* modern infamy has obscured its real role in the evolution of American race relations. Like *DeCuir,* *Plessy* was brought as a test case by members of New Orleans' black community, and it had added interest because Albion Tourgee—a leader of North Carolina's Reconstruction convention, a Reconstruction-era judge, and more recently, an author of several influential books lamenting Reconstruction's failure—served as Plessy's lead counsel. Louisiana's supreme court rejected

Tourgee's argument that the 14th Amendment prohibited segregation. The court noted that segregation was widely accepted both before and after the amendment was enacted: in light of such practice, the amendment could only be interpreted to require "equality, and not identity or community of accommodations." The court could not conceive why blacks and whites would want to mix, believing that racial pride on both sides militated against integration; and it concluded that in any case, segregation laws represented a legitimate exercise of the police power to prevent racial friction and violence. On appeal, the federal Supreme Court agreed. Speaking for the Court, Justice Henry B. Brown emphasized, with a faint air of resignation, the limitations courts faced: they could guarantee civil and political equality, but "If one race be inferior to the other socially, the Constitution of the United States cannot put them upon the same plane."[17]

A dozen years later, the High Court in *Berea College v. Kentucky* approved the extension of segregation laws to private institutions as well as government-operated institutions. Berea College, which was incorporated by John Fee, an abolitionist minister, shortly before the Civil War, had a unique mission of providing education to impoverished students of both races. In 1904, the Kentucky legislature, irritated by the college's integration practices, enacted a law requiring segregation in all private and public schools in the state. Berea College secured the services of an advocate almost as prominent as Tourgee—John Carlisle, a former Kentucky congressman and federal secretary of the treasury—but he fared no better than had Tourgee. The Kentucky supreme court rejected Carlisle's argument that the segregation law interfered with the college's freedom of religion and the right of black and white students to exercise their personal right to associate with whom they pleased. Like its Louisiana counterpart, the Kentucky court upheld segregation laws as a legitimate exercise of police power, and it went further, bluntly arguing that the state had a right to prevent racial amalgamation and protect students from forming dangerous impressions that racial mixing might be acceptable. On appeal, the federal Supreme Court again upheld the law, although it did so primarily on the ground that states have broad power to regulate the conditions under which corporations can do business within their borders.[18]

Justice Harlan dissented in both *Plessy* and *Berea College*. He viewed segregation laws not as a means of fostering natural instincts of separation in both races but as overtly discriminatory measures that imposed a "badge of servitude" on blacks. In *Plessy*, he warned that the majority's decision might encourage the extension of segregation to private as well as public activities, and in *Berea College*, he pointed out that his prophecy had been fulfilled. "Have we become so inoculated with the prejudice of race," asked Harlan, "that an American government . . . can make distinctions between such citizens in the matter of their voluntary meeting for innocent purposes, simply because of their respective races?"[19]

Jim Crow laws also gave rise to one of the sharpest divisions between Northern and Southern states over civil rights during the post-Reconstruction

Justice John Marshall Harlan, United States Supreme Court. Courtesy of the Library of Congress.

years. When the federal Supreme Court struck down the 1875 Civil Rights Act prohibiting racial discrimination in public places, the South viewed the High Court's decision as a victory, but many Northern states responded by enacting state versions of the 1875 Act. Northern and Southern courts also displayed distinctly different attitudes toward Jim Crow laws. Southern courts uniformly upheld the laws, and many took pains to defend them as good social policy.[20] Southern courts took note of, and took pains to cite as supportive of their position, a small group of Northern court decisions, including *Roberts v. City of Boston* (1849) and *Chicago & Northwestern Railroad v. Williams* (1869); but the Northern cases were considerably less supportive of segregation than the Southern courts suggested. All of the Northern cases involved private railroad and streetcar segregation rules, not state laws, and the courts that decided them conspicuously refrained from commending segregation. For example, in *Roberts*, the Massachusetts supreme court upheld a school committee regulation enforcing segregation but took pains to emphasize that it was deferring to local school autonomy rather than approving segregation. In *Williams*, the Illinois supreme court stated in passing that "under some circumstances, [segregation] might not be an unreasonable rule," but it also fined a railroad for refusing to seat a black woman in a passenger car reserved for women and held that absent an explicit segregation rule, segregation would be prohibited.[21]

Jim Crow laws were regularly challenged in Southern state courts, sometimes by disgruntled black passengers and sometimes by railroads that did not want to incur the extra cost of segregated cars; and the laws did not always survive court scrutiny. Several Southern courts looked closely at the *DeCuir* case and concluded that if Reconstruction-era state laws prohibiting segregation could not be applied to interstate commerce, neither could laws mandating segregation. In *Louisville, New Orleans & Texas Railroad v. State* (1889), the Mississippi supreme court held that a law requiring provision of separate cars for each race did not impinge on interstate commerce because it did not require that railroads actually enforce segregation; but the court suggested that if the law had required actual segregation, it would have been unconstitutional. The United States Supreme Court affirmed that such was the case.[22]

Several state courts rebelled against the limits on segregation in interstate commerce. In *Smith v. State* (1898), Tennessee's supreme court tried to get around the *DeCuir* and *Louisville Railroad* cases by invoking the concept of state police power, just then coming into fashion as a way to justify ever-increasing state economic regulation. The court reasoned that segregation laws were police laws because they reduced racial friction and the possibility of violence and disorder, and that the state's use of police powers to protect its citizens could not be limited to intrastate commerce. Rebellion flared again in 1912 when Mississippi's supreme court complained that excluding interstate commerce from the ambit of segregation laws "disregard[s] the reason which underlies this legislation." The court stated with alarm that if segregation laws were invalid as applied to interstate commerce, then "necessarily [they] must be condemned altogether, as the theory upon which [their] wisdom and justice rests will thus be declared fanciful and without foundation in fact."[23] Most Southern courts, however, accepted the intrastate-interstate distinction without complaint. Maryland's supreme court explained that because some states had segregation laws and some did not, the burden on interstate transportation companies of changing their practice as they crossed each state line would be substantial, and "commerce cannot flourish in the midst of such embarrassment." Custom often enforced segregation on interstate trains where the law would not; but Congress never enacted a Jim Crow law, and the interstate beachhead against segregation created in the *Louisville Railroad* case endured.[24]

THE WHITENING OF SOUTHERN JURIES

The issue of whether blacks should be allowed to participate in the legal process as witnesses and jurors had been highly controversial during Reconstruction. With prodding from Congress, most Southern states granted blacks the unrestricted right to testify either at the end of the Restoration period or shortly after Congressional Reconstruction began; but Congress itself did not make any pronouncement on jury service. Many Southerners viewed jury service as conferring a sort of political power closely akin to voting and officeholding; thus as with black suffrage, there was substantial opposition to black jury service. There was a distinct regional difference: the Reconstruction governments of most Deep South states permitted black jury service with little debate, but several border states not subject to Congressional Reconstruction renewed prewar laws barring blacks from jury service. Oddly, the laws were not challenged until the end of the 1870s. The result was mixed: the federal Supreme Court decided that blacks could not legally be excluded from jury service, but as with suffrage laws, it was reluctant to look closely at whether discriminatory enforcement of facially neutral laws violated the 14th Amendment.[25]

The High Court began with two cases from Virginia. In *Ex parte Virginia* (1880), the Court agreed with Alexander Rives, a federal district judge in Virginia and staunch Unionist, that the 14th Amendment prohibited laws that formally excluded blacks from jury service. But in a companion case, *Virginia v. Rives* (1880), the Court concluded Rives had acted wrongly in freeing black defendants in a state murder trial based on their argument that no blacks were permitted to serve on their jury. The Court held there was no constitutional right to have a racially mixed jury; it suggested that discriminatory administration of a jury law that was racially neutral on its face might violate the 14th Amendment, but it did not say just how blatant the discrimination had to be to rise to the level of a constitutional violation.[26]

The Court considered the dilemma of discriminatory administration of facially neutral laws further in *Neal v. Delaware* (1881) and *Bush v. Kentucky* (1883). In *Neal*, local court officials admitted in writing that they systematically excluded black jurors from service. A black defendant presented these admissions to the state court in which he was being tried, but the court held that was not enough: he had to present live testimony of the officials. The Delaware court commented: "That none but white men were selected is in no wise remarkable in view of the fact, too notorious to be ignored, that the great body of black men residing in this state are utterly unqualified by want of intelligence, experience or moral integrity, to sit on juries." This was too much for the Supreme Court: it held that direct exclusion of the sort described in the officials' statements violated the 14th Amendment and that because state officials had not contested the truth of the statements, the Delaware courts should not have required live testimony. But in *Bush*, the Court again held that the mere absence of blacks on jury panels was not enough to show discrimination: direct evidence of discrimination such as that produced in *Neal* would be necessary.[27]

During the decades following the Supreme Court's jury cases, challenges to jury selection procedures came frequently before Southern courts. Unlike the interstate-intrastate distinction the Supreme Court had established in *Louisville Railroad*, Southern states did not resist the Court's standard for jury cases: they either repealed their laws excluding blacks from juries or made clear that such laws would not be enforced. Southern courts did not hesitate to overturn criminal convictions of black defendants if they believed the trial court had denied the defendant a fair chance to show that blacks were systematically excluded from jury panels, but they confirmed that in practice, it was extremely difficult to meet the standard of proof established in *Neal*, and they showed no inclination to help defendants obtain access to court records and officials in order to meet that standard.[28]

PEONAGE LAWS

The straight-out era also witnessed the resurrection of a portion of the Restoration-era black codes in the form of peonage laws. Many black codes had contained harsh vagrancy laws that effectively made refusal to work or refusal to fulfill an employment contract a crime and allowed courts to hire out recalcitrant workers as a means of working off their fines, thus resurrecting slavery in all but name. Between 1880 and 1900, most Deep South states and a few Upper South states enacted new labor control laws, commonly known to their supporters as "false pretences" laws and to their detractors as "peonage" laws. Typically, the laws provided that workers who "willfully" violated labor contracts under which they had received goods or money, for example by attempting to leave their employment, were subject to heavy fines and imprisonment. Given the large number of Southern farmers who operated on a lease or sharecropping basis, the impact of the peonage laws was immense.[29]

The laws were controversial from their inception. Critics charged that the laws improperly injected criminal law into contractual relationships and amounted to resurrection of imprisonment for debt. Southern state courts uniformly agreed that the mere breach of an employment contract could not be made a crime: subjecting workers who broke agreements to imprisonment or hiring-out would come perilously close to reinstituting slavery. But most courts upheld peonage laws by confining their application to cases where the worker had either made the contract knowing he would not fulfill it, or had enticed the employer to hire him by deliberately making false statements. The courts felt little need to preserve a boundary between civil and criminal law in the area of employment relations: when the South Carolina supreme court upheld its state's peonage law in 1890, it stated that it was "unable to discover in the provisions of the constitution anything which forbids . . . [making] the violation of a particular species of civil contracts a criminal offence."[30]

In the late 1890s, as Southern states increased the penalties under peonage laws and accounts of abuses resulting from the laws began to appear in the press, a reaction took place. Alabama's harsh 1901 peonage law became the lightning rod for reaction. The law provided fines and imprisonment for workers and sharecroppers who abandoned their contracts "without sufficient excuse" and made new employment contracts without informing their new employer of the existence of the original contracts. The law offended a number of influential Alabamians, including federal judge Thomas Jones. Jones, a former governor and firm Bourbon, had no objection in principle to laws designed to subordinate blacks or regulate labor, but he recoiled at the thought of restoring any vestige of slavery. In 1903, he delivered a widely publicized set of instructions to a grand jury in which he charged that the 1901 law "places the laborer or renter at the mercy of his employer" and makes him a "serf in all but name." Jones concluded that the law effectively restored imprisonment for debt, discriminated openly against workers in favor of employers and landlords, and was therefore unconstitutional. The following year, the Alabama supreme court formally struck down the law: it did not mention Jones's reasoning, but concluded the law was defective because it deprived workers of a fundamental right to pursue work of their own choosing. Two years later, in *Clyatt v. United States* (1905), the federal Supreme Court indicated that peonage practices were a form of slavery outlawed by the 13th Amendment to the federal Constitution.[31]

State legislatures responded to *Clyatt* and events in Alabama by modifying rather than repealing peonage laws. Some states reduced penalties; others, including Alabama, provided that workers who left employment would be presumed to have acted deceitfully but would be given a chance to prove the presumption wrong. Southern courts divided over the presumption's constitutionality: Georgia's supreme court found the presumption satisfactory but the supreme courts of North Carolina and Missouri indicated that it violated workers' rights to due process and equal protection of the laws, and federal judges in the Carolinas, Florida, and Mississippi agreed.[32]

Alabama again provided the leading test case for this issue. In 1907, a farm worker, Lonzo Bailey, agreed to work for one year at a wage of $15 per month. He received an advance of $15 against his wages, to be repaid by monthly deductions from his pay. After six weeks, he sought other employment, was tried and convicted under Alabama's revised peonage law, and was required to work off his fine and costs by serving his employer for approximately five months without pay. With assistance from several influential white Alabamians who shared Jones's views, Bailey challenged the law and successfully appealed to the United States Supreme Court after Alabama's supreme court rejected his challenge. In *Bailey v. Alabama*, Justice Charles Evans Hughes concluded that the statutory presumption of deceit violated the rule previously settled by the courts that breach of contract, without more, cannot be a criminal offense. Hughes disclaimed any intent to condemn race relations in the South, but the very fact that he felt it necessary to make this disclaimer and his unusually direct condemnation of Alabama's law as "an instrument of compulsion peculiarly effective as against the poor and the ignorant, its most likely victims," were a warning to straight-out lawmakers. Southern legislatures reacted to the *Bailey* case by again modifying but not eliminating peonage laws: presumptions of criminal intent were eliminated, but the possibility of proving deceptive intent in other ways was left open. The peonage laws remained an effective tool for labor control in many parts of the South for the next 50 years. Despite periodic Congressional investigations and unfavorable attention in the press, they were not completely eliminated until well into the modern civil rights revolution of the mid-twentieth century.[33]

RESIDENTIAL SEGREGATION LAWS

A final phenomenon of the straight-out era was the enactment of residential segregation ordinances in numerous Southern cities between 1910 and 1915. The ordinances may have been prompted in part by a rash of urban racial riots that began in Wilmington, North Carolina, in 1898 and flared repeatedly in cities throughout the United States until the 1920s. But in a larger sense, the ordinances were the logical culmination of an era that had been animated largely by a desire to reduce interaction between blacks and whites in as many spheres of life as possible. Inclination led Southerners of both races to live apart from each other, and residential integration occurred only sporadically, but some straight-out era lawmakers again felt a need to formalize custom, as they had for interaction on railroads, streetcars, and in other public places.

Residential segregation ordinances aspired to achieve racial purity block by block. They typically provided that when a majority of a block's residents were of one race, members of the other race would be prohibited from moving onto the block and residents could sell their property only to members of the preponderant race. Some lawmakers were concerned that the ordinances would be seen as infringement of owners' vested property rights, and the fact that most ordinances forced courts to choose between considerations of social order and protection of property rights proved to be their downfall. Four ordinance challenges reached Southern supreme courts between 1913 and 1915, and all but one of the ordinances in question were struck down. Baltimore's segregation ordinance was the first enacted and the first to fall: Maryland's supreme court concluded that a homeowner's right to sell property was fundamental, and that imposing a blanket racial restriction without considering its economic consequences was too much of an infringement on such right. Residential segregation ordinances in Atlanta and Winston, North Carolina, also foundered on the rock of property rights.[34]

In North Carolina, Chief Justice Walter Clark, who had undertaken a long personal journey from service as Robert E. Lee's aide during the Civil War to espousal of a Southern brand of progressivism that earned him appointment to the state's supreme court during a brief period of Republican and Populist control in the 1890s, went further. Clark noted that segregation of European Jews into ghettoes had often led to broader persecutions, and he feared that residential segregation laws aimed at blacks might lead to the same result. "An act . . . so entirely without precedent in the public policy of the state, and so revolutionary in its nature," said Clark, "cannot be deemed to have been within the purview of the Legislature from the use of the words conferring authority to make ordinances for the general welfare." Only Virginia's supreme court was sympathetic to residential segregation ordinances: in upholding Richmond's ordinance, it devoted most of its opinion to describing the usefulness of segregation as a police measure, commenting that segregation was necessary to meet the "grave danger . . . from too close association of the races" and to prevent "breaches of peace, immorality, and danger to the health."[35] Outside Virginia, residential segregation continued to be enforced by custom, but a second beachhead had been created against segregation: courts would not permit segregation laws, even when they were racially neutral in their wording, if the laws impinged on vested property rights of either whites or blacks. Because residence was so closely tied to property ownership, it was unlikely that residential segregation laws could ever be worded so as to withstand a constitutional challenge. With this anticlimax, the legal changes of the straight-out era came to a close.

CHAPTER 12

The Legal Legacy of Reconstruction

He . . . went in with us . . . to try and make this a free country accordin' to Northern notions. It was a grand idee; but there wa'n't material enough to build of, on hand here at that time. There was a good foundation laid, and some time it may be finished off; but not in my day, son,—not in my day.
—Albion W. Tourgee, *A Fool's Errand*, 1879

Above all, [judges] should not give themselves up to the guidance and direction of their feelings and sentiments; for this would unquestionably lead to excessive irregularity, fluctuation, and doubt. They would then realize that the fame which follows is better than that which goes before, and would avoid the supreme folly of mistaking the plaudits and shouts of the multitude of their contemporaries for the trumpet of fame.
—Judge Samuel Hall (Georgia), 1887[1]

At the turn of the twentieth century, it appeared on the surface of things that the Civil War and Reconstruction had made little impact on white Southerners' views of race and region and that in the end, the Civil War had given black Southerners little more than their freedom. There was a vast "submerged link between the antebellum hostility to free Negroes and the Negrophobia which triumphed at the end of the century." Economic conditions for many blacks were little better, and in some cases, worse than during slavery. Custom effectively denied blacks the chance to enjoy many of the basic civil rights they had been granted after the war; their political rights, particularly voting rights, were eroding steadily; and white hostility to the prospect of social equality, which had predominated even during Reconstruction, was now being codified in most Southern states in the form of Jim Crow laws.[2]

But the closer examination attempted in this book supports Judge Tourgee's conclusion that Reconstruction laid an enduring foundation for the next great wave of civil rights reform in the mid-twentieth century. In order to understand the foundation that was laid, it is most useful to look at four themes: first, the extent to which prewar legal differences between the Upper South and the Deep South continued after the war; second, the role the courts played in the process of reconciling the conquered South with the rest of the nation; third, the role that broader national legal currents, particularly economic reform sentiment, played in reuniting the sections; and finally, the extent to which Reconstruction forced white Southerners to change their perception of blacks.

THE ROLE OF LOCAL DIFFERENCES IN POSTWAR SOUTHERN LEGAL HISTORY

Scholars and the public focus on the South as a whole more often than on individual Southern states and subregions; but an analysis of Southern legal history before and after the Civil War is a valuable reminder that Southern culture has never been monolithic. The approaches that Southern and border states took to the challenges posed by war and emancipation contained many common elements, but each state's approach was distinctive. It is sometimes postulated that the most important division in Southern politics and culture is between the Deep South and the Upper South (including the border states), and this line of division is very useful for understanding Southern legal history during the period treated by this book.

By the middle of the nineteenth century, the economics and culture of slavery were moving in different directions in the Deep South and Upper South. The law of slavery followed suit. Much of the Upper South had abandoned cotton and other crops particularly suited to slave labor; as slavery became less important to the Upper South economically, the debate over the proper legal balance between humanity and economic interest tilted more toward humanity than it did in most of the Deep South. Legislators in states such as Tennessee, Kentucky, and Virginia permitted manumission more liberally than did Deep South states, and they created small legal openings for slaves to obtain education and earn independent income if they could. As early as 1810, when the first signs of slavery's impending demise appeared in Maryland and Delaware, those states provided a preview of how the rest of the South would react to emancipation at the end of the Civil War. They foretold that moderates as well as conservatives would gravitate to strict control of blacks for the protection of whites, and that vagrancy and apprenticeship laws would be the most popular and enduring control devices. Maryland and Delaware's prewar laws strikingly resembled the black codes the ex-Confederate states would enact in 1865 and 1866.[3]

The Civil War also produced different legal reactions in the Upper South and Deep South to the postwar order. Close political divisions in the border states produced armed confrontation and guerrilla depredations during the war; this in turn generated deep bitterness and a firm conviction among postwar Unionist lawmakers that victory could be preserved only by close monitoring and restriction of ex-Confederates. Border Unionists tried to accomplish that goal with the blunt legal weapons of oaths and suffrage restrictions. Ironically, such restrictions were a less contentious subject in the Deep South because there, suffrage restrictions were imposed externally by Congress. A related subject was whether ex-Confederate soldiers could be held liable in postwar courts for wartime acts of destruction. This subject raised a more general and fundamental issue: namely, whether the South's memory of the Confederacy should be one of reverence, of shame, or something in between. Several Deep South states enacted amnesty acts and most courts, heeding Richmond Pearson's admonition that "many have errors to regret, and it will be a great public good if the past can be forgiven and forgotten," conferred on Confederate soldiers the legal status of belligerents rather than outlaws, thus insulating them from liability for acts of destruction carried out under military orders. But border Unionists would have none of this: in Tennessee and West Virginia in particular, ex-Confederates were regularly held to account for wartime damages until Redemption governments came to power.[4]

By contrast, there was relatively little difference in the approaches Upper South and Deep South states took toward emancipation and civil rights after the war. The black codes of 1865–66 represented the full flowering of the instinct to preserve racial control that had manifested itself in Maryland and Delaware before the war. The Deep South states of South Carolina, Mississippi, and Texas produced the most restrictive codes and were the main focus of Northern criticism that the South "did but change the form of the slavery," but many Upper South and border states enacted codes that were nearly as restrictive. The codes revealed strong streaks of resistance to racial change along the border: Maryland's use of apprenticeship laws to return thousands of freed children to a state of near-slavery failed only because of the vigorous opposition of Judges Chase and Bond and the Freedmen's Bureau, and from 1867 to 1872, Kentuckians stood virtually alone in the South in refusing to extend testimonial rights to blacks.[5]

Yet a degree of legal difference between the Upper South and Deep South states persisted after Redemption governments came to power. The border states played a less active role in the straight-out movement than their sister states. The Deep South states of Mississippi and South Carolina took the lead in creating devices to limit black suffrage, and every Deep South state felt a need to give its new disfranchising provisions constitutional status. But except for Virginia, Upper South states contented themselves with statutory changes and most of the border states felt no need to change their suffrage laws at all. Upper South states were more active in passing Jim Crow laws, but again there were exceptions: West Virginia resisted all temptation to pass such laws and except for Tennessee, courts in the Upper South were noticeably less hostile than their Deep South counterparts to the *Louisville Railroad* rule prohibiting application of Jim Crow laws to interstate commerce. The two regions saw the rule in very different lights: for example, Mississippi's supreme court viewed it as a threat to racial purity and thus to the core of Southern society, whereas Maryland's supreme court viewed it as a sensible measure designed to save railroads needless bother. The comparative mildness of the Upper South's approach to segregation continued into the twentieth century and provided significant opportunities for leaders of the second civil rights revolution to advance their cause.[6]

SOUTHERN COURTS AS MEDIATORS OF THE TRANSITION TO A POSTWAR SOCIETY

Southern courts played an important role in guiding the process by which their states reassimilated into the Union and adjusted to postwar social and economic changes. Two strong currents shaped Southern judges' actions: their personal journeys, including the impact the war had on them personally, and the surprisingly durable tradition of judicial nationalism and conservatism.

Southern judges' personal journeys were most clearly manifested in their postwar approaches to federalism and states' rights, the postwar issues most closely intertwined with the larger struggle over memory of the Confederacy. Many courts followed the pragmatic course set by Pearson of North Carolina, neither honoring nor condemning the Confederacy but instead looking for ways to promote postwar recovery without unduly disturbing vested property rights and expectations. Centrist courts accepted the federal government's triumph with little misgiving, and they cautioned their constituents against defiance of federal authority, but they felt no need or desire to lecture on the moral virtues of the postwar order. Thus, such courts peremptorily rejected *ab initio* and embraced currency scaling laws as a sensible means of recognizing economic realities. Likewise, centrist courts viewed the flood of postwar lawsuits against former soldiers for war-related damages as tinder that could rekindle the passions of war: they approved of amnesty laws and readily gave former soldiers partial immunity from lawsuits by holding that they had acted as belligerents rather than outlaws.[7]

Most judges gravitated to centrism, for a variety of reasons. Pearson and his North Carolina colleagues were strong Unionists whose beliefs were confirmed by the war and its outcome; but at the same time, they had been members of the state's prewar elite, they understood that most of their opponents had been equally sincere, and they were more concerned with economic recovery than social justice. Native Unionists who served on Reconstruction courts in other states shared many of Pearson's experiences and perspectives; surprisingly, many of the carpetbaggers who served on the courts also shared

Pearson's dedication to recovery and lack of interest in using the courts as a tool for moral education.

A competing school existed, however. Outsider judges such as Hamilton of Texas, Taliaferro of Louisiana, and Peters of Alabama, who had paid for their Unionism with exile during the war, used their new judicial positions to support *ab initio* and occasionally to lecture their constituents on the evils of disunion and the need to embrace the postwar order. In several border states, Reconstruction court judges, like the Radical governments that had appointed them, believed that unless everything possible were done to delegitimize the memory of the Confederacy, Unionist control and the gains of the war would quickly be lost. A few outsider judges tried to drive the point home by refusing to extend belligerent status and immunity for wartime acts to ex-Confederate soldiers, but most took their principal stand on the issue of Confederate money transactions. Outsider-dominated Reconstruction courts in Alabama, Louisiana, Texas, Arkansas, Tennessee, and West Virginia viewed the use of Confederate money not as an act of survival forced upon citizens by the war, but as a gesture of support for the Confederacy that could not be condoned. The symbolic power Confederate currency had for outsider judges is surprising; perhaps it reflects their frustration that so few of their fellow citizens joined them in fighting the apostasy of the Confederacy either during or after the war. Several courts continued the fight against Confederate currency even after the federal Supreme Court adopted Pearson's pragmatic approach in *Thorington;* when Reconstruction ended, exasperated Redemption courts quickly ended the resistance.[8]

Despite these differences, centrist and outsider judges alike carried on elements of nationalism and judicial conservatism that were central to the American judicial tradition. Antebellum judges in the South and elsewhere received their training and information largely from national sources. They were expected to be aware of contemporary political forces but to work largely apart from such forces. They were also deeply imbued with judicial conservatism, which placed high value on equal treatment of all persons protected by the law and on protection of property rights, regardless of whether such persons and rights were politically popular. These ideals survived in the South during Reconstruction, and judicial conservatism was a common thread that explains many seemingly contradictory actions of the courts. When Pearson and other centrists gave effect to Confederate money transactions on a scaled-down basis, they did so partly because they believed that would bring the best practical result but also out of deference to property rights. The fact that Confederate money had served as a prop for the war effort did not lessen the fact that the parties to such transactions had given up things of value in order to obtain a right to something in return, and Southern judges felt strongly that the law must protect such rights and expectations. These sentiments led most judges to treat postwar debt relief measures and proposals to invalidate slave sale contracts with skepticism; only Joseph Brown openly advocated the subordination of property rights to economic necessity after the war.[9]

In following the conservative ideal, Southern courts made little effort to extend the scope of postwar civil rights laws by liberal interpretation, but they likewise declined to narrow such laws. The courts enforced laws regardless of whether they were passed by Republican or conservative legislatures. Reconstruction-era courts took the principle of equal protection of the laws seriously: for example, they were hostile to abuses of apprenticeship laws because such abuses offended the principle that all affected parents, black as well as white, had a right to be heard before their children were bound out. Redemption courts followed suit when the North Carolina and Kentucky supreme courts refused to permit race-based division of school funds unless explicitly authorized by statute, and when the North Carolina court decided that absent a Jim Crow law, a black woman had the same right as other paying passengers to sit where she pleased.[10]

Conversely, Southern courts usually rejected pleas to read laws broadly in the service of civil rights. Except for the Alabama, Mississippi, and Louisiana Reconstruction courts, whose decisions were soon overruled, Southern judges of all political backgrounds firmly rejected any suggestion that federal civil rights acts authorized interracial marriages. Their decisions reflected the social outlook of the time, but also reflected genuine judicial conservatism. Such conservatism was vividly illustrated in *State v. Ross* (1877), when Pearson and his colleagues honored South Carolina's law allowing interracial marriages under traditional principles of comity despite their personal disgust at such marriages. Judicial conservatism also acted as a brake on the advance of married women's property rights in many Southern states: courts were willing to depart from the traditional limits imposed by the marital unity doctrine only to the extent the new married women's property laws clearly required them to do so. During the straight-out era, judicial conservatism impelled most courts to adhere to the *DeCuir* rule prohibiting the application of Jim Crow laws to interstate commerce, but as with antimiscegenation laws, they upheld application of Jim Crow laws within their states without a qualm.[11]

Southern courts performed at least three crucial functions during Reconstruction. First, they put their traditional streak of nationalism to good use in the postwar reconciliation process. Centrist courts set an important example of reconciliation; courts dominated by outsider judges were less successful in this area, but they did impress upon conservatives the point that resistance to the new federalism would ultimately be futile, and they made it easier for their Redemption successors to complete the task of reconciliation that Reconstruction centrist courts had previously accomplished elsewhere. Second, the courts' efforts to preserve property rights and address postwar legal issues through appeals to traditional modes of legal reasoning rather than passion provided much-needed continuity during one of the most turbulent eras of American history. Even in states with deeply divided courts such as Alabama and Georgia, the debate among judges such as Brown, Warner, Peck, Peters, and Saffold permitted controversies over new racial roles and economic reforms to be addressed in a more orderly fashion than would have occurred otherwise.

Finally, the courts played an important if little-noticed role in the long-term evolution of civil rights in the South. They did not come close to creating racial justice: racial customs often prevailed over the law, and court decisions correcting abuses in postwar apprenticeship systems and other instances of blatant discrimination brought little comfort to the many blacks who did not have the resources to pursue their grievances through the legal system. But the courts' consistent application of judicial conservatism and the ideal of equality under the law set examples that remained in place after Reconstruction. Such examples created a small but permanent opening to the prospect of wider justice for Southern blacks at the day that South Carolina's Robert Anderson predicted would eventually come, and which did come in the mid-twentieth century. When white Southerners were ready for increased rights for blacks or when such rights were imposed on them, Southern courts would not stand in the way.

THE ROLE OF NATIONAL REFORMS IN SECTIONAL RECONCILIATION

The South's reassimilation into the Union was made easier by its participation in several national legal movements of the mid-nineteenth century. Southern legislatures attempted to relieve postwar suffering by enacting debtor relief measures similar to laws passed throughout the United States in response to the depressions of 1837–40 and 1857–58, and Reconstruction legislatures completed the national movement for homestead exemptions in the South. The married women's property law movement, which was driven in large part by a desire to protect families of impecunious husbands from their creditors, followed a similar pattern: it began in the North and in southwestern states before the war, and Reconstruction legislatures again completed the process of enacting such laws throughout the South. Homestead and married women's property laws attracted some legal controversy in the Reconstruction South, particularly from judges concerned that they might interfere with vested property rights, but the laws were sufficiently popular that Redemption legislatures and constitutional conventions left them in place virtually untouched.

The South was also in the mainstream of American legal reaction to the advent of railroads and other large-scale internal improvements. Virtually all states North and South went through the same cycle of initial enthusiasm for public subsidy of improvement enterprises, followed by reaction, and eventually by adoption of a compromise that eliminated direct state aid but allowed limited municipal aid to such enterprises. Many states North and South passed through the reactive and municipal phases in the years immediately after the war, and this shared experience created both legal and political bonds between the sections. Sentiment for systematic state regulation of railroads also arose and crested throughout the United States during the Reconstruction era, providing another point of commonality between the Northern and Southern states.[12]

LAW AND THE NEW ROLE OF SOUTHERN BLACKS

The central task of Reconstruction was to decide what role blacks would play in postwar Southern society and how the law would be altered to define that role. It is appropriate to conclude by looking at the part state law played in this process.

Many aspects of Southern law during the postwar period, from the black codes of 1865–66 to the disfranchisement and Jim Crow laws of the straight-out era, have been rightly criticized as an embodiment of white Southerners' determination to keep blacks in a subordinate position at all costs. But it must be remembered that at war's end, Southern whites were asked to abandon a pillar of their social and legal system that had existed for nearly 250 years. It was unrealistic to expect that any such change could be completed smoothly within a period of a few years, but in Judge Tourgee's words, a good foundation was laid.

An enduring if often overlooked success of Reconstruction laws is that they forced white Southerners to view blacks for the first time as fully human beings. This was a fundamental change from slavery, which had sanctioned a view of blacks as subhumans, as property.[13] Benighted as they were, the black codes launched the transition process by conceding that freed blacks were entitled to basic civil rights. The great federal laws of the Reconstruction era, most notably the 1866 Civil Rights Act and the 14th and 15th Amendments, indisputably form the central foundation of Southern blacks' civil and political rights in the postwar era; but state lawmakers played an important role in reinforcing such rights. State courts made clear that although they would not forge new civil rights through creative interpretation of state laws, they would enforce any rights their legislatures chose to create and would enforce such rights for Southerners of all races. The courts alone could not overcome racial prejudices that had built up over centuries, and in some cases, particularly questions of social equality and integration, they shared such prejudices. But their adherence to the conservative ideal of rule of law was genuine, and it preserved an opening for further advances at some future time.[14]

Reconstruction also gave black Southerners their first opportunity to participate directly in shaping American law. Blacks made their largest contribution in the Reconstruction constitutional conventions, taking a variety of positions that illustrated the delicate path of political survival they had to walk even at the height of Reconstruction. A few delegates, most notably Bayne of Virginia, took an uncompromising stand for full civil and social rights. Others, such as Grey of Arkansas, chose a more pragmatic course: they recognized that even white Republicans would not support full social equality, and they signaled that blacks would not press the issue if whites would concede meaningful civil and political rights in return. In South Carolina, the only state in which a majority of delegates were black, leaders such as Whipper and Cardozo led debate on a variety of issues; the high quality of the debate was striking in light of the fact that many of the delegates were only recently out of slavery. At the end of Reconstruction, blacks were largely forced out of lawmaking positions. All they could do was bear witness to the injustice being done, bring it to the attention of those Northerners who were still interested, and hope for better times. The lives of most of the early black lawmakers remain obscure; that is unfortunate, because they offer tantalizing glimpses of drama and tragedy, and if their details were better known, they would certainly cast additional light on the forces behind legal change in the South during Reconstruction.[15]

Reconstruction did not fulfill its supporters' hopes of genuine legal equality for Americans of all races, but neither was it the "fool's errand" that Judge Tourgee suggested in the title of his famous book lamenting the era's failures. The Civil War and the end of slavery, being revolutionary in nature, imposed unprecedented pressure on Southern legal systems. These systems bent under the pressure, but they did not break, primarily because of the enduring strength of judicial nationalism and conservatism and the efforts of Southern judges to reconcile their constituents to the economic and social changes that followed in the wake of slavery's demise. The hardiness and resilience that Southern legal systems displayed in the time and place of their severest testing provide important clues as to why the American system of democratic self-governance has lasted as long as it has.

Furthermore, although Reconstruction did not endure, it left a permanent imprint on Southern law. A core of state civil rights laws remained in effect after the end of Reconstruction; they were largely ignored but were still in place for use when the second great civil rights movement of the mid-twentieth century arrived. Postwar Southern courts could not fully implement the ideal of legal equality for blacks, but they clung tenaciously to the conservative ideal of equal enforcement of existing laws regardless of race. This ideal too was in place when the second civil rights movement arrived.

These are the facts that form the central legal legacy of Reconstruction.

Notes

CHAPTER 1

1. Don E. Fehrenbacher, ed. *Abraham Lincoln: Speeches and Writings* (New York, 1989), 2:221–22; W.E.B. Du Bois, *Black Reconstruction* (New York, 1935), i.

2. *Journal of the Proceedings and Debates in the Constitutional Convention of the State of Mississippi, August 1865*, 76, 152, 156, 215 (1865).

3. See Eric Foner, *Reconstruction: American's Unfinished Revolution, 1863–1877* (New York., 1988), xxv; Du Bois, *Black Reconstruction*, passim.

4. Morton J. Horwitz, *The Transformation of American Law 1870–1960* (New York, 1992), vii–viii.

5. See, for example, Charles Fairman, *History of the Supreme Court of the United States, Vol. 6: Reconstruction and Reunion, Part 1* (New York, 1971), passim; Foner, *Reconstruction*, 274–86.

6. Ira Berlin, *Slaves without Masters: The Free Negro in the Antebellum South* (New York, 1975), 29–35; Christopher Phillips, *Freedom's Port: The African-American Community of Baltimore, 1790–1860* (Urbana, Ill., 1997), 10–24; Patience Essah, *A House Divided: Slavery and Emancipation in Delaware, 1635–1865* (Charlottesville, Va., 1996), passim.

7. David Hackett Fischer, *Albion's Seed: Four British Folkways in America* (New York, 1989), 207–418, 605–782.

8. Berlin, *Slaves without Masters*, 108–30, 178–85; Thomas L. Connelly, "Neo-Confederatism or Power Vacuum: Post-War Kentucky Politics Reappraised," *Register of the Kentucky Historical Society* 64 (1966): 259.

9. Carl N. Degler, *The Other South: Southern Dissenters in the Nineteenth Century* (New York, 1974), 128–37; William E. Parrish, *A History of Missouri, Vol. 3: 1860–1875* (Columbia, Mo., 1973), 26–41, 61–68; E. Merton Coulter, *The Civil War and Readjustment in Kentucky* (Chapel Hill, N.C., 1926), vii and passim; 1864 Tex. Laws (2nd Ex. Sess.), Jt. Res. 1, p. 20.

10. William C. Harris, *With Charity for All: Lincoln and the Restoration of the Union* (Lexington, Ky., 1997), passim; Theodore B. Wilson, *The Black Codes of the South* (University, Ala., 1965), passim; Foner, *Reconstruction*, 250–86.

11. Foner, *Reconstruction*, 255–68; Fairman, *History of the Supreme Court*, 1:1169–1201.

12. James McPherson, *Battle Cry of Freedom: The Civil War Era* (New York, 1988), 323–25, 442–48, 859–62; James E. Bond, *No Easy Walk to Freedom: Reconstruction and the Ratification of the Fourteenth Amendment* (Westport, Conn., 1997), passim.

13. 14 U.S. Stats. 428, 15 U.S. Stats. 2,14,41 (1867); Richard L. Hume, "Carpetbaggers in the Reconstruction South: A Group Portrait Outside Whites in the 'Black and Tan' Constitutional Conventions," *Journal of American History* 64 (1977), 313.

14. Foner, *Reconstruction*, 322–28, 366–74; see Chapters 6 and 11.

15. See generally Chapter 4; Robert Kaczorowski, *The Politics of Judicial Interpretation: The Federal Courts, Department of Justice and Civil Rights, 1866–1876* (Dobbs Ferry, N.Y., 1985); Everette Swinney, *Suppressing the Ku Klux Klan: The Enforcement of the Reconstruction Amendments, 1870–1874* (New York, 1987).

16. See Chapter 3; Fairman, *History of the Supreme Court*, 1:615–20; Foner, *Reconstruction*, 445–48, 499–505.

17. Foner, *Reconstruction*, 549–86; Michael Perman, *Struggle for Mastery: Disfranchisement in the South, 1888–1908* (Chapel Hill, N.C., 2001), passim.

18. See generally Chapter 10.

19. See generally Chapter 11.

CHAPTER 2

1. Pearson in *Raleigh Standard*, August 11, 1868, quoted in Horace Raper, *William W. Holden: North Carolina's Political Enigma* (Chapel Hill, N.C., 1985), 109; Bond in *Baltimore American*, July 1, 1867, quoted in Richard Paul Fuke, "Hugh Lennox Bond and Radical Republican Ideology," *Journal of Southern History* 45 (1979): 581.

2. Brown quoted in Joseph H. Parks, *Joseph E. Brown of Georgia* (Baton Rouge, La., 1977), 116–17; *Shorter v. Cobb*, 39 Ga. 285, 288–89, 296 (1869).

3. See George M. Fredrickson, *The Black Image in the White Mind: The Debate on Afro-American Character and Destiny, 1817–1914* (New York, 1971), 132.

4. Thomas R .R. Cobb, *An Inquiry into the Law of Negro Slavery in the United States of America* (Philadelphia, 1858), § 97; compare George M. Stroud, *A Sketch of the Laws Relating to Slavery in the Several States of the United States of America* (1856; reprint, 1968). See also Mark V. Tushnet, *The American Law of Slavery, 1810–1860* (Princeton, N.J., 1981); William Wiethoff, *A Peculiar Humanism: The Judicial Advocacy of Slavery in the High Courts of the Old South, 1820–1850* (Athens, Ga., 1996); A. E. Keir Nash, "Reason of Slavery: Understanding the Judicial Role in the Peculiar Institution," *Vanderbilt Law Review* 32 (1979), all passim.

5. Cobb, *Law of Negro Slavery*, § 105; *State v. Mann*, 13 N.C. 263, 266–67 (1829).

6. Cobb, *Law of Negro Slavery*, § 93; *Fields v. State*, 1 Yerg. 126 (Tenn. 1836); *State v. Caesar*, 31 N.C. 191 (1849); Nash, "Reason of Slavery," 74 n. 227; *State v. Will*, 1 Dev. & Bat. 121 (N.C. 1834); *Kelly v. State*, 3 S.&M. 426 (Miss. 1842); *Dave v. State*, 22 Ala. 33 (1833); *Loftin v. Espy*, 12 Tenn. 68, 78 (1833).

7. Joe Gray Taylor, *Negro Slavery in Louisiana* (Baton Rouge, La., 1963), 106–10, 153–57, 195–200; Judith Kelleher Schaefer, *Slavery, the Civil Law and the Supreme Court of Louisiana* (Baton Rouge, La., 1994), 1–10.

8. Cobb, *Law of Negro Slavery*, § 328.

9. St. George Tucker, *Blackstone's Commentaries: With Notes of Reference to the Constitution and Laws of the Federal Government of the United States and of the Commonwealth of Virginia* (1803; reprint 1996), 1:Appendix 76–79; James C. Ballagh, *A History of Slavery in Virginia* (Baltimore, 1902; reprint, 1968), 139–43; Ralph B. Flanders, *Plantation Slavery in Georgia* (Chapel Hill, N.C., 1933), 248–50; Robert M. Ireland, *The Kentucky State Constitution: A Reference Guide* (Westport, Conn., 1999), 3–5; Caleb P. Patterson, *The Negro in Tennessee, 1790–1865* (Austin, Tex., 1922), 190–91.

10. Flanders, *Slavery in Georgia*, 248; Taylor, *Slavery in Louisiana*, 153; H. M. Henry, *The Police Control of the Slave in South Carolina* (Emory, Va., 1914), 171; Patterson, *Negro in Tennessee*, at 153.

11. See 1831 Tenn. Laws, 102; 1830 La. Laws, 46; 1852 La. Laws, 315; Julia Floyd Smith, *Slavery and Plantation Growth in Antebellum Florida 1821–1860* (Gainesville, Fla., 1973), 111–13; Henry, *Slave in South Carolina*, 170–73; Ivan E. McDougle, *Slavery in Kentucky, 1792–1865* (Westport, Conn., 1970), 64; 1858–59 Ark. Laws, 69, 175 (effective date later postponed by legislature); 1847 Fla. Laws, 155; 1858 Fla. Laws, 860; 1858 Tenn. Laws, 45.

12. See McDougle, *Slavery in Kentucky*, 64–66; Patience Essah, *A House Divided: Slavery and Emancipation in Delaware, 1635–1865* (Charlottesville, Va., 1996), 105; Patterson, *Negro in Tennessee*, 80–94; Christopher Phillips, *Freedom's Port: The African-American Community of Baltimore, 1790–1860* (Urbana, Ill., 1997), 36–44; David S. Bogen, "The Maryland Context of Dred Scott: The Decline in the Legal Status of Maryland Free Blacks, 1776–1810," *American Journal of Legal History* 34 (1990): 381.

13. *Carmille v. Carmille's Executors*, 2 Mc.Mul. 454, 470 (S.C. 1842); A. E. Keir Nash, "Negro Rights, Unionism, and Greatness on the South Carolina Court of Appeals: The Extraordinary Chief Justice John Belton O'Neall," *S.C. Law Review* 21 (1969): 160–66.

14. Nash, "John Belton O'Neall," 162–66; S.C. Stats. (1841), 2836; see *Drane v. Beall*, 21 Ga. 21 (1857); *Bivens v. Crawford*, 26 Ga. 225 (1858); compare *Foster's Administrator v. Foster*, 51 Va. 537 (1853) with *Bailey v. Poindexter's Executor*, 55 Va. 132 (1858).

15. Henry, *Slave in South Carolina*, 4–10; 1831 Va. Laws, 39; 1830 La. Laws, 96–97.

16. McDougle, *Slavery in Kentucky*, 79; Orville W. Taylor, *Negro Slavery in Arkansas* (Durham, N.C., 1958), 82–83, 187–90.

17. See S.C. Stats. at Large (1822), 3; *id.* (1849), 3075; 1835 Ga. Laws, 268; 1845 Ga. Laws, 49; 1856 Fla. Laws, 790.

18. 1810 Del. Laws, 124; see Ira Berlin, *Slaves without Masters: The Free Negro in the Antebellum South* (New York, 1975), 46–54; *Allen v. Negro Sarah*, 2 Del. 454, 435 (1837); *State v. Dillahunt*, 3 Del. 551 (1843).

19. 1811 Del. Laws, 150; 1849 Del. Laws, 412; Essah, *Slavery in Delaware*, 111–15.

20. Bogen, "Maryland Context of Dred Scott"; 1796 Md. Laws, 67 (vagrancy); 1805 Md. Laws, 80 (product sales certificate); 1806 Md. Laws, 81 (certificate to keep hunting weapons); 1808 Md. Laws, 54 (apprenticeship).

21. Tucker, *Blackstone's Commentaries*, 1:Appendix 79.

22. Daniel Crofts, *Reluctant Confederates: Upper South Unionists in the Secession Crisis* (Chapel Hill, N.C., 1989), 107–10; William C. Harris, *With Charity for All: Lincoln and the Restoration of the Union* (Lexington, Ky., 1997), 5–10, 81–83; Carl N. Degler, *The Other South: Southern Dissenters in the Nineteenth Century* (New York, 1974), 108–140.

23. Crofts, *Reluctant Confederates*, 104–7; Harris, *With Charity for All*, 7–10.

24. Harris, *With Charity for All*, 83, 87–90; John L. Waller, *Colossal Hamilton of Texas: A Biography of Andrew Jackson Hamilton* (El Paso, Tex., 1968), 34–46.

25. Dumas Malone, ed., *Dictionary of American Biography* (New York, 1934), 13:84 (Moncure); Lyon Gardiner Tyler, ed., *Encyclopedia of Virginia Biography* (New York, 1915; reprint 1998), 5:622–24 (Moncure), 3:17–21; John J. Kneebone et al., eds., *Dictionary of Virginia Biography* (Richmond, Va., 1998), 1:133–34.

26. William Draper Lewis, ed., *Great American Lawyers* (Philadelphia, 1908), 5:233; William S. Powell, ed., *Dictionary of North Carolina Biography* (Chapel Hill, N.C., 1994), 5:49–51; A. E. Keir Nash, "A More Equitable Past? Southern Supreme Courts and the Protection of the Antebellum Negro," *N.C. Law Review* 48 (1970): 225.

27. Jeffrey J. Crow, "Thomas Settle, Jr., Reconstruction, and the Memory of the Civil War," *Journal of Southern History* 62 (1996): 690; Powell, *Dictionary of North Carolina Biography*, 5:317.

28. Crow, "Thomas Settle," 698–725; Powell, *Dictionary of North Carolina Biography*, 5:243–44, 2:63, 5:316–17 (Settle).

29. John Ray Skates, Jr., *A History of the Mississippi Supreme Court, 1817–1948* (Jackson, Miss., 1973), 79 (Handy), 79, 85–86, 93–94 (Simrall), 98; Dunbar Rowland, *Courts, Judges and Lawyers of Mississippi 1798–1935* (Jackson, Miss., 1935), 94–96 (Handy).

30. Timothy S. Huebner, *The Southern Judicial Tradition: State Judges and Sectional Distinctiveness, 1790–1890* (New York, 1999), 77–99 (Lumpkin); Paul D. Hicks, *Joseph Henry Lumpkin: Georgia's First Chief Justice* (Athens, Ga., 2002), 98–113; John B. Harris, ed. *A History of the Supreme Court of Georgia* (Macon, Ga., 1948), 48–49, 90–93; Henry S. Marks, ed., *Who Was Who in Alabama* (Huntsville, Ala., 1972), 138 (Peck), 140 (Peters); John W. DuBose, *Alabama's Tragic Decade: Ten Years of Alabama, 1865–1874* (Birmingham, Ala., 1940), 267 n. 32 (Peters), 59 n. 19 (Judge); *National Cyclopedia of American Biography* (1922), 18:145 (Walker); George H. Thompson, *Arkansas and Reconstruction: The Influence of Geography, Economics and Personality* (Port Washington, N.Y., 1976), 52–58 (Walker).

31. T. R. Fehrenbach, *Lone Star: A History of Texas and the Texans* (New York, 1968), 487; Ron Tyler, ed., *The New Handbook of Texas* (Austin, Tex., 1996), 2:427–28 (Hamilton); 4:842 (Morrill); 2:906 (Evans); 4:1115 (Ogden); Marks, *Who Was Who in Alabama*, 140 (Peters); Ted Tunnell, *Crucible of Reconstruction: War, Radicalism and Race in Louisiana, 1862–1877* (Baton Rouge, La., 1984), 16, 24, 115, 135 (Ludeling, Taliaferro).

32. Waller, *Hamilton*, at 34–46; Tyler, *New Handbook of Texas*, 2:427–28.

33. Waller, *Hamilton*, at 59–95, 105–22; *Donley v. Tindall*, 32 Tex. 43, 57–58 (1869).

34. Walter W. Manley, ed., *The Supreme Court of Florida and Its Predecessor Courts, 1821–1917* (Gainesville, Fla., 1997), 224–27 (Westcott), 221–24 (Hart); Tyler, *New Handbook of Texas*, 4:102 (Latimer).

35. Parks, *Joseph E. Brown*, 24–30, 90–93, 195–220, 268–73, 311–34, 348–49, 369–77, 395–406.

36. Harris, *Supreme Court of Georgia*, 48–49; John W. Akin, *Hiram Warner: A Sketch Read before the Georgia Bar Association at Its 14th Annual Session, July 2, 1897* (Atlanta, Ga., 1897); see Chapter 5.

37. Skates, *Mississippi Supreme Court*, 98; Rowland, *Courts of Mississippi*, 97, 98; see *Donnell v. State*, 48 Miss. 661 (1873).

38. Francis B. Simkins and Robert H. Woody, *South Carolina during Reconstruction* (Chapel Hill, N.C., 1932), 143 (Willard); Manley, *Florida Supreme Court*, 217–19 (Randall); Tyler, *New Handbook of Texas*, 6:797 (Walker); Skates, *Mississippi Supreme Court*, 98 (Tarbell).

39. *National Cyclopedia of American Biography*, 19:224; Thompson, *Arkansas and Reconstruction*, 110–15, 149–52, 85–89; Cortez A. M. Ewing, "Arkansas Reconstruction Impeachments," *Arkansas Historical Quarterly* 13 (1954): 137, 148–51.

40. DuBose, *Alabama's Tragic Decade*, 115–16 (Peck); Marks, *Who Was Who in Alabama*, 138 (Peck); Skates, *Mississippi Supreme Court*, 85–86 (Peyton); Rowland, *Courts of Mississippi*, 97 (Peyton); Tunnell, *Crucible of Reconstruction*, 16, 21–22 (Ludeling).

41. See generally William R. Parrish, *Missouri under Radical Rule, 1865–70* (Columbia, Mo., 1965); Thomas B. Alexander, *Political Reconstruction in Tennessee* (Nashville, Tenn., 1950); Milton Gerofsky, "Reconstruction in West Virginia," *West Virginia History* 6 (1944); all passim.

42. John W. Green, *Lives of the Judges of the Supreme Court of Tennessee, 1796–1947* (Knoxville, Tenn., 1947), 137–40, 145–54, 158–63, 168–73; James W. Ely, Jr., *A History of the Tennessee Supreme Court* (Knoxville, Tenn., 2002), 97–105, 119–24; 1 W.Va. 83–96 (1863) (biographies of early West Virginia Supreme Court judges); Jim Comstock, ed., *The West Virginia Heritage Encyclopedia* (Richwood, W. Va., 1976), 10:2235 (Haymond); see also Gerald T. Dunne, *The Missouri Supreme Court: From Dred Scott to Cruzan* (Columbia, Mo., 1993), 60–67.

43. Bond in *American Missionary*, 2d Ser., IX (April 1, 1865), 80, quoted in Fuke, "Bond and Radical Republican Ideology," 571; *id.*, 573–76; W. Augustus Low, "The Freedmen's Bureau and Civil Rights in Maryland," *Journal of Negro History* 37 (1952): 231–32, 241–42; Baker, *Politics of Continuity*, 56–107; Richard P. Fuke, *Imperfect Equality: African Americans and the Confines of White Racial Attitudes in Post-Emancipation Maryland* (New York, 1999), 69–79.

44. 1867 Md. Laws, ch. 144; *Dictionary of American Biography*, 2:431–32; see also Lou Falkner Williams, *The Great South Carolina Ku Klux Klan Trials, 1871–1872* (Athens, Ga., 1996), 50–54, 70–74.

45. Loren P. Beth, *John Marshall Harlan: The Last Whig Justice* (Lexington, Ky., 1992), 21–67, 68–131, 227–36; *Civil Rights Cases*, 109 U.S. 3 (1883); *Plessy v. Ferguson*, 163 U.S. 537 (1896); *Berea College v. Kentucky*, 211 U.S. 45 (1908).

46. Roscoe Pound, *The Formative Era of American Law* (Boston, 1938), 82–83. A perusal of Southern supreme court decisions both before and after the Civil War shows that judges in all states routinely cited decisions of other state courts in all regions of the United States.

47. Pound, *Formative Era of American Law*, 92–93, 138–41; Francis R. Aumann, *The Changing American Legal System: Some Selected Phases* (Columbus, Ohio, 1940; reprint, 1969), 92–103; Huebner, *Southern Judicial Tradition*, 8–9.

48. For example, among the judges cited in this chapter, Lumpkin attended Princeton, Brown attended Yale, and Simrall attended Transylvania. Huebner, *Southern Judicial Tradition*, 14–21; Parks, *Joseph E. Brown*, 4, 221; Skates, *Mississippi Supreme Court*, 93–94; Rowland, *Courts of Mississippi*, 98.

CHAPTER 3

1. *Hedges v. Price*, 2 W.Va. 192, 240–41 (1867); *State v. Blalock*, 61 N.C. 242, 244–45 (1867). Loomis, a circuit judge, was temporarily substituting for an absent supreme court justice.

2. 1861 (Sept.) Ky. Laws, 145; 1865–66 Ky. Laws, 3; *Louisville & Nashville R. Co. v. Buckner*, 71 Ky. 277 (1871).

3. Albert B. Moore, *Conscription and Conflict in the Confederacy* (New York, 1924), 163–66, 301–3; William M. Robinson, *Justice in Grey: A History of the Judicial System of the Confederate States of America* (Cambridge, Mass., 1941), 83–85, 209–14.

4. *Ex parte Coupland*, 26 Tex. 387 (1862); *Jeffers v. Fair*, 33 Ga. 347, 364–65 (1862); *Ex parte Hill*, 38 Ala. 429, 455 (1863).

5. *In Matter of Bryan*, 60 N.C. 1 (1863); *Ex parte Walton*, 60 N.C. 350 (1864); *Gatlin v. Walton*, 60 N.C. 325, 350 (1864).

6. Moore, *Conflict in the Confederacy*, 167–89; *In Matter of Kirk*, 60 N.C. 186 (1863); *Burroughs v. Peyton*, 57 Va. 470 (1864); *Cobb v. Stallings*, 34 Ga. 72 (1864); *Simmons v. Miller*, 40 Miss. 19 (1864).

7. James M. McPherson, *Battle Cry of Freedom: The Civil War Era* (New York, 1988), 501–3; Daniel E. Sutherland, *Guerrillas, Unionists and Violence on the Confederate Home Front* (Fayetteville, Ark., 1997), 4–11, 127–30; Noel C. Fisher, *War at Every Door: Partisan Politics and Guerrilla Violence in East Tennessee, 1860–1869* (Chapel Hill, N.C., 1997), 3–4; Thomas B. Alexander, *Political Reconstruction in Tennessee* (Nashville, Tenn., 1950), 7–35; E. Merton Coulter, *The Civil War and Readjustment in Kentucky* (Chapel Hill, N.C., 1926), 84–135; Richard O. Curry, ed., *Radicalism, Racism, and Party Realignment: The Border States during Reconstruction* (Baltimore, 1969), 82–83.

8. 1861 Ky. Laws, 145; 1862 Ky. Laws, 627; 1863 Ky. Laws, 548, 570.

9. Coulter, *Civil War in Kentucky*, 140–43, 146–54; 1861 Ky. Laws, Res. 32; Aug. 1862 Ky. Laws, Res. 89; Jan. 1863 Ky. Laws, Res. 98; 1864 Ky. Laws, Res. 49; 1865–66 Ky. Laws, 3; 1867 Ky. Laws, 981, 1561.

10. 1867 N.C. Laws, 6, 8, 221; 1866–67 Miss. Laws, 403; 1866 Fla. Laws, 66; *State v. Blalock*, 61 N.C. 242, 244–45 (1867); *State v. Shelton*, 65 N.C. 294, 297 (1871); *Ford v. Surget*, 46 Miss. 130 (1871).

11. *Eastern Lunatic Asylum v. Garrett*, 68 Va. 163 (1876); see *Miller v. Gould*, 38 Ga. 465 (1868).

12. 1865 Tenn. Laws, 19; 1861 W.Va. Laws, 16; 1865–66 W.Va. Laws, 72; 1865 Mo. Const., XI:4; *Yost v. Stout*, 44 Tenn. 205 (1867); *Merritt v. Mayor of Nashville*, 45 Tenn. 95 (1867); *Weatherspoon v. Wodey*, 45 Tenn. 149 (1867).

13. *Drehman v. Stifel*, 41 Mo. 184 (1867); *Clark v. Mitchell*, 64 Mo. 564 (1877); 1865–66 Ky. Laws, 3, 25; 1867 Ky. Laws, 981, 1561; *Christian County Court v. Rankin & Tharp*, 63 Ky. 502 (1866); *Farmer v. Lewis*, 64 Ky. 66 (1866); *Bell v. Louisville & Nashville R. Co.*, 64 Ky. 404, 409 (1866); *Ferguson v. Loar*, 68 Ky. 689 (1869); *Dills v. Hatcher*, 69 Ky. 505 (1870); *Edgerton v. Commonwealth*, 70 Ky. 142 (1870); *Commonwealth v. Holland*, 62 Ky. 182 (1864); see also, for example, *Price v. Poynter*, 64 Ky. 387 (1866); *Bell v. Louisville & Nashville R. Co.*, 64 Ky. 404 (1866); *Witherspoon v. Farmer's Bank of Kentucky*, 63 Ky. 496 (1866).

14. *Railroad v. Hurst*, 58 Tenn. 625, 635 (1872); *Pierce v. Carskadon*, 83 U.S. 234 (1873); *Carskadon v. Williams*, 7 W.Va. 1 (1873). Arkansas followed an unusual pattern: postwar violence became sufficiently acute that in 1868, Reconstruction Governor Powell Clayton declared martial law and raised a special militia force that was anathema to conservatives but effectively quelled the violence. In order to support Clayton, the state's Reconstruction legislature ratified his acts and repealed an amnesty law the Restoration legislature had enacted in 1866; the law was never reinstated. 1864–65 Ark. Laws, 51–52; 1866–67 Ark. Laws, 169; 1868 Ark. Laws, 213; 1868–69 Ark. Laws, 124; Eric Foner, *Reconstruction: America's Unfinished Revolution, 1863–1877* (New York, 1988), 440.

15. Harold M. Hyman, *Era of the Oath: Northern Loyalty Tests during the Civil War and Reconstruction* (Philadelphia, 1954), 5–33; 12 U.S. Stats. 326–27 (August 6, 1861), 430 (June 17, 1862), 502 (July 2, 1862).

16. Hyman, *Era of the Oath*, 34–46; Sutherland, *Confederate Home Front*, 4–6; Fisher, *War at Every Door*, 160–65.

17. William E. Parrish, *A History of Missouri, Vol. 3: 1860–1875* (Columbia, Mo., 1973), 69–70; 1862 Mo. Laws, 12; 1865 Mo. Const., II: 5–7, 9, 11.

18. 1865 Tenn. Const., Schedule; 1865 Tenn. Laws, 32; 1864 Md. Const., I:4; 1861–62 W.Va. Laws, 46; 1862 W.Va. Laws, 9; 1865 W.Va. Laws (Ex. Sess.), 6; 1865–66 W.Va. Laws, 778.

19. 1865 Tenn. Const., Schedule; Parrish, *History of Missouri*, 135–39; Hyman, *Era of the Oath*, 95–100; 1865 Tenn. Laws, 32; 1865–66 Mo. Laws, 117.

20. *State v. Cummings*, 36 Mo. 264 (1865), *reversed*, *Cummings v. Missouri*, 4 Wall. (71 U.S.) 277 (1867).

21. *Blair v. Ridgely*, 41 Mo. 63 (1867). On appeal, the United States Supreme Court divided equally as to whether to affirm the *Blair* decision; therefore the decision stood. Charles Fairman, *History of the Supreme Court of the United States, Vol. 6: Reconstruction and Reunion, Part 1* (New York, 1971), 616. See also *State v. Garesche*, 36 Mo. 256 (1865) (upholding requirement that attorneys take a loyalty oath); *State v. McAdoo*, 36 Mo. 452 (1865) (same as to officeholders).

22. *Ex parte Faulkner*, 1 W.Va. 269 (1866); *Ex parte Hunter*, 2 W.Va. 122 (1867); *Anderson v. Baker*, 23 Md. 531 (1865); *Ridley v. Sherbrook*, 43 Tenn. 569 (1866). See also *Ex parte Quarrier*, 2 W.Va. 569 (1867) (holding that attorneys who took the federal amnesty oath could be admitted to practice in West Virginia).

23. 1864 Va. Const., IV:1; 1865–66 Va. Laws, 226; 1869–70 Va. Laws, 78; 1864–65 Ark. Laws, 48; *Rison v. Farr*, 24 Ark. 161 (1866).

24. Foner, *Reconstruction*, 323–34; 1868 N.C. Const., VI:2; 1865 S.C. Const., IV; 1868 S.C. Const., II:30, VIII:2; 1868 S.C. Laws (Spec. Sess.), 95; 1865 Ga. Const., V:1; 1868 Ga. Const., II:2; 1865 Fla. Const., VI:1; 1868 Fla. Const., XV:1, XVII:1; 1868 Fla. Laws, 1; 1865 Ala. Const., VII:6, VIII:1; 1867 Ala. Const. VII:2–4; 1868 Ala. Laws, 203, 269; 1868 Miss. Const., VII:2; 1865 Miss. Laws, 274; 1868 La. Const., 98, 99; 1868 La. Laws, 21, 46; 1868 Ark. Const., VIII:2.

25. *Ex parte Law*, 15 Fed. Cas. 3 (No. 8,126), 35 Ga. 285 (Appendix) (D.Ga. 1866); *In re Baxter*, 2 Fed. Cas. 1043 (No. 1,118) (W.D. Tenn. 1866); *In re Shorter*, 22 Fed. Cas. 16 (No. 12,811) (D. Ala. 1865); *Ex parte Garland*, 71 U.S. 333 (1867). Mississippi's federal district judge, Robert Hill, enforced the test oath in his court. Hyman, *Era of the Oath*, 46.

26. Chase letter to Alexander Long, February 10, 1869, quoted in Fairman, *Reconstruction and Reunion*, 616; Parrish, *History of Missouri*, 253–58.

27. 1870 Mo. Laws, 502, 503; 1875 Mo. Const., XIV:6; 1874–75 Va. Laws, 200; 1876–77 Va. Laws, 297; 1875–76 Ala. Laws, 103; 1879 La. Const., 185; 1871 Ark. Laws, 351; 1873 Ark. Laws, 483; 1874 Ark. Const., II:1; 1869–70 Tenn. Laws, 25, 134; 1870 Tenn. Const., IV:1, X:1; 1872 W.Va. Const., III:11, IV:1; 1870 W.Va. Laws, 16, 34, 158; 1871 W.Va. Laws, 17; 1872–73 W.Va. Laws, 7, 343, 372; 1867 Md. Const., I:1; 1867 Md. Laws, 17.

28. 1872 W.Va. Const., III:11.

CHAPTER 4

1. *White v. Clements*, 39 Ga. 232, 248, 251 (1869); *1868 Ark. Convention Debates*, 95–96.

2. *1864 Md. Convention Debates*, 664, 666, 710.

3. Charles Fairman, *History of the Supreme Court of the United States, Vol. 6: Reconstruction and Reunion, Part 1* (New York, 1971), 105–12; Eric Foner, *Reconstruction: America's Unfinished Revolution, 1863–1877* (New York, 1988), 182–91.

4. 1865 S.C. Const., IX:11; 1865 Ga. Const., I:20, II:5, V:1; 1865 Fla. Const., XVI:1–2; 1865 Ala. Const., IV: 36; 1865 Miss. Const., VIII; 1866 Tex. Const., VIII:1; *1865 Miss. Convention Journal*, 75–76, 152.

5. See Theodore B. Wilson, *The Black Codes of the South* (University, Ala., 1965), 135–40; 1865 S.C. Laws, 271; 1865–66 Ga. Laws, 239; 1865–66 Ala. Laws, 98; 1865 Miss. Laws, 82; 1866–67 Ark. Laws, 98; 1866 Tex. Laws, 128; 1865–66 Ky. Laws, 38; 1863 Del. Laws, 330. Other states simply repealed portions of their prewar codes without directly articulating blacks' new rights. See, for example, 1867 Md. Laws, 64.

6. Donald Nieman, *To Set the Law in Motion: The Freedmen's Bureau and the Legal Rights of Blacks, 1865–1868* (Millwood, N.Y., 1979), passim; Miller quoted in Fairman, *History of the Supreme Court*, 1:125.

7. 1865 S.C. Laws, 271, 291; 1865 Miss. Laws, 82; 1866 Tex. Laws, 80.

8. Lawrence M. Friedman, *Crime and Punishment in American History* (New York, 1993), 102–4; 1865 Miss. Laws, 90, 165; 1865 S.C. Laws, 291; 1865 Va. Laws, 9; 1865 N.C. Laws, 111; 1865 Ala. Laws, 119; 1865 La. Laws, 16; 1865–66 W. Va. Laws, 28; 1861 Del. Laws, 145.

9. Gilbert T. Stephenson, *Race Distinctions in American Law* (New York, 1910; reprint, 1970), 59–63; see 1793 Md. Laws, 45; 1865 Miss. Laws, 82; 1865 S.C. Laws, 29, 34; 1866 N.C. Laws, 99, 101; 1865 Ga. Laws, 6; 1866 Tex. Laws, 63; 1865 Va. Laws, 86; 1865 Ky. Laws, 43; 1866 Miss. Laws, 44; 1864 Va. Const., IV:20; 1865 Mo. Const., XI:11.

10. Md. Code (1865), 6; 1867 Md. Laws, 144; *Brown v. State*, 23 Md. 503 (1865); *In re Turner*, 24 F.Cas. 337, 339 (No. 14,247) (D. Md. 1867); Richard P. Fuke, *Imperfect Equality: African Americans and the Confines of White Racial Attitudes in Post-Emancipation Maryland* (New York, 1999), 69–85; W. Augustus Low, "The Freedmen's Bureau and Civil Rights in Maryland," *Journal of Negro History* 37 (1952): 239–41.

11. *Comas v. Reddish*, 35 Ga. 236, 237 (1866); *Adams v. Adams*, 36 Ga. 236 (1867); *Alfred v. McKay*, 36 Ga. 440 (1867); *Jack v. Thompson*, 41 Miss. 49 (1866); *Howey v. Callaway*, 48 Miss. 587 (1873); *Beard v. Hudson*, 61 N.C. 180, 183 (1867); *In Matter of Ambrose*, 61 N.C. 91 (1867); *Mitchell v. Mitchell*, 67 N.C. 307 (1872); *Lamb v. Lamb*, 67 Ky. 213 (1868).

12. *Daniel v. Swearengen*, 6 S.C. (N.S.) 297, 303 (1875); *Murrell v. State*, 44 Ala. 367 (1870).

13. Ira Berlin, *Slaves without Masters: The Free Negro in the Antebellum South* (New York, 1975), 186–98; 1865 S.C. Laws, 271; 1865 Fla. Laws, 37; 1863 Del. Laws, 330; 1865 Ga. Const., II:5.

14. Leon Litwack, *Been in the Storm So Long: The Aftermath of Slavery* (New York, 1979), 286–87, 521–24; Jenkins quoted in Wilson, *Black Codes*, 141; *1868 Ark. Convention Journal*, 95–96.

15. 1865 Miss. Laws, 82; 1865 S.C. Laws, 28; 1865 Ala. Laws, 98; 1865 Fla. Const., XVI:2; 1865 Va. Laws, 89; 1866 N.C. Laws, 99; 1865 Ga. Laws, 239; 1866 Tex. Laws, 59; 1865 Tenn. Laws, 24; 1865 Mo. Const., I:3; 1865 W.Va. Laws, 24; 1863 Del. Laws, 330; 1865 Md. Laws, 109.

16. 14 U.S. Stats. 27 (1866); Fairman, *History of Supreme Court*, 1:125–30.

17. David G. Sansing, "The Failure of Johnsonian Reconstruction in Mississippi, 1865–1866," *Journal of Mississippi History* 34 (1972): 373, 383; Victor B. Howard, "The Black Testimony Controversy in Kentucky, 1865–1872," reprinted in Donald

G. Nieman, ed. *Black Southerners and the Law 1865–1900* (New York, 1994), 162–88; *United States v. Rhodes*, 27 Fed. Cas. 785 (No. 16,151) (D. Ky. 1867); *Bowlin v. Commonwealth*, 65 Ky. 5, 8 (1867).

18. *Clarke v. State*, 35 Ga. 75, 80 (1866); *Handy v. Clark*, 9 Del. 16 (1869); *State v. Underwood*, 63 N.C. 98 (1869); *Crim v. State*, 43 Ala. 53, 56 (1869).

19. Howard, "Black Testimony in Kentucky"; 1871–72 Ky. Laws, ch. 139; *United States v. Blyew*, 80 U.S. 581 (1872).

20. 1866–67 Miss. Laws, 232; 1865 Fla. Const., XVI:3; 1866 Tex. Laws, 128; 1866 Ark. Laws, 98; 1865–66 Tenn. Laws, 24; 1868 Va. Const., III:3; 1870 S.C. Laws, 690; 1868 Ga. Const., V:13; 1868 Fla. Const., XV:1; 1870 Miss. Laws, 88; 1868 La. Laws, 142; 1869 Tex. Const., XII:45; 1867–68 Tenn. Laws, 85.

21. 1865 N.C. Const., Ord. 39; 186 N.C. Laws, 99; 1865 S.C. Laws, 271; 1865–66 Ga. Laws, 233; 1865 Fla. Laws, 23; 1865 Miss. Laws, 82; 1865–66 W.Va. Laws, 17; 1867 Md. Laws, 64.

22. Litwack, *Been in the Storm So Long*, 265; *Charge to Grand Jury—The Civil Rights Act*, 30 F.Cas. 999 (No. 18,258) (W.D.N.C. 1875).

23. *1868 Ark. Convention Journal*, 372 (Montgomery), 498 (Grey).

24. *Scott v. State*, 39 Ga. 321, 323 (1869); 1865 N.C. Laws, 99; 1865 S.C. Laws, 291; 1865 Ga. Const., V:1; 1865 Fla. Laws, 30.

25. *State v. Ross*, 76 N.C. 242, 242–43, 250 (1877); *State v. Kennedy*, 76 N.C. 251 (1877).

26. *State v. Hairston*, 63 N.C. 451, 452–53 (1869); *State v. Reinhardt*, 63 N.C. 547 (1869); *Scott v. State*, 39 Ga. 321 (1869). In Texas, federal district judge Thomas Duval held the state's discriminatory penalties violated the 1866 Act and the 14th Amendment, but in 1877, a state appellate court disagreed with him, holding that the United States Supreme Court's recent decision in the *Slaughter House Cases*, 83 U.S. 36 (1873) made clear that the states had exclusive control over domestic institutions such as marriage. In 1879 Texas extended its miscegenation penalties to blacks as well as whites and Duval upheld the amended law. *Frasher v. State*, 3 Tex. App. 263 (1877): *Ex parte Francois*, 9 F.Cas. 699 (No. 5,047) (W.D. Tex. 1879).

27. *Dickerson v. Brown*, 49 Miss. 357, 374–75 (1873); *Hart v. Hoss & Elder*, 26 La. Ann. 90 (1874); *Ellis v. State*, 42 Ala. 525 (1868); *Burns v. State*, 48 Ala. 195, 197 (1872); *Green v. State*, 58 Ala. 190 (1877); Stephenson, *Race Distinctions*, 80–82; *Loving v. Virginia*, 388 U.S. 1 (1967).

28. 18 U.S. Stats. 335 (1875); C. Vann Woodward, *The Strange Career of Jim Crow* (New York, 1966), 24–27; 1865 Fla. Laws, 23; 1865 Miss. Laws, 229; 1866 Tex. Laws, 102.

29. Fairman, *History of Supreme Court*, 156–72; 1870 Miss. Laws, 104; 1873 Miss. Laws, 66; 1873 Fla. Laws, 25; 1870 Ga. Laws, 398; 1868 La. Const., XIII; 1873 Ark. Laws, 15.

30. *Donnell v. State*, 48 Miss. 661 (1873); *DeCuir v. Benson*, 27 La. Ann. 1, 6 (1875), *reversed sub nom. Hall v. DeCuir*, 95 U.S. 485 (1878). As to Southern reaction to the Sumner bill, see 1874 Va. Laws, 3; 1874 N.C. Laws, 367; 1873 Del. Laws, 686 (all opposing the bill). Only Louisiana's legislature endorsed the bill. 1872 La. Laws, 29.

31. Sefton, *U.S. Army and Reconstruction*, 35–42, 90–92, 122–29; Low, "Freedmen's Bureau in Maryland," 232–42; Walter L. Fleming, *Civil War and Reconstruction in Alabama* (New York, 1905), 425–28.

32. Simrall quoted in James E. Bond, *No Easy Walk to Freedom: Reconstruction and the Ratification of the Fourteenth Amendment* (Westport, Conn., 1997), 39.

33. 1867 W.Va. Laws, 173; 1867 Mo. Laws, 196; 1866 Tenn. Laws (Ex. Sess.), 5, 23; 1867 Ky. Laws, Res. 37; 1867 Md. Laws, Jt. Res. 18; 1867 Del. Laws, 303.

34. 1868 Ala. Laws, 29; 1870 Miss. Laws, 89; 1868 Tenn. Laws, 18; 1868 N.C. Laws, 613; 1870 S.C. Laws, 559; 1868–69 Ark. Laws, 63; 1873 Ky. Laws, 729, 767.

35. Robert Kaczorowski, *The Politics of Judicial Interpretation: The Federal Courts, Department of Justice and Civil Rights, 1866–1876* (Dobbs Ferry, N.Y., 1985), 59–62, 108–11; Everette Swinney, *Suppressing the Ku Klux Klan: The Enforcement of the Reconstruction Amendments, 1870–1874* (New York, 1987), passim; *Walpole v. State*, 68 Tenn. 370, 373 (1878). Arkansas and Tennessee repealed portions of their anti-Klan laws after the end of Reconstruction. 1875 Ark. Laws, 84; 1869–70 Tenn. Laws, 131.

36. See E. Merton Coulter, *The Civil War and Readjustment in Kentucky* (Chapel Hill, N.C., 1926), 247, 258–61; William E. Parrish, *A History of Missouri, Vol. 3: 1860–1875* (Columbia, Mo., 1973), 102–7; Jean H. Baker, *The Politics of Continuity: Maryland Political Parties from 1858 to 1870* (Baltimore, 1973), 85–90.

37. 13 U.S. Stats. 6, § 24 (1864); 13 U.S. Stats. 387, § 14 (1864).

38. 1865 Mo. Const., I:2; *1865 Mo. Convention Journal*, 65–70, 198; 1864 Md. Const., I:24; *1864 Md. Convention Debates*, 634, 666–71, 712–15, 742; Richard O. Curry, ed., *Radicalism, Racism, and Party Realignment: The Border States during Reconstruction* (Baltimore, 1969), 82–83.

39. *Corbin v. Marsh*, 63 Ky. 193, 197–98 (1865) (Robertson); *Hughes v. Todd*, 63 Ky. 188, 202, 205–11 (1865) (Williams); 1865 Ky. Laws, 157, 161; 1865–66 Ky. Laws, 64.

40. 1864 Md. Const., III:36; *1864 Md. Convention Debates*, 662–74, 720–26, 924–28, 943–44; 1867 Md. Laws, 189, 327; 1867 Md. Const., Decl. of Rights, § 24; *1867 Md. Convention Debates*, 141–49, 273–78; 1865 Tenn. Laws, Jt. Res. 10; 1870 W.Va. Laws, 146.

41. *1865 Miss. Convention Journal*, 215; 1870–71 N.C. Laws, 119; 1869–70 Tenn. Laws (1st Sess.), 27, 57.

42. 1868 S.C. Const., IV:34; 1868 Ga. Const., V:17; 1868 La. Const., 128; 1868 Ark. Const., XV:14; *Bradford v. Jenkins*, 41 Miss. 328 (1867); *Jacoway v. Denton*, 25 Ark. 625 (1870); *Young v. Thompson*, 42 Tenn. 596 (1865); *Mathews v. Dunbar*, 3 W.Va. 138 (1869); *Williams v. Johnson*, 30 Md. 500 (1869); *Armstrong v. Lecomte*, 21 La. Ann. 527, 529 (1869); *Rodriquez v. Bienvenu*, 22 La. Ann. 300 (1870); *Emancipation Proclamation Cases*, 31 Tex. 504 (1868).

43. *White v. Hart*, 39 Ga. 306 (1869), *reversed* 80 U.S. 646 (1873); *Clark v. Jennings*, 41 Ga. 182 (1870); see *Grier v. Wallace*, 7 S.C. (N.S.) 182 (1876) (following the United States Supreme Court's decision in *White v. Hart*); *McMath v. Johnson*, 41 Miss. 439 (1867); *Whitfield v. Whitfield*, 44 Miss. 456 (1870); *Emancipation Proclamation Cases*, 31 Tex. 504 (1868); *Rodriquez v. Bienvenu*, 22 La. Ann. 300 (1870).

44. See *State v. Ross*, 76 N.C. 242 (1877); *Britton v. Atlanta & Charlotte Air-Line R. Co.*, 88 N.C. 536 (1883).

CHAPTER 5

1. *Griswold v. Hepburn*, 63 Ky. 20, 23 (1865), *reversed in part and affirmed in part*, 75 U.S. (8 Wall.) 603 (1870), *overruled by Second Legal Tender Cases*, 79 U.S. (12 Wall.) 457 (1871).

2. See James M. McPherson, *Battle Cry of Freedom: The Civil War Era* (New York, 1988), 323–25, 442–48, 859–62.

3. *Federalist* No. 82 (Hamilton); 1 U.S. Stat. 577 (1798); Leonard W. Levy, ed., *The Virginia Report of 1799–1800 Touching Alien and Sedition Laws* (New York, 1970), 22; Forrest McDonald, *States' Rights and the Union: Imperium in Imperio, 1776–1876* (Lawrence, Kan., 2000), 41.

4. *Martin v. Hunter's Lessee*, 14 U.S. 304 (1816); *Green v. Biddle*, 21 U.S. 1 (1823); *Worcester v. Georgia*, 31 U.S. 515; McDonald, *States' Rights and the Union*, 79–80, 98–103; Herman W. Ames, *State Documents on Federal Relations: The States and the United States* (Philadelphia, 1911; reprint, 1970), 105–13; Joseph Desha, "Message to Kentucky Legislature, November 7, 1825," reprinted in Ames, *State Documents*, at 113; Tim Alan Garrison, *The Legal Ideology of Removal: The Southern Judiciary and the Sovereignty of Native American Nations* (Athens, Ga., 2002), 103–14; Joseph A. Ranney, "This New and Beautiful Organism: The Evolution of American Federalism in Three State Supreme Courts." *Marquette Law Review* 87 (2003): 253, 266–67.

5. *Bodley v. Gaither*, 19 Ky. 57 (1825); *Beall v. Beall*, 8 Ga. 210, 216 (1850); *Campbell v. State*, 11 Ga. 353, 366 (1852); Ranney, "New and Beautiful Organism," 266–67.

6. *Congressional Globe*, 37th Cong. 2d sess., 736–37 (February 11, 1862); U.S. Const. IV:4; "Our Domestic Relations," reprinted in Charles Sumner, *Works of Sumner* (Boston, 1875–83), 7:493, 523, 527, 540; *id.*, 6:309; Joel S. Parker, *Revolution and Reconstruction* (New York, 1866), 40; Orestes Brownson, *The American Republic: Its Constitution, Tendencies, and Destiny* (New York, 1866), 195, 203.

7. *Texas v. White*, 74 U.S. 700, 725, 733, 735–36 (1869).

8. 1866 N.C. Laws, 97–98; *Thorington v. Smith*, 75 U.S. 1, 11 (1869).

9. *In Matter of Hughes*, 61 N.C. 58 (1867); *Phillips v. Hooker*, 62 N.C. 193, 202–03, 205 (1867).

10. *Turner v. North Carolina R. Co.*, 63 N.C. 522 (1869); *Leak v. Commissioners of Richmond County*, 64 N.C. 133, 135, 137 (1870).

11. *Scott v. Bilgerry*, 40 Miss. 119, 134–35 (1866); *Hill v. Boyland*, 40 Miss. 618, 627, 639 (1866).

12. *Cassell v. Backrack*, 42 Miss. 56, 69 (1868).

13. *Green v. Sizer*, 40 Miss. 530, 553–55 (1866); *Beauchamp v. Comfort*, 42 Miss. 94 (1868); *Cowan v. McCutchen*, 43 Miss. 207 (1870); *Thomas v. Taylor*, 42 Miss. 651, 697, 708 (1869); *Shattuck v. Daniel*, 52 Miss. 834, 837 (1876).

14. *Griffin's Executor v. Cunningham*, 61 Va. 31, 71, 121; *Antoni v. Wright*, 63 Va. 833, 864, 885–86 (1872); *Bilgerry v. Branch & Sons*, 60 Va. 393, 401–02 (1869); *Dearing's Administrator v. Rucker*, 59 Va. 426 (1868); *Hilb v. Peyton*, 62 Va. 550, 555 (1872); *Dinwiddie County v. Stuart, Buchanan & Co.*, 69 Va. 526 (1877).

15. See Walter W. Manley, ed., *The Supreme Court of Florida and Its Predecessor Courts, 1821–1917* (Gainesville, Fla., 1997), 161–226; Robert H. Woody, "Jonathan Jasper Wright, Associate Justice of the Supreme Court of South Carolina," *Journal of Negro History* 18 (1933): 14; Francis B. Simkins and Robert H. Woody, *South Carolina during Reconstruction* (Chapel Hill, N.C., 1932), 93, 142–43; *Austin v. Kinsman*, 13 Rich. Eq. 259 (S.C. 1867); *Rutland v. Copes*, 15 Rich. L. 84 (S.C. 1867); *Rutland v. Copes*, 15 Rich. L. 42 (S.C. 1867); *Bobo v. Goss*, 1 S.C. (N.S.) 262 (1870); *Randall v. Pettes*, 12 Fla. 517 (1868); *Forcheimer v. Holly*, 14 Fla. 239 (1872).

16. *Calhoun v. Calhoun*, 2 S.C. (N.S.) 283, 298 (1870).

17. *Scheible v. Bacho*, 41 Ala. 423, 442, 461 (1868); *Watson v. Stone*, 41 Ala. 451, 464 (1867); *Chancely v. Bailey*, 37 Ga. 532, 541–42, 554 (1868).

18. *Cutts & Johnson v. Hardee*, 38 Ga. 350, 358 (1868) (jury scaling law); *Shorter v. Cobb*, 39 Ga. 285, 288–89, 304 (1869) (prohibition of enforcement of slave contracts);

White v. Hart, 39 Ga. 306 (1869); *Hardeman v. Downer*, 39 Ga. 425, 460 (1869) (homestead exemption); *Miller v. Gould*, 38 Ga. 465 (1868) (Confederate currency transactions); *Nicholas v. Hovenor*, 42 Ga. 514, 516 (1871).

19. *Noble & Brother v. Cullom & Co.*, 44 Ala. 554, 564 (1870); *Powell v. Boon & Booth*, 43 Ala. 459, 486, 567, 584 (1869); *Hale v. Huston, Sims & Co.*, 44 Ala. 134, 138 (1870); *Newman v. Reed*, 50 Ala. 297 (1874); *Whitfield v. Riddle*, 52 Ala. 467 (1875); see also *Van Hoose v. Bush*, 54 Ala. 342 (1875).

20. Texas had two Reconstruction courts. The Military Court (1868–70) consisted of justices appointed by the military officials who administered the state under the federal Reconstruction Acts. The Semicolon Court (1870–73) consisted of justices appointed by the governor under the state's 1869 constitution. It earned its name and ended its existence in dramatic fashion in 1873 when Texas's Reconstruction governor, Edmund Davis, was defeated for reelection by conservative Richard Coke. The 1869 constitution provided that all state elections "shall be held at the county seats of the several counties until otherwise provided by law; and the polls shall be opened for four days." A Houston voter charged with fraudulent repeat voting asserted as a defense that the election was invalid because the law authorizing it stated that the polls were to be open only one day. The court decided the case on a point of grammar: it held that because the constitution employed a semicolon rather than a comma to separate the phrases "until otherwise provided by law" and "four days," the four-day requirement could not be modified by the legislature and as a result the election was invalid. Davis then attempted to retain the governor's office but backed down after President Grant made clear that the federal government would not support him. 1869 Tex. Const., III:6; *Ex Parte Rodriguez*, 39 Tex. 706 (1874); Carl H. Moneyhon, *Republicanism in Reconstruction Texas* (Austin, Tex., 1980), 191–94.

21. *Luter v. Hunter*, 30 Tex. 688, 702–04 (1868); *Donley v. Tindall*, 32 Tex. 43, 57–58 (1869); *Grant v. Ryan*, 37 Tex. 37, 40 (1872); *Cundiff v. Campbell*, 40 Tex. 142, 146 (1874); *San Patricio County v. McClane*, 44 Tex. 392 (1876).

22. *Hawkins v. Filkins*, 24 Ark. 286, 303, 310 (1867); *Penn v. Tollison*, 26 Ark. 545, 561 (1871). McClure and his colleagues responded to Walker's argument that some government must exist in wartime by conceding only that Arkansas could be allowed belligerent rights, the minimum rights necessary "for the sake of humanity" during the war. *Thompson v. Mankin*, 26 Ark. 586, 588 (1871).

23. *Latham v. Clark*, 25 Ark, 574, 589–90 (1870); *Berry v. Bellows*, 30 Ark. 198, 204 (1876); see also *Hendry v. Cline*, 29 Ark. 414 (1875).

24. *Hunley v. Scott*, 19 La. Ann. 161 (1867); *McCracken v. Poole*, 19 La. Ann. 359 (1867); *Norton v. Dawson*, 19 La. Ann. 467 (1867).*Bowman v. Gonegal*, 19 La. Ann. 328 (1867); *Barrow v. Pike*, 21 La. Ann. 14 (1869); *Delmas v. Merchants Mutual Insurance Co.*, 81 U.S. (14 Wall.) 661 (1872); *Henderson v. Merchants Mutual Insurance Co.*, 25 La. Ann. 343 (1873).

25. *Smith v. Stewart*, 21 La. Ann. 67, 71–72 (1869).

26. See Thomas B. Alexander, *Political Reconstruction in Tennessee* (Nashville, Tenn., 1950), passim; James W. Ely, Jr., ed., *A History of the Tennessee Supreme Court* (Knoxville, Tenn., 2002), 74–150; Richard O. Curry, ed., *Radicalism, Racism, and Party Realignment: The Border States during Reconstruction* (Baltimore, 1969), 80–104; Milton Gerofsky, "Reconstruction in West Virginia," *West Virginia History* 6 (1944): passim.

27. *Wright & Cantrell v. Overall*, 42 Tenn. 336, 339, 344 (1865); *Thornburg v. Harris*, 43 Tenn. 57 (1866).

28. *Burkhart v. Jennings*, 2 W.Va. 242, 262 (1867).

29. *Wright & Cantrell*, 42 Tenn. at 339; *Thornburg; Robertson v. Shores*, 47 Tenn. 164, 169 (1869); *Brown v. Wylie*, 2 W.Va. 502 (1867); *Washington v. Burnett*, 4 W.Va. 84 (1870). However, like other courts that supported *ab initio*, Tennessee and West Virginia balked at reversing completed transactions involving Confederate currency. *Henly v. Franklin*, 43 Tenn. 472 (1866); *Washington v. Burnett*, 4 W.Va. 84 (1870).

30. *Frierson v. General Assembly of the Presbyterian Church in the United States*, 54 Tenn. 683, 700 (1872); *Sherfy v. Argenbright*, 48 Tenn. 128, 132–34 (1870); *Naff v. Crawford*, 48 Tenn. 11, 121–27 (1870); *Doublas v. Neil*, 54 Tenn. 437, 445 (1872); *Stewart v. Smith*, 62 Tenn. 231 (1874); *Clay v. Robinson*, 7 W.Va. 348, 358 (1874); *Harrison v. Farmers Bank of Virginia*, 6 W.Va. 1, 6 (1873).

31. See Thomas L. Connelly, "Neo-Confederatism or Power Vacuum: Post-War Kentucky Politics Reappraised," *Register of the Kentucky Historical Society* 64 (1966): 258–59; E. Merton Coulter, *The Civil War and Readjustment in Kentucky* (Chapel Hill, N.C., 1926), passim.

32. *Bowlin v. Commonwealth*, 65 Ky. 5, 9 (1867); *Corbin v. Marsh*, 63 Ky. 193 (1865); *Griswold v. Hepburn*, 63 Ky. at 23.

33. 63 Ky. at 67 (Williams). For the response of Williams's colleagues, see *Hoskins & Hughes v. Gentry*, 63 Ky. 284, 286 (1865).

34. 1 U.S. Stats. 79, § 12 (1789); 12 U.S. Stats. 756 (1863); 14 U.S. Stats. 306, 307 (1866); 15 U.S. Stats. 227 (1868); 18 U.S. Stats. 114 (1875).

35. Shortly before the war, the Wisconsin supreme court gained national notoriety by declaring the federal Fugitive Slave Act unconstitutional and holding that it had an equal right with the United States Supreme Court to pass judgment on federal laws. *In re Booth*, 3 Wis. 1 (1854), *reversed, Ableman v. Booth*, 62 U.S. 506 (1859); *Ableman v. Booth*, 11 Wis. 498 (1859) (refusing to accept and file the United States Supreme Court's decision); see generally Alfons J. Beitzinger, "Federal Law Enforcement and the Booth Cases," *Marquette Law Review* 41 (1957): 7.

36. *In re Tarble*, 25 Wis. 390, 391–92 (1870), *reversed*, 80 U.S. 397 (1871); *Morse v. Home Ins. Co. of New York City*, 30 Wis. 496, 504–05 (1872), *reversed*, 87 U.S. 445 (1874); see also *Whiton v. Chicago & Northwestern R. Co.*, 25 Wis. 424 (1870) and *State ex rel. Drake v. Doyle*, 40 Wis. 175 (1876), *affirmed*, 94 U.S. 535, 541 (1876), *overruled by Terral v. Burke Construction Co.*, 257 U.S. 529 (1922).

37. *Continental Insurance Co. v. Kasey*, 68 Va. 222, 224; *Bell v. Bell*, 3 W.Va. 183 (1869); *Williams v. Adkins*, 46 Tenn. 614 (1869); *Jones v. Davenport*, 47 Tenn. 145 (1869); *Mayor of Macon v. Cummins*, 47 Ga. 321, 327 (1872).

38. John F. Dillon, *Removal of Causes from State Courts to Federal Courts* (St. Louis, 1881), § 1, p. 2.

CHAPTER 6

1. *1868 S.C. Convention Proceedings*, 706; *1868 Ark. Convention Debates*, 370.

2. Thomas M. Cooley, *A Treatise on the Constitutional Limitations Which Rest upon the Legislative Power of the States of the American Union* (Boston, 1868), 203; see G. Alan Tarr, *Understanding State Constitutions* (Princeton, N.J., 1998), 29–32.

3. Tarr, *Understanding State Constitutions*, 97.

4. *Charleston Mercury*, February 5, 1868, quoted in Eric Foner, *Reconstruction: America's Unfinished Revolution, 1863–1877* (New York, 1988), 333.

5. James D. Dilts, *Great Road: The Building of the Baltimore & Ohio* (Stanford, Calif., 1993), 30–47, 114–26, 154–75, 210–16, 250–55, 270–74, 300–11; *Md. 1851 Convention Debates*, 413; 1851 Md. Const., II:22, 47; 1834 Tenn. Const., XI:7; 1845 La. Const., VI:113, 121–24; 1845 Tex. Const., VII:31; 1851 Ky. Const., II:33–36, 48–52, 59; 1851 Va. Const., IV:27–30.

6. Charles Fairman, *History of the Supreme Court of the United States, Vol. 6: Reconstruction and Reunion, Part 1* (New York, 1971), 107–11; Roberta Sue Alexander, *North Carolina Faces the Freedmen: Race Relations during Presidential Reconstruction, 1865–67* (Durham, N.C., 1985), 36–41. Only Alabama and Louisiana preserved significant restrictions on state aid to enterprise. 1864 La. Const., VII:112–14; 1867 Ala. Const., IV:38, 41.

7. See generally Richard L. Hume, "Carpetbaggers in the Reconstruction South: A Group Portrait of Outside Whites in the 'Black and Tan' Constitutional Conventions," *Journal of American History* 64 (1977): 313; Hume, "Negro Delegates to the State Constitutional Conventions of 1867–69," in Howard N. Rabinowitz, ed., *Southern Black Leaders of the Reconstruction Era* (Urbana, Ill., 1982).

8. *1868 La. Convention Journal*, 71, 189, 259, 291.

9. *1867 Va. Convention Debates*, 230, 580 (Bayne), 364, 458–61 (Underwood), 547–550; John J. Kneebone et al., eds., *Dictionary of Virginia Biography* (Richmond, Va., 1998), 1:409–10 (Bayne); Fairman, *History of the Supreme Court*, 558–59, 598–600; 16 U.S. Stats. 44 (1869); Patricia Hickin, "John C. Underwood and the Antislavery Movement in Virginia, 1847–1860," *Virginia Magazine of History and Biography* 73 (1965): 156.

10. Craig M. Simpson, *A Good Southerner: The Life of Henry A. Wise of Virginia* (Chapel Hill, N.C., 1985), 34–36; Joseph M. St. Hilaire, "The Negro Delegates in the Arkansas Constitutional Convention of 1868: A Profile," *Arkansas Historical Quarterly* 33 (1974): 38; Paul Palmer, "Miscegenation as an Issue in the Arkansas Constitutional Convention of 1868," *Arkansas Historical Quarterly* 24 (1965): 99; *1868 Ark. Convention Debates*, 373 (McClure).

11. *1868 S.C. Convention Proceedings*, 55.

12. Francis B. Simkins and Robert H. Woody, *South Carolina during Reconstruction* (Chapel Hill, N.C., 1932), 116–17, 131–33; Thomas Holt, *Black Over White: Negro Political Leadership in South Carolina During Reconstruction* (Urbana, Ill., 1977), 82–84; Robert H. Woody, "Jonathan Jasper Wright, Associate Justice of the Supreme Court of South Carolina," *Journal of Negro History* 18 (1933): 14.

13. *1868 S.C. Convention Proceedings*, 109–17, 137, 216–17, 221–28, 686–707.

14. Ellwood P. Cubberley, *The History of Education* (Boston, 1948), passim; Lawrence A. Cremin, *The American Common School* (New York, 1951), 176; David Hackett Fischer, *Albion's Seed: Four British Folkways in America* (New York, 1989), 130–34 (citation omitted).

15. Charles W. Dabney, *Universal Education in the South, Vol. 1* (New York, 1936; reprint, 1969), 314–18; 1865 Fla. Laws, 1475; 1865 Ark.Laws, 30.

16. See, for example, 1868 Va. Const., VIII; 1902 Va. Const., IX; 1868 N.C. Const., IX:2; 1868 S.C. Const., X:3; 1895 S.C. Const., XI:5; 1867 Ala. Const., XI; 1874 Ala. Const., XII:1; 1868 Miss. Const., VIII:1; 1890 Miss. Const., VIII; 1868 Ark. Const., IX:1; 1874 Ark. Const., XIV:1.

17. *1867 Va. Convention Debates*, 89; see, for example, 1868 Va. Const., XI:1; 1902 Va. Const., XIV:190; 1868 N.C. Const., X:2; 1868 S.C. Const., II:32; 1895 S.C. Const., III:28; 1868 Ala. Const., XIV:1,3; 1874 Ala. Const., XIV:1–2; 1868 Ark. Const., XII:1–2; 1874 Ark. Const., IX:1–5; 1870 Tenn. Const., XI:11; 1872 W.Va. Const., VI:48.

18. 1845 Tex. Const., VII:19–20; 1851 Md. Const., II:38; see generally Chapter 9.

19. *1868 S.C. Convention Proceedings*, 783; see, for example, 1868 N.C. Const., X:6; 1868 S.C. Const., XIII:8; 1895 S.C. Const., XVII:9; 1868 Ala. Const., XIV:6; 1874 Ala. Const., XIV:6; 1868 Miss. Const., I:16; 1890 Miss. Const., IV:94; 1868 Ark. Const., XII:6; 1874 Ark. Const., IX:7–8; 1872 W.Va. Const., VI:29.

20. *1895 S.C. Convention Journal*, 2; Malcolm McMillan, *Constitutional Development in Alabama, 1798–1901: A Study in Politics, the Negro and Sectionalism* (Chapel Hill, N.C., 1955), 210.

21. *Proceedings of 1877 Georgia Convention*, 298; *Galveston Daily News*, January 28, 1874, quoted in John Walker Mauer, "State Constitutions in a Time of Crisis: The Case of the Texas Constitution of 1876," *Texas Law Review* 68 (1990): 1643; 1877 Ga. Const., VII:3; 1876 Tex. Const., III:50–52; *1875 Mo. Convention Journal*, 25–30; 1875 Mo. Const., IV:44–53. General incorporation provisions: see, for example, 1877 Ga. Const., III:7; 1874 Ala. Const., II:23; 1876 Tex. Const., XII:1; 1874 Ark. Const., XII:2; 1870 Tenn. Const., XI:8,11; 1863 W.Va. Const., XI:5; 1872 W.Va. Const., VI:49, XI:1.

CHAPTER 7

1. *Gunn v. Hendry*, 43 Ga. 556, 560 (1871); John T. Trowbridge, *The South: A Tour of Its Battlefields and Ruined Cities* (New York, 1866), 580.

2. Eric Foner, *Reconstruction: America's Unfinished Revolution, 1863–1877* (New York, 1988), xxv; Harold Woodman, *New South, New Law: The Legal Foundations of Credit and Labor Relations in the Postbellum Agricultural South* (Baton Rouge, La., 1995), passim.

3. 1865 N.C. Const., Ord. 19; 1866 N.C. Laws, 100; 1866–67 N.C. Laws, 56; Kenneth E. St. Clair, "Debtor Relief in North Carolina during Reconstruction," *North Carolina Historical Review* 18 (1941): 215, 216–17; 1865 S.C. Laws, 304 (debtor must pay 10% within a year); 1865–66 Ga. Laws, 241 (25%); 1866 Ga. Laws, 157 (33%); 1866 Tex. Laws, 125 (33%); 1862–63 W.Va. Laws, 34; 1863–64 W.Va. Laws, 3 (debtor must pay interest); 1864 Md. Laws, 268 (graduated scale starting at 25%; payments within 4 months).

4. 1818 Ala. Const, Ord. 29; 1868 Ala. Laws, 179; 1865 Miss. Laws, 236; 1864–65 Ark. Laws, 45; 1861 Mo. Laws, 46; 1862 Mo. Laws, 30.

5. *Bronson v. Kinzie*, 42 U.S. 311 (1843); *Taylor v. Stearns*, 59 Va. 244, 275 (1866).

6. *Crawford v. Bank of Wilmington*, 61 N.C. 136 (1867); *Parker v. Shannonhouse*, 61 N.C. 209 (1867); St. Clair, "Debtor Relief in North Carolina," 215, 223; *Jacobs v. Smallwood*, 63 N.C. 112, 115–17, 126–27; *Farnsworth & Reaves v. Vance*, 42 Tenn. 108 (1865); *Webster & Mann v. Rose*, 53 Tenn. 93 (1871).

7. 1864–65 Ark. Laws, ch. 45; 1865–66 W.Va. Laws, 69; *Oliver v. McClure*, 28 Ark. 555 (1874); *Turner v. Watkins*, 31 Ark. 429 (1876); *Ex parte Pollard*, 40 Ala. 77 (1866); *State v. Carew*, 12 Rich. Eq. 498, 520 (1866); *Barry v. Iseman*, 14 Rich. Law 148 (1867); *Townsend v. Quinan*, 36 Tex. 548 (1872); *Jones v. McMahan*, 30 Tex. 719 (1868); *Taylor v. Stearns*, 59 Va. 244, 274 (1868); *Coffman v. Bank of Kentucky*, 40 Miss. 29 (1866).

8. 1867 N.C. Laws, 85; 1868 S.C. Const., I:20; *Ware v. Miller*, 9 S.C. (N.S.) 13 (1877).

9. 1865–66 W. Va. Laws, 69; John Cornyn, "The Roots of Texas Constitution: Settlement to Statehood," *Texas Tech Law Review* 26 (1995): 1089, 1185–88; see, for example, 1851 Md. Const., II:39; 1868 Va. Const., XI:1; 1868 Ga. Const., VII:1; 1868 Ark. Const., I:14.

10. *The Homestead Cases*, 62 Va. 266, 297 (1872); *Pryor v. Smith*, 67 Ky. 379 (1868); *Knight v. Whitman*, 69 Ky. 51 (1869).

11. *Hardeman v. Downer*, 39 Ga. 425, 447 (Brown), 460 (Warner) (1869); *Gunn v. Hendry*, 43 Ga. 556 (1871), *reversed*, *Gunn v. Barry*, 82 U.S. 610 (1873); *Chambliss v. Jordan*, 50 Ga. 81 (1873).

12. 1868 Ga. Laws, 148; 1870 Ga. Laws, 401; *Butler v. Weathers*, 39 Ga. 524 (1869); *Connell v. Vaughn*, 40 Ga. 154 (1869); *Graham v. Clark*, 40 Ga. 660 (1869); *Walker v. Whitehead*, 43 Ga. 539 (1871), *reversed* 83 U.S. 314 (1873); *Gunn v. Hendry*, 43 Ga. 556 (1871); *Gunn v. Barry*, 44 Ga. 351 (1871), *reversed*, 82 U.S. 610 (1873).

13. *Alexander v. Kilpatrick*, 14 Fla. 450 (1874); *Douglass v. Gregg*, 66 Tenn. 384 (1874); *Lincoln v. Rowe*, 64 Mo. 138 (1876). Tennessee apparently applied the no-retroactivity rule in a case decided before *Gunn*. See reporter's note to *Deatherage v. Walker*, 58 Tenn. 45 (1872).

14. *Hill v. Kessler*, 63 N.C. 437, 440, 446 (1869); *Dellinger v. Tweed*, 66 N.C. 206 (1872); *Garrett v. Cheshire*, 69 N.C. 396 (1873); *Edwards v. Kearzey*, 79 N.C. 664 (1878), *reversed*, 96 U.S. 595 (1878).

15. *Robert v. Coco*, 25 La. Ann. 199 (1873); *Doughty v. Sheriff*, 27 La. Ann. 355 (1875); *Martin v. Kilpatrick*, 30 La. Ann. 1214 (1878) (reversing the *Coco* rule); *Sneider v. Heidelberger*, 45 Ala. 126 (1871); *Webb v. Edwards*, 46 Ala. 17, 27–28 (1871) (dissent and criticism of homestead law by Chief Justice Elisha Peck); *Alabama Conference v. Vaughn*, 54 Ala. 443 (1876); *Stephenson v. Osborne*, 41 Miss. 119 (1866); *Lessley v. Phipps*, 49 Miss. 790 (1874); *Johnson v. Fletcher*, 54 Miss. 628 (1877).

16. See, for example, James Agee and Walker Evans, *Let Us Now Praise Famous Men: Three Tenant Families* (Boston, 1941); Nicholas Lemann, *Promised Land: The Great Black Migration and How It Changed America* (New York, 1991); Foner, *Reconstruction*, 170.

17. See, for example, *Brazier v. Ansley*, 33 N.C. 12, 14 (1850).

18. Foner, *Reconstruction*, 405–6; for a more pessimistic view, see Woodman, *New South, New Law*, 109–10.

19. *Saulsbury, Respess & Co. v. Eason*, 47 Ga. 617 (1873).

20. 1866 S.C. Laws, 380; 1866 Ga. Laws, 141; 1866 Ala. Laws, 44 ; 1866–67 Miss. Laws, 569; 1861–62 La. Laws, 77; 1866 Tex. Laws, 64; 1867 N.C. Laws, 3, 89; *Bain v. Brooks*, 46 Miss. 537 (1872); *Dunn v. Spears*, 5 S.C. (N.S.) 17 (1873); *Visanka v. Bradley*, 4 S.C. (N.S.) 288 (1873).

21. 1868–69 N.C. Laws, 305; 1868–69 S.C. Laws, 227; 1873–74 S.C. Laws, 88; 1872 Fla. Laws, 54; 1868 Ala. Laws, 252, 455; 1872 Miss. Laws, 131; 1868 Ark. Laws, 224; 1872 Miss. Laws, 131; 1873 Miss. Laws, 79; 1868 Ark. Laws, 245; 1868–69 S.C. Laws, 227; 1868 Ga. Const., I:30.

22. 1874 Tex. Laws, 55; 1874–75 Ark. Laws, 84; 1876–77 N.C. Laws, 551; 1876 Miss. Laws, 109; 1876–77 Ala. Laws, 74; 1879 Fla. Laws, 72; 1886 La. Laws, 127; Woodman, *New South, New Law*, 45–75.

23. 1858 Tenn. Code, 3539; 1869–70 Tenn. Laws (2nd Sess.), 191; 1875 Tenn. Laws, 206; 1831 Md. Laws, 171; 1868 Md. Laws, 292; 1870 Md. Laws, 279; 1857–58 Ky. Laws, 488, 674; *McLean v. McLean*, 73 Ky. 167, 158 (1873); 1835 Mo. Rev. Stats, 377, § 14; *Knox v. Hunt & Porter*, 18 Mo. 243 (1853); 1877 Mo. Laws, 285; Woodman, *New South, New Law*, 67.

24. *Stamps v. Gilman & Co.*, 43 Miss. 456, 471 (1870); see also *Upham v. Dodd*, 24 Ark. 544 (1867) and *Treadway v. Treadway's Executors*, 56 Ala. 390 (1877) (same); *DeBardeleben v. Crosby*, 53 Ala. 33 (1875) (lien statutes to be construed narrowly); *McLester v. Somerville & McEachin*, 54 Ala. 670 (1876) (refusing to extend lien to items that were necessary to make a crop but were not specified in lien statute); *Davis v. Meyers*, 41 Ga. 95 (1870); *Harrell v. Fagan*, 43 Ga. 339 (1871).

25. *Christian v. Crocker,* 25 Ark. 327, 329 (1869); *Bres & O'Brien v. Cowan,* 22 La. Ann. 438 (1870); *Holloway v. Brinkley,* 42 Ga. 226 (1871); *Mann v. Taylor,* 52 Tenn. 267 (1871); Woodman, *New South, New Law,* 76–77.

CHAPTER 8

1. *Commissioners of Columbia County v. King,* 13 Fla. 451, 477–78 (1871).
2. *Whiting v. Sheboygan & Fond du Lac R. Co.,* 25 Wis. 167, 196–97, 219–20 (1871); *Attorney General v. Chicago & Northwestern R. Co.,* 35 Wis. 425, 530 (1874); Carter Goodrich, *Government Promotion of American Canals and Railroads, 1800–1890* (New York, 1960), 208–45.
3. Goodrich, *Promotion of Canals and Railroads,* 102–63; James D. Dilts, *Great Road: The Building of the Baltimore & Ohio* (Stanford, Calif., 1993), 210–12, 250–55, 270–74, 300–11, quoting *Baltimore American,* March 11, 1836.
4. William E. Connelley and E. Merton Coulter, *History of Kentucky* (Chicago, 1922), 2:721–38; *1849–50 Ky. Convention Debates,* 758; 1850 Ky. Const., II:33, 35–36; *1850 Md. Convention Debates,* 413; 1851 Md. Const., II:22; 1845 Tex. Const., VII:31, 33; 1851 Va. Const., IV:28–31.
5. *Louisville & Nashville R. Co. v. County Court of Davidson,* 33 Tenn. 637, 665 (1856); *Cotten v. Commissioners of Leon County,* 6 Fla. 610, 623 (1856); *Police Jury v. Succession of McDonough,* 8 La. Ann. 341 (1853); *Caldwell v. Justices of County of Burke,* 50 N.C. (4 Jones) 323, 329 (1858); *Taylor v. Commissioners of New Berne,* 55 N.C. (2 Jones Eq.) 141 (1855); see also *Goddin v. Crump,* 35 Va. (8 Leigh) 120 (1837), *Nichol v. Mayor of Nashville,* 28 Tenn. 252, 270 (1848); compare *Slack v. Maysville & Lexington R. Co.,* 52 Ky. 7, 15 (1852) (doubting the wisdom of subsidies).
6. Mark W. Summers, *Railroads, Reconstruction and the Gospel of Prosperity: Aid under the Radical Republicans, 1865–1877* (Princeton, N.J., 1984), 5–10.
7. See Goodrich, *Promotion of Canals and Railroads,* 245–55; 1870 Va. Const., X:14–15; 1868 Ga. Const., III:6; 1868 Ark. Const., X:6, 9–10; 1870 Tenn. Const., II:31; 1874 Ala. Const., II:54; 1890 Miss. Const., IV:95; 1877 Ga. Const., VII:3; 1868 N.C. Const., V:5; 1869–70 Tenn. Laws, 39.
8. 1902 Va. Const., VIII:127; 1868 Ga. Const., III:6; 1874 Ga. Laws, 16; 1869 Fla. Laws, 29; 1868 Ala. Laws, 514; 1874 Ala. Const., II:55; 1872 Miss. Laws, 101, 120; 1869 Miss. Const., XII:14; 1879 La. Const., 56; 1866 Tex. Const., Ord. 10; 1869 Tex. Const., XII:40; 1871 Tex. Laws, 37; 1874 Tex. Laws, 118; 1870 Tenn. Const., II:29; 1870–71 Tenn. Laws, 58; 1871 Tenn. Laws, 142; 1872–73 W. Va. Laws, 288; 1872 W.Va. Const., X:7–8; 1865 Mo. Const., XI:14; 1868 Mo. Laws, 92; 1875 Mo. Const., IV:47.
9. William E. Parrish, *A History of Missouri, Vol. 3: 1860–1875* (Columbia, Mo., 1973), 196–98, 208–9; 1865 Mo. Const., XI:13–15; 1865 Convention Ordinance (March 10, 1865); 1869 Mo. Laws, p. 73; 1871 Mo. Laws, 52; 1875 Mo. Const., X:12.
10. *Smith v. County of Clark,* 54 Mo. 58, 78 (1873); *Osage Valley & Southern Kansas R. Co. v. County Court of Morgan County,* 53 Mo. 156, 158 (1873); *New Orleans, Mobile & Chattanooga R. Co. v. Dunn,* 51 Ala. 128, 138 (1874); *Fielder v. Montgomery & Eufaula R. Co.,* 51 Ala. 178 (1874); *East Tennessee University v. Mayor and Aldermen of Knoxville,* 64 Tenn. 166 (1874); 1871–72 Mo. Laws, 56; 1875 Mo. Const., IV:47, IX:6.
11. *City of San Antonio v. Jones,* 28 Tex. 19 (1866); *City of San Antonio v. Lane,* 32 Tex. 405 (1869), overruled on other grounds by *City of San Antonio v. Gould,* 34 Tex.

49 (1870–71); *Giddings v. City of San Antonio,* 47 Tex. 548 (1877); *Peck v. City of San Antonio,* 51 Tex. 490 (1879). The Redemption court gave little weight to the Military Court's decision because that court was not "regularly constituted" under Texas law, but it decided the Restoration and Semicolon Court decisions were well reasoned and the need for judicial consistency was strong enough that the earlier decisions should stand. See *Peck,* 51 Tex. at 492–93; James R. Norvell, "The Reconstruction Courts of Texas, 1867–1873," *Southwest Historical Quarterly* 62 (1958): 151.

12. 1868 Ky. Laws, 992; see also 1869 Ky. Laws, 1815; *Shelby County Court v. Cumberland & Ohio R. Co.,* 71 Ky. 209, 216 (1871); *Mercer County Court v. Kentucky River Navigation Co.,* 71 Ky. 300, 321–24 (1871); 1868 N.C. Const., V:5, VII:7; *University R. Co. v. Holden,* 63 N.C. 410 (1869).

13. Alfred D. Chandler, *The Visible Hand: The Managerial Revolution in American Business* (Cambridge, Mass., 1977), 122–27, 133–37, 145–48; Summers, *Railroads, Reconstruction and the Gospel of Prosperity,* 69–95.

14. 1863 Mo. Laws, 48; 1871–72 Mo. Laws, 69; 1875 Mo. Laws, 112; 1866–67 W.Va. Laws, 294; 1869 W.Va. Laws, 13; 1872–73 W.Va. Laws, 213, 710; 1866–67 Va. Laws, 725; 1876–77 Va. Laws, 254; 1872–73 Ala. Laws, 62; 1873 Ark. Laws, 425; 1867 Ky. Laws, Res. 41; 1877 Tenn. Laws, 98; 1871–72 N.C. Laws, 186.

15. 1872 W.Va. Const., XI:9; 1874 Ala. Const., XIII:22; 1874 Ark. Const., XVII:3, 6; 1875 Mo. Const., XII:12, 14, 24; 1877 Ga. Const., IV:2; see 1879 La. Const., 235; 1885 Fla. Const., XV:30–31; 1890 Ky. Const., 209, 213–15; 1890 Miss. Const., VII:186–88; 1895 S.C. Const., IX:14; 1902 Va. Const., XII:155–56, 160–61.

16. *Trustees of Dartmouth College v. Woodward,* 17 U.S. 518 (1819); John W. Cadman, *The Corporation in New Jersey: Business and Politics, 1791–1875* (Cambridge, Mass., 1949), 191–93.

17. *Alabama & Florida R. Co. v. Burkett,* 46 Ala. 569 (1871); *Mississippi, Red River & Ouachita R. Co. v. Gaster,* 24 Ark. 96 (1863); *Hamilton v. Keith,* 68 Ky. 458 (1869); *Philadelphia, Wilmington & Baltimore R. Co. v. Bowers,* 9 Del. 506 (1873); *Sloan v. Pacific R. Co.,* 61 Mo. 24 (1875); *Raleigh & Gaston R. Co. v. Reid,* N.C. 155, 158 (1870).

18. *Mississippi Society of Arts & Sciences v. Musgrove,* 44 Miss. 820 (1870); *Moore v. State,* 48 Miss. 147 (1873); *Atlantic & Gulf R. Co. v. Allen,* 15 Fla. 637, 663 (1876), citing *Wilmington v. Reid,* 80 U.S. 264 (1872); *Knoxville & Ohio R. Co. v. Hicks,* 68 Tenn. 442 (1877); *State v. Bank of Smyrna,* 7 Del. 99 (1859) (applying the *Dartmouth* doctrine to a bank taxation law); *North Missouri R. Co. v. Maguire,* 49 Mo. 490, 498–99 (1872); *Central Railroad & Banking Co. v. State,* 54 Ga. 401 (1875); *State v. Georgia Railroad & Banking Co.,* 54 Ga. 423 (1875).

19. 1851 Md. Const., II:47; 1864 Md. Const., III:51; 1863 W.Va. Const., XI:5; 1902 Va. Const., XII:158; 1874 Ala. Const., XIII:10; 1875 Mo. Const., XII:21; 1879 La. Const., 234; 1890 Miss. Const., VII:178; 1895 S.C. Const., IX:17; see *Louisville, Cincinnati & Lexington R. Co. v. Commonwealth,* 73 Ky. 43 (1873); *Sprigg v. Western Telegraph Co.,* 46 Md. 67 (1877). Kentucky enacted its anti-*Dartmouth* clause as a statute rather than a constitutional provision. 1856 Ky. Laws, 15.

20. Cadman, *Corporation in New Jersey,* 6–14; *Proprietors of Charles River Bridge v. Proprietors of Warren Bridge,* 36 U.S. 420 (1837).

21. Cadman, *Corporation in New Jersey,* 15–17, 135–50; 1845 La. Const., VI:123; 1834 Tenn. Const., XI:7; 1845 Tex. Const., VII:3; 1851 Md. Const., II:47; 1854 Ky. Laws, 179; 1863 Mo. Laws, 19.

22. 1868 N.C. Const., VIII:1; 1871–72 N.C. Laws, 186, 347; 1869–70 S.C. Laws, 295; 1876 Ga. Laws, 118; 1868 Ala. Laws, 34, 462; 1868–69 Ark. Laws, 102, 179; 1867

Ky. Laws, 1787; 1870 Ky. Laws, 644–45; 1872–73 W.Va. Laws, 213; 1869 Mo. Laws, 26, 45; *Horst v. Moses*, 48 Ala. 128, 142 (1872).

CHAPTER 9

1. *Felkner v. Tighe*, 39 Ark. 357, 364–65 (1882); Merrick quoted in Armantine Smith, "The History of the Woman's Suffrage Movement in Louisiana," *Louisiana Law Review* 62 (2002): 542.

2. William Blackstone, *Commentaries on the Laws of England*, 430, quoted in Mary Lynn Salmon, *Women and the Law of Property in Early America* (Chapel Hill, N.C., 1986), 200 n. 1.

3. Salmon, *Women and Law of Property*, 5–45, 88–111; Norma Basch, *In the Eyes of the Law: Women, Marriage and Property in Nineteenth-Century New York* (Ithaca, N.Y., 1982), 51–55; see *Tabb v. Archer*, 13 Va. 399 (1809); *Boatright v. Wingate*, 3 Brevard 423 (S.C. Const. Ct. 1814); *Bell v. Bell*, 1 Ga. 637 (1846); *Kimball v. Kimball*, 2 Howard 532 (Miss. 1837); *Powell v. Powell*, 28 Tenn. 480 (1848); *Sharp v. Wickliffe & McKinney*, 13 Ky. 10 (1823).

4. Salmon, *Women and Law of Property*, 112–35; Basch, *In the Eyes of the Law*, 74–78, 110–37; *Methodist Episcopal Church v. Jaques*, 1 Johns. Ch. 450 (N.Y. Ch. 1815).

5. *Lindsay v. Platt*, 9 Fla. 150 (1860); *Dollner, Potter & Co. v. Snow*, 16 Fla. 86 (1877).

6. 1835 Ark. Terr. Laws, p. 34; 1839 Miss. Laws, p. 72; 1842 Md. Laws, 161; 1845 Ala. Laws, 24–25;1846 Ky. Laws, 42 (separate property limited to real estate and slaves); 1847 Ala. Laws, 79; 1849–50 Tenn. Laws, 111; 1849 Mo. Laws, 67; 1851 Md. Const., III: 38; Richard Chused, "Married Women's Property Law: 1800–1850," *Georgetown Law Journal* 71 (1983): 1398–1401.

7. Chused, "Married Women's Property Law," 1360–67; Basch, *In the Eyes of the Law*, 115–17.

8. Sandra Moncrief, "The Mississippi Married Woman's Property Act of 1839," *Journal of Mississippi History* 47 (1985): 110; Elizabeth Gaspar Brown, "Husband and Wife—Memorandum on the Mississippi Women's Law of 1839," *Michigan Law Review* 42 (1944): 1110.

9. 1847 Ala. Laws, 79; *Wilkinson v. Cheatham*, 45 Ala. 337, 339–40 (1871); 1860 Md. Code, Art. 45; *Barton v. Barton*, 32 Md. 214, 223 (1870); see *Cooke v. Husbands*, 11 Md. 492 (1857).

10. Harriet Spiller Daggett, *The Community Property System of Louisiana* (Baton Rouge, La., 1931), passim; Kathleen E. Lazarou, *Concealed under Petticoats: Married Women's Property and the Law of Texas, 1840–1913* (New York, 1986), 43–62; 1840 Repub. Tex. Laws, chs. 3–4; 1845 Tex. Const., VII: 19–20; Timothy S. Huebner, *The Southern Judicial Tradition: State Judges and Sectional Distinctiveness, 1790–1890* (New York, 1999), 99 (Hemphill); *Cartwright v. Hollis*, 5 Tex. 152 (1849); *Christmas v. Smith*, 10 Tex. 123 (1853); *Milburn v. Walker*, 11 Tex. 329 (1854).

11. Lee Ann Whites, *The Civil War as a Crisis in Gender: Augusta, Georgia, 1860–1890* (Athens, Ga., 1995), 73, 136, quoting *Augusta Chronicle & Sentinel*, April 4, 1865; Anne Firor Scott, *The Southern Lady: From Pedestal to Politics, 1830–1930* (Charlottesville, Va., 1995), 92–97; Sally G. McMillen, *Southern Women: Black and White in the Old South*, 2d ed. (Wheeling, Ill., 2002), 164–67, 182–85.

12. See Suzanne D. Lebsock, "Radical Reconstruction and the Property Rights of Southern Women," *Journal of Southern History* 43 (1977): 19; Smith, "Woman's Suffrage Movement in Louisiana," 544.

13. 1865–66 Ga. Laws, 226; 1868 N.C. Const., X:6; 1868 S.C. Const., XIII:8; 1868 Ga. Const., VII:1; *1868 South Carolina Convention Proceedings*, 785–86; Lebsock, "Property Rights of Southern Women," 202–4.

14. 1868 Fla. Const., V:25; 1868 Ala. Const., XIV:6; 1868 Miss. Const., I:16; 1868 Ark. Const., XII:6; see 1864 Md. Const., III:42; 1867 Md. Const., III:43.

15. 1895 S.C. Const., XVII:9; 1877 Ga. Const., III:11; 1885 Fla. Const., XI:1; 1875 Ala. Const., XIV:6; 1890 Miss. Const., IV:94; 1874 Ark. Const., IX:7; see 1866 Tex. Const., VII:19; 1869 Tex. Const., Art. XII:14; 1876 Tex. Const., XVI:15; 1872 W.Va. Const., VI:49.

16. 1868 Ky. Laws, 146; 1869–70 Tenn. Laws (1st Sess.), 113; 1876–77 Va. Laws, 333; 1875 Mo. Laws, 61.

17. See Joan Hoff, *Law, Gender and Injustice: A Legal History of U.S. Women* (New York, 1991), 380–83; Lazarou, *Concealed under Petticoats*, 91–95; Daggett, *Community Property System of Louisiana*, 40.

18. 1860 Md. Code, Art. 45; 1871–72 N.C. Laws, 328; 1873 Miss. Laws, 78; 1873 Ark. Laws, 382; 1873 Ky. Laws, 36; 1887 Ala. Laws, 80; 1891 W.Va. Laws, 324.

19. 1871–72 N.C. Laws, 328; 1871–72 Ga. Laws, 49; 1879 Fla. Laws, 3130; 1873 Ark. Laws, 382.

20. 1871–72 Ga. Laws, 48; 1866–67 Miss. Laws, 725; 1873 Del. Laws, 638; 1873 Ark. Laws, 382; 1872 Md. Laws, 270; 1869–70 S.C. Laws, 488; 1875–76 Ala. Laws, 159; 1872–73 W.Va. Laws, 273; 1889 Mo. Laws, 164, § 3468.

21. *Shuler v. Millsaps*, 71 N.C. 297, 298 (1874); *Jordan v. Baker*, 73 N.C. 145, 146–47 (1875); *Pippen v. Wesson*, 74 N.C. 437 (1876); *Kirkman v. Bank of Greensboro*, 77 N.C. 394 (1877); *Manning v. Manning*, 79 N.C. 293 (1878).

22. *Hardin v. Pelan*, 41 Miss. 112 (1866); *Whitworth v. Carter*, 43 Miss. 61, 72 (1870); *Foxworth v. Magee*, 44 Miss. 430 (1870); *Apple v. Ganong*, 47 Miss. 189 (1872); *Dibrell v. Carlisle*, 48 Miss. 691, 706 (1873); *Netterville v. Barber*, 52 Miss. 167, 172–73 (1876); *Dollner, Potter & Co. v. Snow*, 16 Fla. 86 (1877); compare *King v. Hooton & Watson*, 56 Fla. 805, 47 So. 394 (1908) (discussing the 1885 Redemption constitution's role in expanding married women's rights in Florida).

23. *Wilkinson v. Cheatham*, 45 Ala. 337, 339, 341 (1871); *Nunn's Administrator v. Givhan's Administrator*, 45 Ala. 370, 376; *O'Neal v. Robinson*, 45 Ala. 526, 534 (1871).

24. *Witsell v. Charleston*, 7 S.C. (N.S.) 88, 101 (1876); *Oliver v. Grimball*, 14 S.C. 556 (1881); see also *Dunn v. Dunn*, 1 S.C. (N.S.) 350 (1870) (applying common-law rules to separate property acquired before 1868).

25. *Huff v. Wright*, 39 Ga. 41, 43 (1869); *Urquhart v. Oliver*, 56 Ga. 344, 346, 349 (1876). As to separate-estate laws, see, for example, 1895 W.Va. Laws, 21; 1913 Tex. Laws, 61.

26. Elizabeth Cady Stanton, Susan B. Anthony, and Matilda Joslyn Gage, *History of Woman Suffrage*, 6 vols. (New York, 1881–1922), 3:604.

27. Stanton et al., *History of Woman Suffrage*, 2:314–40; Malcolm S. Feely, *Frederick Douglass* (New York, 1991), 249–50, 265–69.

28. Stanton et al., *History of Woman Suffrage*, 3:824, 828; Paul E. Fuller, *Laura Clay and the Women's Rights Movement* (Lexington, Ky., 1975), 22–26; *1867 Va. Convention Debates*, 467–68; *1868 S.C. Convention Proceedings*, 838.

29. Stanton et al., *History of Woman Suffrage*, 3:825; Fuller, *Laura Clay*, 54–56; *1895 S.C. Convention Journal*, 343, 371–73, 412–14; Smith, "Woman's Suffrage Movement in Louisiana," 542–43.

30. Stanton et al., *History of Woman Suffrage*, 2:407–13, 3:594; *Minor v. Happersett*, 53 Mo. 58 (1872), *affirmed*, 88 U.S. 162 (1875); Lee Ann Whites, "The Tale of Two Minors: Women's Rights on the Border," in *Women in Missouri History: In Search of Power and Influence*, ed. Lee Ann Whites et al. (Columbia, Mo., 2004), 101; National American Woman Suffrage Association, *Victory: How Women Won It* (New York, 1940), 161–63.

CHAPTER 10

1. 40 Tex. v (1874).

2. Eric Foner, *Reconstruction: America's Unfinished Revolution, 1863–1877* (New York, 1988), 561–87; C. Vann Woodward, *Origins of the New South, 1877–1913* (Baton Rouge, La., 1951), 1–22, 51–74; William Gillette, *Retreat from Reconstruction, 1869–1879* (Baton Rouge, La., 1979), 104–236.

3. Post-Reconstruction leaders were denominated "Bourbons" because of a perceived similarity to the Bourbon family that ruled France up to the time of the French Revolution (1793) and again after the Napoleonic era (1815–48). After Restoration, the French Bourbons were said to have forgotten nothing and learned nothing. The first part of the gibe was perhaps true of the Southern Bourbons, but the second clearly was not.

4. Foner, *Reconstruction*, 587–98; Michael J. Klarman, "The Plessy Era," *Supreme Court Review* (1998): 306–12; C. Vann Woodward, *The Strange Career of Jim Crow* (New York, 1966), 33–35; Albert D. Kirwan, *Revolt of the Rednecks: Mississippi Politics, 1876–1925* (Lexington, Ky., 1951), 9–19; William Ivy Hair, *Bourbanism and Agrarian Protest: Louisiana Politics, 1877–1900* (Baton Rouge, La., 1969), 107–8.

5. Robert H. Woody, "Jonathan Jasper Wright, Associate Justice of the Supreme Court of South Carolina," *Journal of Negro History* 18 (1933): 114–15, 122–27; *Ex parte Norris*, 8 S.C. (N.S.) 408 (1876); *Ex parte Smith*, 8 S.C. (N.S.) 495 (1877).

6. Walter W. Manley, ed. *The Supreme Court of Florida and Its Predecessor Courts, 1821–1917* (Gainesville, Fla., 1997), 217–19, 235; John B. Harris, ed., *A History of the Supreme Court of Georgia* (Macon, Ga., 1948), 91, 97–98, 114; Dunbar Rowland, *Courts, Judges and Lawyers of Mississippi 1798–1935* (Jackson, Miss., 1935), 81, 97–98; *Missouri Reports*, Vols. 57–63; John W. Green, *Lives of the Judges of the Supreme Court of Tennessee, 1796–1947* (Knoxville, Tenn., 1947), 150–54; Thomas Alexander, "Thomas A. R. Nelson as an Exemplar of Whig Conservatism in Tennessee," *Tennessee Historical Quarterly* 15 (1956): 17.

7. *Plowman v. Thornton*, 52 Ala. 559, 569 (1875); *Giddings v. San Antonio*, 47 Tex. 548, 557 (1877); *Berry v. Bellows*, 30 Ark. 198, 204 (1876). See also James R. Norvell, "The Reconstruction Courts of Texas, 1867–1873," *Southwest Historical Quarterly* 62 (1958): 141; *Atcheson v. Scott*, 51 Tex. 213, 220 (1879).

8. 1876–77 N.C. Laws, 589–90.

9. *Britton v. Atlanta & Charlotte Air-Line Railway Co.*, 88 N.C. 536, 545–46 (1883).

10. See *Ex parte Francois*, 9 F.Cas. 699, 701 (W.D. Tex. 1879) (No. 5,047); *Frasher v. State*, 3 Tex. Ct. App 263 (1877).

11. Ellwood P. Cubberley, *The History of Education* (Boston, 1948), passim; Lawrence A. Cremin, *The American Common School* (New York, 1951), 176; David

Hackett Fischer, *Albion's Seed: Four British Folkways in America* (New York, 1989), 130–34 (citation omitted); Charles W. Dabney, *Universal Education in the South, Vol. 1* (New York, 1936; reprint, 1969), 1:23–34, 125–35, 262, 290, 344–46, 362–70; Horace Mann Bond, *The Education of the Negro in the American Social Order* (New York, 1934), 36–41.

12. See, for example, 1868 S.C. Const., X:3, 5, 10; 1868 Ga. Const., I:29, VI:1; 1868 Fla. Const., IX:1, 4, 7; 1868 Miss. Const., VIII:1, 10; 1868 Ark. Const., IX:1, 5; 1895 S.C. Const., XI:5–6; 1885 Fla. Const., XII; 1890 La. Const., 224–25; 1874 Ark. Const., XIV:1, 3; 1872 W.Va. Const., XII:1.

13. 1874 Ky. Laws, 63; *Claybrook v. Owensboro*, 16 F. 297 (D. Ky. 1883); *Dawson v. Lee*, 83 Ky. 49, 56 (1884); 1883 N.C. Laws, 37; *Puitt v. Commissioners of Gaston County*, 94 N.C. 709, 715–16 (1886); *Riggsbee v. Town of Durham*, 94 N.C. 800 (1886).

14. *Board of Education of Richmond County v. Cumming*, 103 Ga. 641, 29 S.E. 488 (Ga. 1898), *affirmed sub nom. Cumming v. Georgia*, 175 U.S. 528 (1899).

15. *Home Ins. Co. of New York v. Morse*, 87 U.S. (20 Wall.) 445 (1874), *reversing Morse v. Home Ins. Co. of New York*, 30 Wis. 496 (1872); 1870 Wis. Laws, 56.

16. *Doyle v. Continental Ins. Co.*, 94 U.S. 535 (1876); *State ex rel. Drake v. Doyle*, 40 Wis. 175 (1876); 1872 Wis. Laws, 64, 67.

17. *Reece v. Newport News & Mississippi Valley R. Co.*, 9 S.E.212 (W.Va. 1889); *Debnam v. Southern Bell Telephone & Telegraph Co.*, 36 S.E. 269 (N.C. 1900); *Commonwealth v. East Tennessee Coal Co.*, 30 S.W. 608 (Ky. 1895); *Prewitt v. Security Mut. Life Ins. Co.*, 83 S.W. 611 (Ky. 1904); *State ex rel. Louisville & Nashville R. Co.*, 51 So. 918 (Miss. 1910); *Louisville & Nashville R. Co. v. State*, 65 So. 881 (Miss. 1914); see also *State ex rel. Kimberlite Diamond Mining & Washing Co. v. Hodges*, 169 S.W. 942 (Ark. 1914) (upholding an antiremoval revocation law but limiting its application to companies that did not transact business outside Arkansas); *Terral v. Burke Construction Co.*, 257 U.S. 529 (1922).

18. Woodward, *Origins of the New South*, 107–41, 175–204; Paul D. Escott, *Many Excellent People: Power and Privilege in North Carolina, 1850–1900* (Chapel Hill, N.C., 1985), 197–205, 220–30.

19. See John Walker Mauer, "State Constitutions in a Time of Crisis: The Case of the Texas Constitution of 1876," *Texas Law Review* 68 (1990): 1619–22.

20. See Chapter 8.

21. 1868–69 N.C. Laws, 305; 1876–77 N.C. Laws, 551; 1874 Tex. Laws, 55; 1874–75 Ark. Laws, 84; 1876–77 N.C. Laws, 551; 1876 Miss. Laws, 109; 1876–77 Ala. Laws, 74; 1879 Fla. Laws, 72; 1886 La. Laws, 127; Harold Woodman, *New South, New Law: The Legal Foundations of Credit and Labor Relations in the Postbellum Agricultural South* (Baton Rouge, La., 1995), 45–75.

22. Steven Hahn, "Hunting, Fishing, and Foraging: Common Rights and Class Relations in the Postbellum South," in *Black Southerners and the Law 1865–1900*, ed. Donald G. Nieman (New York, 1994); St. George Tucker, *Blackstone's Commentaries: With Notes of Reference to the Constitution and Laws of the Federal Government of the United States and of the Commonwealth of Virginia* (Philadelphia, 1803; reprint 1996), 3:170, 212–13.

23. 1880–81 Ala. Laws, 175, 223, 260; 1872 Ga. Laws, 34; 1872–73 N.C. Laws, 314; 1874–75 N.C. Laws, 70; 1879 N.C. Laws, 252; 1877 S.C. Laws, 251; 1878 S.C. Laws, 689; 1897 S.C. Laws, 41, 101, 243, 247; 1880 S.C. Laws, 323, 401; 1881 S.C. Laws, 591; 1876 Miss. Laws, 294; 1878 Miss. Laws, 305; 1880 Miss. Laws, 376; Hahn, "Hunting, Fishing, and Foraging."

24. Alwyn Barr, *Reconstruction to Reform: Texas Politics, 1876–1906* (Austin, Tex., 1971), 81–84; see 1881 Tex. Laws, 103–4.

CHAPTER 11

1. *Chiles v. Chesapeake & Ohio R. Co.*, 101 S.W. 386, 388 (Ky. 1907); *New York World*, September 27, 1895.

2. Michael J. Klarman, "The Plessy Era," *Supreme Court Review* (1998): 317–20; Michael Perman, *Struggle for Mastery: Disfranchisement in the South, 1888–1908* (Chapel Hill, N.C., 2001), 25–29; Francis B. Simkins, *Pitchfork Ben Tillman: South Carolinian* (Baton Rouge, La., 1944), 286–87; George M. Fredrickson, *The Black Image in the White Mind: The Debate on Afro-American Character and Destiny, 1817–1914* (New York, 1971), 276.

3. 1877 Ga. Const., VII:2; 1882 S.C. Laws, 1117; C. Vann Woodward, *Origins of the New South, 1877–1913* (Baton Rouge, La., 1951), 81–87; Perman, *Struggle for Mastery*, 6–18.

4. Perman, *Struggle for Mastery*, 56–68; 1889 Tenn. Laws, 414, 864; 1891 Ark. Laws, 45.

5. Albert D. Kirwan, *Revolt of the Rednecks: Mississippi Politics, 1876–1925* (Lexington, Ky., 1951), 67–71, 82–84; Frank Johnston, "Suffrage and Reconstruction in Mississippi," *Publications of Mississippi Historical Society* 6 (1902): 141, 214–17, 223–24; J. S. McNeilly, "History of the Measures Submitted to the Committee on Elective Franchise, Apportionment and Election in the Constitutional Convention of 1890," *id.*, 129, 139.

6. Perman, *Struggle for Mastery*, 74–91; Kirwan, *Revolt of the Rednecks*, 67–75.

7. Simkins, *Tillman*, 231; *Mills v. Green*, 67 F. 818 (C.C.D.S.C. 1895), *reversed*, 69 F. 852 (4th Cir. 1895), appeal dismissed as moot, 159 U.S. 651 (1895).

8. Simkins, *Tillman*, 291; Edward A. Miller, *Gullah Statesman: Robert Smalls from Slavery to Congress, 1838–1915* (Columbia, S.C., 1995), 204–14; Willard B. Gatewood, Jr., "'The Remarkable Misses Rollin'": Black Women in Reconstruction South Carolina," *South Carolina History Magazine* 92 (1991): 172 (Whipper).

9. George B. Tindall, "The Question of Race in the South Carolina Convention of 1895," *Journal of Negro History* 37 (1952): 227, 288–90; *New York World*, October 29, 1895; *1895 S.C. Convention Journal*, 463.

10. *New York World*, October 29, 1895; *1895 S.C. Convention Journal*, 111, 319–30, 468–69, 727.

11. Perman, *Struggle for Mastery*, 129–46; 1898 La. Const., 197–98.

12. *1901–2 Va. Convention Proceedings*, 2:3076–77; Perman, *Struggle for Mastery*, 150–221; 1868 N.C. Const. (1901), VI:4; 1901 Ala. Const., VIII:178, 180–81; 1902 Va. Const., II:19–22.

13. Perman, *Struggle for Mastery*, 233–41, 271–85; 1876 Tex. Const. (1902), VI:2; 1907 Ga. Laws, 47; 1904 Md. Laws, 109; *Hart v. State*, 60 A. 457 (Md. 1905).

14. *Ratliff v. State*, 20 So. 865 (Miss. 1896); *Williams v. Mississippi*, 170 U.S. 213, 225 (1898); *Giles v. Harris*, 189 U.S. 475 (1903).

15. *Hall v. DeCuir*, 95 U.S. 485 (1878); C. Vann Woodward, *The Strange Career of Jim Crow* (New York, 1966), 33–35, 91–103; *Civil Rights Cases*, 109 U.S. 3 (1883).

16. See, for example, 1878 Miss. Laws, 103; 1881–82 Va. Laws, 37; 1885 Fla. Const., XII:12; 1890 Ky. Const., 187; 1898 La. Const., 248 (schools); 1887 Fla. Laws,

3743; 1888 Miss. Laws, 46; 1890–91 Ala. Laws, 412; 1890 La. Laws, 152; 1891 Ark. Laws, 15; 1891 Tex. Laws, 44; 1891 Tenn. Laws, 135; 1892 Ky. Laws, 63 (railroads); 1899 N.C. Laws, 540; 1905 Fla. Laws, 5420 (streetcars).

17. *Plessy v. Ferguson*, 163 U.S. 537, 551–52 (1896); *Brown v. Board of Education of Topeka*, 347 U.S. 483 (1954).

18. 1904 Ky. Laws, 181; *Commonwealth v. Berea College*, 94 S.W. 622 (Ky. 1906), *affirmed*, 211 U.S. 45 (1908).

19. *Plessy*, 163 U.S. at 552; *Berea College*, 211 U.S. at 58.

20. *Ex parte Plessy*, 11 So. 948 (La. 1893), *affirmed*, 163 U.S. 537 (1896); *Smith v. State*, 46 S.W. 566, 568 (Tenn. 1898); *Ohio Valley Ry's Receiver v. Lander*, 47 S.W. 344 (Ky. 1898); *Morrison v. State*, 95 S.W. 494 (Tenn. 1906); *Alabama & Vicksburg R. Co. v. Morris*, 60 So. 11, 14 (Miss. 1912).

21. *Roberts v. City of Boston*, 59 Mass. 198 (1849); *Chicago & Northwestern R. Co. v. Williams*, 55 Ill. 185 (1870). The only exception was *West Chester & Philadelphia R. Co. v. Miles*, 55 Pa. 209 (1867), in which the Pennsylvania supreme court approved a private segregation rule as conducive to social order and expressed horror at the prospect of racial amalgamation.

22. *Ex parte Plessy*, 11 So. 948 (La. 1893), *affirmed*, 163 U.S. 537 (1896); *Louisville, New Orleans & Texas R. Co. v. Mississippi*, 6 So. 203 (Miss. 1889), *affirmed*, 133 U.S. 587 (1890).

23. *Smith v. State*, 46 S.W. 666 (Tenn. 1898); *Alabama & Vicksburg R. Co. v. Morris*, 60 So. 11, 14 (Miss. 1912).

24. *State ex rel. Abbott v. Hicks*, 11 So. 74 (La. 1892); *Pullman Palace Car Co. v. Cain*, 40 S.W. 220 (Tex. Civ. App. 1897); *Southern Kansas R. Co. of Texas v. State*, 99 S.W. 166 (Tex. Civ. App. 1906); *Hart v. State*, 60 A. 457, 460 (Md. 1905), quoting *DeCuir*.

25. Klarman, "Plessy Era," 371–79; see Chapter 4.

26. *Virginia v. Rives*, 100 U.S. 313 (1880); *Ex parte Virginia*, 100 U.S. 339 (1880). In a West Virginia jury case, *Strauder v. West Virginia*, 100 U.S. 303, 310 (1880), the Court reaffirmed that blacks could not be formally excluded from jury service but made clear that states could "confine the selection to males, to freeholders . . . or to persons having educational qualifications." This opened the way for Southern states to enact laws worded neutrally but designed to exclude persons with traits thought to be associated with blacks, such as poverty and illiteracy, from jury service.

27. *Neal v. Delaware*, 103 U.S. 370 (1881); *Bush v. Kentucky*, 107 U.S. 110 (1883).

28. See, for example, *Commonwealth v. Johnson*, 78 Ky. 511 (1880); *State v. Brownfield*, 39 S.E. 2 (S.C. 1901); *State v. Peoples*, 42 S.E. 814 (N.C. 1902); *Montgomery v. State*, 42 So. 894 (Fla. 1907); *Carter v. State*, 48 S.W. 508 (Tex. Crim. App. 1898), *reversed* 177 U.S. 442 (1900).

29. Daniel A. Novak, "Peonage: Negro Contract Labor, Sharecropping, Tenantry and the Law in the South, 1865–1970" (PhD diss., Brandeis University, 1975), 76–79; see, for example, 1891 Fla. Laws, 4032; 1892 La. Laws, 516; 1894 Ark. Laws, 78; 1900 Miss. Laws, 101.

30. *State v. Williams*, 10 S.E. 876, 877 (S.C. 1890); *Edge v. State*, 39 S.E. 889 (Ga. 1901); *Lamar v. State*, 47 S.E. 958 (Ga. 1904).

31. 1900–1 Ala. Laws, 1208; *Peonage Cases*, 123 F. 671, 686–88 (M.D. Ala. 1903); *Clyatt v. United States*, 197 U.S. 207, 218 (1905).

32. See, for example, 1903 Ga. Laws, 345; 1903 Ala. Laws, 345; 1907 Ala. Laws, 636; 1907 Fla. Laws, 5678; *Vance v. State*, 57 S.E. 889 (Ga. 1907) (upholding presumption); *State v. Williams*, 63 S.E. 949 (N.C. 1909) (suggesting presumption was

unconstitutional); *State v. Kingsley*, 18 S.W. 994 (Mo. 1891). Arkansas federal judge Jacob Trieber also echoed Jones's general criticisms of peonage laws. *Peonage Cases*, 136 F. 707 (E.D. Ark. 1905).

33. *Bailey v. Alabama*, 219 U.S. 219, 244–45 (1911), *reversing Bailey v. State*, 48 So. 498 (Ala. 1908); see generally Pete Daniel, *Shadow of Slavery: Peonage in the South, 1901–1969* (Urbana, Ill., 1972).

34. *State v. Gurry*, 88 A. 546 (Md. 1913); *Carey v. City of Atlanta*, 84 S.E. 856 (Ga. 1915).

35. *State v. Darnell*, 81 S.E. 338 (N.C. 1914); *Hopkins v. City of Richmond*, 86 S.E. 139 (Va. 1915); see Aubrey L. Brooks, *Walter Clark: Fighting Judge* (Chapel Hill, N.C., 1944).

CHAPTER 12

1. Albion W. Tourgee, *A Fool's Errand*, ed. John Hope Franklin (Cambridge, Mass., 1971), vii, xvi-xvii, 403; *Smith v. DuBose*, 3 S.E. 309, 317 (Ga. 1887).

2. George M. Fredrickson, *The Black Image in the White Mind: The Debate on Afro-American Character and Destiny, 1817–1914* (New York, 1971), 221.

3. See Chapter 2.

4. *Ex parte Garland*, 71 U.S. 333 (1867); *Cummings v. Missouri*, 71 U.S. 277 (1867), *reversing State v. Cummings*, 36 Mo. 24 (1865); *State v. Blalock*, 61 N.C. 242, 244–45 (1867); see Chapter 3.

5. See Chapters 4 and 12.

6. *Louisville, New Orleans & Texas R. Co. v. Mississippi*, 6 So. 203 (Miss. 1889), *affirmed*, 133 U.S. 587 (1890); *Alabama & Vicksburg R. Co. v. Morris*, 60 So. 11, 14 (Miss. 1912); *Hart v. State*, 60 A. 457 (Md. 1905).

7. See Chapter 5.

8. *Thorington v. Smith*, 75 U.S. 1 (1869); see Chapter 5.

9. See Chapters 2 and 7.

10. *Britton v. Atlanta & Charlotte Air-Line Railway Co.*, 88 N.C. 536, 545–46 (1883); *Dawson v. Lee*, 83 Ky. 49, 56 (1884); *Puitt v. Commissioners of Gaston County*, 94 N.C. 709 (1886); *Riggsbee v. Town of Durham*, 94 N.C. 800 (1886).

11. *State v. Ross*, 76 N.C. 242, 242–43, 250 (1877); *State v. Kennedy*, 76 N.C. 251 (1877).

12. See Chapters 7–9.

13. See Chapters 1 and 4.

14. See Chapter 4.

15. See Chapters 4 and 11.

Bibliography

BOOKS

Agee, James, and Walker Evans. *Let Us Now Praise Famous Men: Three Tenant Families.* Boston, 1941.

Akin, John W. *Hiram Warner: A Sketch Read before the Georgia Bar Association at Its 14th Annual Session, July 2, 1897.* Atlanta, Ga., 1897.

Alexander, Roberta Sue. *North Carolina Faces the Freedmen: Race Relations during Presidential Reconstruction, 1865–67.* Durham, N.C., 1985.

Alexander, Thomas B. *Political Reconstruction in Tennessee.* Nashville, Tenn., 1950.

Ames, Herman W. *State Documents on Federal Relations: The States and the United States.* Philadelphia, 1911; reprint, 1970.

Aumann, Francis R. *The Changing American Legal System: Some Selected Phases.* Columbus, Ohio, 1940; reprint, 1969.

Baker, Jean H. *The Politics of Continuity: Maryland Political Parties from 1858 to 1870.* Baltimore, 1973.

Ballagh, James C. *A History of Slavery in Virginia.* Baltimore, 1902; reprint, 1968.

Barr, Alwyn. *Reconstruction to Reform: Texas Politics, 1876–1906.* Austin, Tex., 1971.

Basch, Norma. *In the Eyes of the Law: Women, Marriage and Property in Nineteenth-Century New York.* Ithaca, N.Y., 1982.

Berlin, Ira. *Slaves without Masters: The Free Negro in the Antebellum South.* New York, 1975.

Beth, Loren P. *John Marshall Harlan: The Last Whig Justice.* Lexington, Ky., 1992.

Bond, Horace Mann. *The Education of the Negro in the American Social Order.* New York, 1934.

Bond, James E. *No Easy Walk to Freedom: Reconstruction and the Ratification of the Fourteenth Amendment.* Westport, Conn., 1997.

Brooks, Aubrey L. *Walter Clark: Fighting Judge.* Chapel Hill, N.C., 1944.

Brownson, Orestes. *The American Republic: Its Constitution, Tendencies, and Destiny.* New York, 1866.

Cadman, John W. *The Corporation in New Jersey: Business and Politics, 1791–1875.* Cambridge, Mass., 1949.

Chandler, Alfred D. *The Visible Hand: The Managerial Revolution in American Business.* Cambridge, Mass., 1977.

Cobb, Thomas R. R. *An Inquiry into the Law of Negro Slavery in the United States of America.* Philadelphia, 1858.

Coleman, Peter J. *Debtors and Creditors in America: Insolvency, Imprisonment for Debt, and Bankruptcy, 1607–1900.* Madison, Wis., 1974.

Comstock, Jim, ed., *The West Virginia Heritage Encyclopedia.* Richwood, W. Va., 1976.

Connelley, William E., and E. Merton Coulter. *History of Kentucky.* Chicago, 1922.

Cooley, Thomas M. *A Treatise on the Constitutional Limitations Which Rest upon the Legislative Power of the States of the American Union.* Boston, 1868.

Coulter, E. Merton. *The Civil War and Readjustment in Kentucky.* Chapel Hill, N.C., 1926.

Cremin, Lawrence A. *The American Common School.* New York, 1951.

Crofts, Daniel. *Reluctant Confederates: Upper South Unionists in the Secession Crisis.* Chapel Hill, N.C., 1989.

Cubberley, Ellwood P. *The History of Education.* Boston, 1948.

Curry, Richard O., ed. *Radicalism, Racism, and Party Realignment: The Border States During Reconstruction.* Baltimore, 1969.

Dabney, Charles W. *Universal Education in the South. Vol. 1.* New York, 1936; reprint, 1969.

Daggett, Harriet Spiller. *The Community Property System of Louisiana.* Baton Rouge, La., 1931.

Daniel, Pete. *Shadow of Slavery: Peonage in the South, 1901–1969.* Urbana, Ill., 1972.

Degler, Carl N. *The Other South: Southern Dissenters in the Nineteenth Century.* New York, 1974.

Dillon, John F. *Removal of Causes from State Courts to Federal Courts.* St. Louis, 1881.

Dilts, James D. *Great Road: The Building of the Baltimore & Ohio.* Stanford, Calif., 1993.

Du Bois, W.E.B. *Black Reconstruction.* New York, 1935.

DuBose, John W. *Alabama's Tragic Decade: Ten Years of Alabama, 1865–1874.* Birmingham, Ala., 1940.

Dunne, Gerald T. *The Missouri Supreme Court: From Dred Scott to Cruzan.* Columbia, Mo., 1993.

Ely, James W., Jr., ed. *A History of the Tennessee Supreme Court.* Knoxville, Tenn., 2002.

Escott, Paul D. *Many Excellent People: Power and Privilege in North Carolina, 1850–1900.* Chapel Hill, N.C., 1985.

Essah, Patience. *A House Divided: Slavery and Emancipation in Delaware, 1635–1865.* Charlottesville, Va., 1996.

Fairman, Charles. *History of the Supreme Court of the United States. Vol. 6: Reconstruction and Reunion, Part 1.* New York, 1971.

Feely, Malcolm S. *Frederick Douglass.* New York, 1991.

Fehrenbach, T. R. *Lone Star: A History of Texas and the Texans.* New York, 1968.

Fehrenbacher, Don E., ed. *Abraham Lincoln: Speeches and Writings. Vol. 2.* New York, 1989.

Fischer, David Hackett. *Albion's Seed: Four British Folkways in America.* New York, 1989.

Fisher, Noel C. *War at Every Door: Partisan Politics and Guerrilla Violence in East Tennessee, 1860–1869.* Chapel Hill, N.C., 1997.

Flanders, Ralph B. *Plantation Slavery in Georgia.* Chapel Hill, N.C., 1933.

Fleming, Walter L. *Civil War and Reconstruction in Alabama.* New York, 1905.

Foner, Eric. *Reconstruction: America's Unfinished Revolution, 1863–1877.* New York, 1988.

Fredrickson, George M. *The Black Image in the White Mind: The Debate on Afro-American Character and Destiny, 1817–1914.* New York, 1971.

Friedman, Lawrence M. *Crime and Punishment in American History.* New York, 1993.

Fuke, Richard P. *Imperfect Equality: African Americans and the Confines of White Racial Attitudes in Post-Emancipation Maryland.* New York, 1999.

Fuller, Paul E. *Laura Clay and the Women's Rights Movement.* Lexington, Ky., 1975.

Garrison, Tim Alan. *The Legal Ideology of Removal: The Southern Judiciary and the Sovereignty of Native American Nations.* Athens, Ga., 2002.

Gillette, William. *Retreat from Reconstruction, 1869–1879.* Baton Rouge, La., 1979.

Goodrich, Carter. *Government Promotion of American Canals and Railroads, 1800–1890.* New York, 1960.

Green, John W. *Lives of the Judges of the Supreme Court of Tennessee, 1796–1947.* Knoxville, Tenn., 1947.

Hair, William Ivy. *Bourbonism and Agrarian Protest: Louisiana Politics, 1877–1900.* Baton Rouge, La., 1969.

Harris, John B., ed. *A History of the Supreme Court of Georgia.* Macon, Ga., 1948.

Harris, William C. *With Charity for All: Lincoln and the Restoration of the Union.* Lexington, Ky., 1997.

Henry, H. M. *The Police Control of the Slave in South Carolina.* Emory, Va., 1914.

Hicks, Paul D. *Joseph Henry Lumpkin: Georgia's First Chief Justice.* Athens, Ga., 2002.

Hoff, Joan. *Law, Gender and Injustice: A Legal History of U.S. Women.* New York, 1991.

Holt, Thomas. *Black Over White: Negro Political Leadership in South Carolina During Reconstruction.* Urbana, Ill., 1977.

Horwitz, Morton J. *The Transformation of American Law 1870–1960.* New York, 1992.

Huebner, Timothy S. *The Southern Judicial Tradition: State Judges and Sectional Distinctiveness, 1790–1890.* New York, 1999.

Hyman, Harold M. *Era of the Oath: Northern Loyalty Tests during the Civil War and Reconstruction.* Philadelphia, 1954.

Ireland, Robert M. *The Kentucky State Constitution: A Reference Guide.* Westport, Conn., 1999.

Kaczorowski, Robert. *The Politics of Judicial Interpretation: The Federal Courts, Department of Justice and Civil Rights, 1866–1876.* Dobbs Ferry, N.Y., 1985.

Kirwan, Albert D. *Revolt of the Rednecks: Mississippi Politics, 1876–1925.* Lexington, Ky., 1951.

Kneebone, John J., et al., eds. *Dictionary of Virginia Biography.* Richmond, Va., 1998.

Lazarou, Kathleen E. *Concealed under Petticoats: Married Women's Property and the Law of Texas, 1840–1913.* New York, 1986.

Lemann, Nicholas. *Promised Land: The Great Black Migration and How It Changed America.* New York, 1991.

Levy, Leonard W., ed., *The Virginia Report of 1799–1800 Touching Alien and Sedition Laws.* New York, 1970.

Lewis, William Draper, ed. *Great American Lawyers.* Philadelphia, 1908.

Litwack, Leon. *Been in the Storm So Long: The Aftermath of Slavery.* New York, 1979.

Malone, Dumas, ed. *Dictionary of American Biography.* New York, 1934.

Manley, Walter W., ed. *The Supreme Court of Florida and Its Predecessor Courts, 1821–1917.* Gainesville, Fla., 1997.

Marks, Henry S., ed. *Who Was Who in Alabama.* Huntsville, Ala., 1972.

McDonald, Forrest. *States' Rights and the Union: Imperium in Imperio, 1776–1876.* Lawrence, Kan., 2000.

McDougle, Ivan E. *Slavery in Kentucky, 1792–1865.* Westport, Conn., 1970.

McMillan, Malcolm. *Constitutional Development in Alabama, 1798–1901: A Study in Politics, the Negro and Sectionalism.* Chapel Hill, N.C., 1955.

McMillen, Sally G. *Southern Women: Black and White in the Old South.* 2d ed. Wheeling, Ill., 2002.

McPherson, James M. *Battle Cry of Freedom: The Civil War Era.* New York, 1988.

Miller, Edward A. *Gullah Statesman: Robert Smalls from Slavery to Congress, 1838–1915.* Columbia, S.C., 1995.

Moneyhon, Carl H. *Republicanism in Reconstruction Texas.* Austin, Tex., 1980.

Moore, Albert B. *Conscription and Conflict in the Confederacy.* New York, 1924.

National American Woman Suffrage Association. *Victory: How Women Won It.* New York, 1940.

Nieman, Donald. *To Set the Law in Motion: The Freedmen's Bureau and the Legal Rights of Blacks, 1865–1868.* Millwood, N.Y., 1979.

Nieman, Donald G., ed. *Black Southerners and the Law 1865–1900.* New York, 1994.

Parker, Joel S. *Revolution and Reconstruction.* New York, 1866.

Parks, Joseph H., *Joseph E. Brown of Georgia.* Baton Rouge, La., 1977.

Parrish, William E. *A History of Missouri. Vol. 3: 1860–1875.* Columbia, Mo., 1973.

Parrish, William E. *Missouri under Radical Rule, 1865–70.* Columbia, Mo., 1965.

Patterson, Caleb P. *The Negro in Tennessee, 1790–1865.* Austin, Tex., 1922.

Perman, Michael. *Struggle for Mastery: Disfranchisement in the South, 1888–1908.* Chapel Hill, N.C., 2001.

Phillips, Christopher. *Freedom's Port: The African-American Community of Baltimore, 1790–1860.* Urbana, Ill., 1997.

Pound, Roscoe. *The Formative Era of American Law.* Boston, 1938.

Powell, William S., ed. *Dictionary of North Carolina Biography.* Chapel Hill, N.C., 1994.

Rabinowitz, Howard N., ed., *Southern Black Leaders of the Reconstruction Era.* Urbana, Ill., 1982.

Raper, Horace. *William W. Holden: North Carolina's Political Enigma.* Chapel Hill, N.C., 1985.

Robinson, William M. *Justice in Grey: A History of the Judicial System of the Confederate States of America.* Cambridge, Mass., 1941.

Rowland, Dunbar. *Courts, Judges and Lawyers of Mississippi 1798–1935.* Jackson, Miss., 1935.

Salmon, Mary Lynn. *Women and the Law of Property in Early America.* Chapel Hill, N.C., 1986.

Schaefer, Judith Kelleher. *Slavery, the Civil Law and the Supreme Court of Louisiana.* Baton Rouge, La., 1994.

Scott, Anne Firor. *The Southern Lady: From Pedestal to Politics, 1830–1930.* Charlottesville, Va., 1995.

Simkins, Francis B., and Robert H. Woody. *South Carolina during Reconstruction.* Chapel Hill, N.C., 1932.

Simpson, Craig M. *A Good Southerner: The Life of Henry A. Wise of Virginia.* Chapel Hill, N.C., 1985.

Skates, John Ray, Jr. *A History of the Mississippi Supreme Court, 1817–1948.* Jackson, Miss., 1973.

Smith, Julia Floyd. *Slavery and Plantation Growth in Antebellum Florida 1821–1860.* Gainesville, Fla., 1973.

Stanton, Elizabeth Cady, Susan B. Anthony, and Matilda Joslyn Gage. *History of Woman Suffrage.* 6 vols. New York, 1881–1922.

Stephenson, Gilbert T. *Race Distinctions in American Law.* New York, 1910; reprint, 1970.

Stroud, George M. *A Sketch of the Laws Relating to Slavery in the Several States of the United States of America.* Philadelphia, 1856; reprint, 1968.

Summers, Mark W. *Railroads, Reconstruction and the Gospel of Prosperity: Aid under the Radical Republicans, 1865–1877.* Princeton, N.J., 1984.

Sumner, Charles. *Works of Sumner.* Boston, 1875–83.

Sutherland, Daniel E. *Guerrillas, Unionists and Violence on the Confederate Home Front.* Fayetteville, Ark., 1997.

Swinney, Everette. *Suppressing the Ku Klux Klan: The Enforcement of the Reconstruction Amendments, 1870–1874.* New York, 1987.

Tarr, G. Alan. *Understanding State Constitutions.* Princeton, N.J., 1998.

Taylor, Joe Gray. *Negro Slavery in Louisiana.* Baton Rouge, La., 1963.

Taylor, Orville W. *Negro Slavery in Arkansas.* Durham, N.C., 1958.

Thompson, George H. *Arkansas and Reconstruction: The Influence of Geography, Economics and Personality.* Port Washington, N.Y., 1976.

Tourgee, Albion W. *A Fool's Errand.* Edited by John Hope Franklin. Cambridge, Mass., 1971.

Trowbridge, John T. *The South: A Tour of Its Battlefields and Ruined Cities.* New York, 1866.

Tucker, St. George. *Blackstone's Commentaries: With Notes of Reference to the Constitution and Laws of the Federal Government of the United States and of the Commonwealth of Virginia.* Philadelphia, 1803; reprint 1996.

Tunnell, Ted. *Crucible of Reconstruction: War, Radicalism and Race in Louisiana, 1862–1877.* Baton Rouge, La., 1984.

Tushnet, Mark V., *The American Law of Slavery, 1810–1860.* Princeton, N.J., 1981.

Tyler, Lyon Gardiner, ed. *Encyclopedia of Virginia Biography.* New York, 1915; reprint 1998.

Tyler, Ron, ed., *The New Handbook of Texas.* Austin, Tex., 1996.

Waller, John L. *Colossal Hamilton of Texas: A Biography of Andrew Jackson Hamilton.* El Paso, Tex., 1968.

Whites, Lee Ann. *The Civil War as a Crisis in Gender: Augusta, Georgia, 1860–1890.* Athens, Ga., 1995.

Whites, Lee Ann, et al., eds. *Women in Missouri History: In Search of Power and Influence.* Columbia, Mo., 2004.

Wiethoff, William. *A Peculiar Humanism: The Judicial Advocacy of Slavery in the High Courts of the Old South, 1820–1850.* Athens, Ga., 1996.

Williams, Lou Falkner. *The Great South Carolina Ku Klux Klan Trials, 1871–1872.* Athens, Ga., 1996.

Wilson, Theodore B. *The Black Codes of the South.* University, Ala., 1965.

Woodman, Harold. *New South, New Law: The Legal Foundations of Credit and Labor Relations in the Postbellum Agricultural South.* Baton Rouge, La., 1995.

Woodward, C. Vann. *Origins of the New South, 1877–1913.* Baton Rouge, La., 1951.

Woodward, C. Vann. *The Strange Career of Jim Crow.* New York, 1966.

ARTICLES AND THESES

Alexander, Thomas. "Thomas A. R. Nelson as an Exemplar of Whig Conservatism in Tennessee." *Tennessee Historical Quarterly* 15 (1956): 17.

Beitzinger, Alfons J. "Federal Law Enforcement and the Booth Cases." *Marquette Law Review* 41 (1957): 7.

Bogen, David S. "The Maryland Context of Dred Scott: The Decline in the Legal Status of Maryland Free Blacks, 1776–1810." *American Journal of Legal History* 34 (1990): 381.

Brown, Elizabeth Gaspar. "Husband and Wife—Memorandum on the Mississippi Women's Law of 1839." *Michigan Law Review* 42 (1944): 1110.

Chused, Richard. "Married Women's Property Law: 1800–1850." *Georgetown Law Journal* 71 (1983): 1359.

Connelly, Thomas L. "Neo-Confederatism or Power Vacuum: Post-War Kentucky Politics Reappraised." *Register of the Kentucky Historical Society* 64 (1966): 257.

Cornyn, John. "The Roots of Texas Constitution: Settlement to Statehood." *Texas Tech Law Review* 26 (1995): 1089.

Crow, Jeffrey J. "Thomas Settle, Jr., Reconstruction, and the Memory of the Civil War." *Journal of Southern History* 62 (1996): 689.

Ewing, Cortez A. M. "Arkansas Reconstruction Impeachments." *Arkansas Historical Quarterly* 13 (1954): 137.

Fuke, Richard Paul. "Hugh Lennox Bond and Radical Republican Ideology." *Journal of Southern History* 45 (1979): 569.

Gatewood, Jr., Willard B. "'The Remarkable Misses Rollin': Black Women in Reconstruction South Carolina." *South Carolina History Magazine* 92 (1991): 172.

Gerofsky, Milton. "Reconstruction in West Virginia." *West Virginia History* 6 (1944): 295; 7 (1945): 5.

Hickin, Patricia. "John C. Underwood and the Antislavery Movement in Virginia, 1847–1860." *Virginia Magazine of History and Biography* 73 (1965): 156.

Hume, Richard L. "Carpetbaggers in the Reconstruction South: A Group Portrait of Outside Whites in the 'Black and Tan' Constitutional Conventions." *Journal of American History* 64 (1977): 313.

Johnston, Frank. "Suffrage and Reconstruction in Mississippi." *Publications of Mississippi Historical Society* 6 (1902): 141.

Klarman, Michael J. "The Plessy Era." *Supreme Court Review* (1998): 303.

Lebsock, Suzanne D. "Radical Reconstruction and the Property Rights of Southern Women." *Journal of Southern History* 43 (1977): 195.

Low, W. Augustus. "The Freedmen's Bureau and Civil Rights in Maryland." *Journal of Negro History* 37 (1952): 221.

Mauer, John Walker. "State Constitutions in a Time of Crisis: The Case of the Texas Constitution of 1876." *Texas Law Review* 68 (1990): 1615.

McNeilly, J. S. "History of the Measures Submitted to the Committee on Elective Franchise, Apportionment and Election in the Constitutional Convention of 1890." *Publications of Mississippi Historical Society* 6 (1902): 129.

Moncrief, Sandra. "The Mississippi Married Woman's Property Act of 1839." *Journal of Mississippi History* 47 (1985): 110.

Nash, A. E. Keir. "A More Equitable Past? Southern Supreme Courts and the Protection of the Antebellum Negro." *North Carolina Law Review* 48 (1970): 197.

Nash, A. E. Keir. "Negro Rights, Unionism, and Greatness on the South Carolina Court of Appeals: The Extraordinary Chief Justice John Belton O'Neall." *South Carolina Law Review* 21 (1969): 141.

Nash, A. E. Keir. "Reason of Slavery: Understanding the Judicial Role in the Peculiar Institution." *Vanderbilt Law Review* 32 (1979): 7.

Norvell, James R. "The Reconstruction Courts of Texas, 1867–1873." *Southwest Historical Quarterly* 62 (1958): 141.

Novak, Daniel A. "Peonage: Negro Contract Labor, Sharecropping, Tenantry and the Law in the South, 1865–1970." PhD diss., Brandeis University, 1975.

Palmer, Paul. "Miscegenation as an Issue in the Arkansas Constitutional Convention of 1868." *Arkansas Historical Quarterly* 24 (1965): 99.

Ranney, Joseph A. "This New and Beautiful Organism: The Evolution of American Federalism in Three State Supreme Courts." *Marquette Law Review* 87 (2003): 254.

Sansing, David G. "The Failure of Johnsonian Reconstruction in Mississippi, 1865–1866." *Journal of Mississippi History* 34 (1972): 373.

Smith, Armantine. "The History of the Woman's Suffrage Movement in Louisiana." *Louisiana Law Review* 62 (2002): 509.

St. Clair, Kenneth E. "Debtor Relief in North Carolina during Reconstruction." *North Carolina Historical Review* 18 (1941): 215.

St. Hilaire, Joseph M. "The Negro Delegates in the Arkansas Constitutional Convention of 1868: A Profile." *Arkansas Historical Quarterly* 33 (1974): 38.

Tindall, George B. "The Question of Race in the South Carolina Convention of 1895." *Journal of Negro History* 37 (1952): 277.

Woody, Robert H. "Jonathan Jasper Wright, Associate Justice of the Supreme Court of South Carolina." *Journal of Negro History* 18 (1933): 14.

FEDERAL LEGAL PUBLICATIONS

Federal Cases (cited as "- F.Cas.– (No. -.")

Federal Reporter (cited as "- F. –.")

United States Reports (cited as "- U.S. –"). Most state and federal case reports and federal statutes are cited by placing the volume number to the left of the title and the page number to the right. (Example: Volume 1, page 1 of the *United States Reports* is "1 U.S. 1.")

United States Statutes at Large (cited as "- U.S. Stats. -").

STATE LEGAL PUBLICATIONS

State constitutions are cited by placing the year of enactment to the left of the state's name and the article and section numbers to the right. The article and section number are separated by a colon. (Example: Article I, § 1 of the 1867 Alabama constitution is cited as "1867 Ala. Const., I:1.")

State statutes are cited by placing the year of the legislative session to the left of the state's name and the page or chapter number to the right. (Example: A statute that begins at page 1 of the laws for the 1866 session of the Alabama legislature is "1866 Ala. Laws, 1.")

State supreme court reports. All states except Louisiana published decisions of their state supreme courts during the late nineteenth century as "Reports" (for example, "Alabama Reports," "Arkansas Reports," and so forth), cited as "- Ala. -," "- Ark. -," and so forth. Louisiana published "Reports Annotated," cited as "- La. Ann. -." The citation format is the same as for federal court decisions. (Example: Volume 1, page 1 of the Alabama Reports is "1 Ala. 1.")

REPORTS OF CONSTITUTIONAL CONVENTIONS

Debates and Proceedings of the Constitutional Convention of the State of Virginia Assembled at the City of Richmond, Tuesday, December 3, 1867. Richmond, Va., 1868.

Debates and Proceedings of the Convention Which Assembled at Little Rock, January 7, 1868 to Form a Constitution for the State of Arkansas. Little Rock, Ark., 1868.

Debates and Proceedings of the Maryland Reform Convention to Revise the State Constitution. Annapolis, Md., 1851.

Debates in the Convention for Revision and Amendment of the Constitution of the State of Louisiana. New Orleans, La., 1864.

Debates of the Constitutional Convention of the State of Maryland. Annapolis, Md., 1864.

Journal of the Constitutional Convention of the State of Alabama Assembled in the City of Montgomery, September 6, 1875. Montgomery, Ala., 1875.

Journal of the Constitutional Convention of the State of South Carolina. Columbia, S.C., 1895.

Journal of the Convention of Delegates of the People of Arkansas Assembled at the Capitol, January 4, 1864. Little Rock, Ark., 1870.

Journal of the Missouri State Convention, Held at the City of St. Louis, January 6–April 10, 1865. St. Louis, Mo., 1865.

Journal of the Proceedings and Debates in the Constitutional Convention of the State of Mississippi, August 1865, Jackson, Miss., 1865.

Journal of the Proceedings of the Constitutional Convention of the People of Georgia. Augusta, Ga., 1868.

Loeb, Isidor, and Floyd C. Shoemaker. *Debates of the Missouri Constitutional Convention of 1875.* Columbia, Mo., 1930–44.

Official Journal of the Proceedings of the Convention for Framing a Constitution for the State of Louisiana. New Orleans, La., 1868.

Perlman, Philip B. *Debates of the Maryland Constitutional Convention of 1867.* Baltimore, 1923.

Proceedings of the Constitutional Convention of South Carolina, Held at Charleston, S.C., Beginning January 14 and ending March 17, 1868. Charleston, S.C., 1868.

Report of the Debates and Proceedings of the Convention for the Revision of the Constitution of the State of Kentucky. Frankfort, Ky., 1849.

Report of the Proceedings and Debates of the Constitutional Convention of Virginia, Held in the City of Richmond, June 12, 1901 to June 26, 1902. Richmond, Va., 1906.

Small, Samuel W., ed. *A Stenographic Report of the Proceedings of the Constitutional Convention Held in Atlanta, 1877.* Atlanta, Ga., 1877.

Index

About the Author

JOSEPH A. RANNEY teaches legal history as an adjunct professor at Marquette University Law School and is a partner in the Madison, Wisconsin, law firm of DeWitt Ross & Stevens S.C., practicing commercial and intellectual property litigation.

X